Richard Attenborough

BRITISH FILM MAKERS

Manchester University Press

BRIAN MCFARLANE, NEIL SINYARD series editors
ALLEN EYLES, PHILIP FRENCH, SUE HARPER,
TIM PULLEINE, JEFFREY RICHARDS, TOM RYALL
series advisers

BRITISH FILM MAKERS

already published

Lindsay Anderson   JOHN IZOD, KARL MAGEE, KATHRYN MACKENZIE, ISABELLE GOURDIN-SANGOUARD

Anthony Asquith   TOM RYALL

Roy Ward Baker   GEOFF MAYER

Sydney Box   ANDREW SPICER

Jack Clayton   NEIL SINYARD

Lance Comfort   BRIAN MCFARLANE

Terence Davies   WENDY EVERETT

Terence Fisher   PETER HUTCHINGS

Terry Gilliam   PETER MARKS

Derek Jarman   ROWLAND WYMER

Launder and Gilliat   BRUCE BABINGTON

Mike Leigh   TONY WHITEHEAD

Richard Lester   NEIL SINYARD

Joseph Losey   COLIN GARDNER

Carol Reed   PETER WILLIAM EVANS

Michael Reeves   BENJAMIN HALLIGAN

Karel Reisz   COLIN GARDNER

Tony Richardson   ROBERT SHAIL

J. Lee Thompson   STEVE CHIBNALL

Michael Winterbottom   BRIAN MCFARLANE and DEANE WILLIAMS

Richard Attenborough

BRITISH FILM MAKERS

SALLY DUX

Manchester University Press
MANCHESTER AND NEW YORK

distributed exclusively in the USA by Palgrave Macmillan

Copyright © Sally Dux 2013

The right of Sally Dux to be identified as the author of this work has been asserted by her in accordance with the Copyright, Designs and Patents Act 1988.

Published by Manchester University Press
Oxford Road, Manchester M13 9NR, UK
and Room 400, 175 Fifth Avenue, New York, NY 10010, USA
www.manchesteruniversitypress.co.uk

Distributed exclusively in the USA by
Palgrave Macmillan, 175 Fifth Avenue, New York, NY 10010, USA

Distributed exclusively in Canada by
UBC Press, University of British Columbia, 2029 West Mall, Vancouver, BC, Canada V6T 1Z2

British Library Cataloguing-in-Publication Data
A catalogue record for this book is available from the British Library

Library of Congress Cataloging-in-Publication Data applied for

ISBN 978 0 7190 8764 6 hardback

First published 2013

The publisher has no responsibility for the persistence or accuracy of URLs for any external or third-party internet websites referred to in this book, and does not guarantee that any content on such websites is, or will remain, accurate or appropriate.

Typeset in Scala with Meta display by
Koinonia, Manchester
Printed in Great Britain by
TJ International Ltd, Padstow

In loving memory of my parents
Harry Garth Edmonds and Dorothy Edmonds
(1919–2007)

Contents

LIST OF PLATES	*page* ix
SERIES EDITORS' FOREWORD	xi
ACKNOWLEDGEMENTS	xiii
INTRODUCTION	1
1 On-screen: Attenborough as actor	5
2 Attenborough as producer: Beaver Films and Allied Film Makers	20
3 New directions: *Oh! What a Lovely War* (1969)	37
4 Anglo-American alliances: *Young Winston* (1972), *A Bridge Too Far* (1977) and *Magic*	62
5 Race, nation and conflict: *Gandhi* (1982), *A Chorus Line* (1985) and *Cry Freedom* (1987)	105
6 Public and private identities: *Chaplin* (1992) and *Grey Owl* (1999)	138
7 Brief encounters: *Shadowlands* (1993), *In Love and War* (1996) and *Closing the Ring* (2007)	168
CONCLUSION	198
FILMOGRAPHY	201
BIBLIOGRAPHY	207
INDEX	218

List of plates

1. Richard Attenborough (Tom Curtis) in *The Angry Silence* (1960) (Studio Canal – KinoWelt–Beaver Films/British Lion)   *page* 99
2. Bryan Forbes (Porthill), Richard Attenborough (Lexy) and Kieron Moore (Stevens) in *The League of Gentlemen* (1960) (Granada Ventures–Allied Film Makers/Rank)   99
3. Michael Redgrave (General Sir Henry Wilson) and Laurence Olivier (Field-Marshal Sir John French) in *Oh! What a Lovely War* (1969) (Paramount–Accord/Paramount)   100
4. Simon Ward (Winston Churchill) in *Young Winston* (1972) (Sony Pictures Home Entertainment–Open Road/Hugh French/Columbia-Warner)   100
5. Dirk Bogarde (Lieutenant-General Frederick Browning) and Sean Connery (Major-General 'Roy' Urquhart) in *A Bridge Too Far* (1977) (Metro-Goldwyn Mayer Studios–Joseph E. Levine Presents/United Artists)   101
6. 'Fats' and Anthony Hopkins (Corky Withers) in *Magic* (1978) (IDT Entertainment–Joseph E. Levine Presents/20th Century-Fox)   101
7. Ben Kingsley (Mahatma Gandhi) in *Gandhi* (1982) (Columbia Tristar – Indo-British Films in association with International Film Investors, Goldcrest Films International, National Film Development Corporation of India/Columbia–EMI–Warner)   102
8. Denzel Washington (Steve Biko) in *Cry Freedom* (1987) (Universal–Marble Arch Productions/Universal)   102
9. Robert Downey Jr (Charles Chaplin) in *Chaplin* (1992) (Studio Canal–Kinowelt Home Entertainment – Carolco–Le Studio Canal + RSC Video Japan Satellite Broadcasting/Lambeth Production/Guild)   103
10. Anthony Hopkins (C.S. 'Jack' Lewis) and Debra Winger (Joy Gresham) in *Shadowlands* (1993) (Paramount–Shadowlands Productions/Spelling Films International in association with Price Entertainments/Savoy Pictures)   103

X LIST OF PLATES

11 Pierce Brosnan (Archie) and Annie Galipeau (Pony) in *Grey Owl* (1999) (20th Century Fox–Largo Entertainment/Transfilm/Beaver Productions/20th Century-Fox)   104

12 Pete Postlethwaite (Quinlan) and Martin McCann (Jimmy) in *Closing the Ring* (2007) (Universal–Closing the Ring/Prospero Pictures and Scion Films)   104

Series editors' foreword

The aim of this series is to present in lively, authoritative volumes a guide to those film-makers who have made British cinema a rewarding but still under-researched branch of world cinema. The intention is to provide books which are up to date in terms of information and critical approach, but not bound to any one theoretical methodology. Though all books in the series will have certain elements in common – comprehensive filmographies, annotated bibliographies, appropriate illustration – the actual critical tools employed will be the responsibility of the individual authors.

Nevertheless, an important recurring element will be a concern for how the oeuvre of each filmmaker does or does not fit certain critical and industrial contexts, as well as for the wider social contexts which helped to shape not just that particular filmmaker but the course of British cinema at large.

Although the series is director oriented, the editors believe that reference to a variety of stances and contexts is more likely to reconceptualise and reappraise the phenomenon of British cinema as a complex, shifting field of production. All the texts in the series will engage in detailed discussion of major works of the filmmakers involved, but they all consider as well the importance of other key collaborators, of studio organisation, of audience reception, of recurring themes and structures: all those other aspects which go towards the construction of a national cinema.

The series explores and charts a field which is more than ripe for serious excavation. The acknowledged leaders of the field will be reappraised; just as important, though, will be the bringing to light of those who have not so far received any serious attention. They are all part of the very rich texture of British cinema, and it will be the work of this series to give them all their due.

Acknowledgements

This book owes its completion to the efforts of many people. It began as a doctoral thesis, based at the Open University, which was completed in 2009 under the supervision of Professor James Chapman and examined by Professor Jeffrey Richards. Both suggested that the thesis should be made into a book. I am very grateful to Manchester University Press and Matthew Frost for agreeing to do this. The project would not have been possible without its subject Lord Attenborough, who has supported my work from its inception, granting me a succession of interviews and providing me with much additional information. Lord Attenborough's associate, Diana Hawkins, has been helpful in obtaining answers to obscure questions that I posed, while Gabriel Clare-Hunt his personal assistant, has been diligent in arranging meetings. I owe my initial introduction to Lord and Lady Attenborough to my mother-in-law, Margot Dux.

Film historians have played an important role, particularly those regular attendees of the Issues in Film History seminars, held at the Institute of Historical Research. I am particularly grateful to Professor Anthony Aldgate, Dr Mark Glancy, Professor Sue Harper, Dr James C. Robertson, Dr Robert James and Dr Myra Cross for their help and advice. I have also benefited from colleagues Dr Guy Barefoot and Philip Kemp of the Department of History of Art and Film at the University of Leicester. Other individuals have also played important roles. Particular mention must be made of Professor Bert Hogenkamp, who translated several Dutch reviews of *A Bridge Too Far*. Terence Clegg, Charles Chilton and the late Major-General Ian Gill, all willingly imparted their knowledge, experiences and opinions giving me their valuable time for interviews.

Acknowledgement must also be made to the facilities made available from the British Library (including the Colindale Newspaper Library), the National Archives at Kew and the library at the University of Leicester. In particular, the British Film Institute Reading Room and Special Collections Department have offered expert advice within a friendly and encouraging environment. I am also grateful to the administrators of the BECTU History Project for allowing me access to their tapes.

I am especially indebted to James Chapman, who has continued to offer advice and also provide constructive comments on draft chapters. His continued support, academic guidance and generosity of time have all been invaluable.

Family members have remained a backbone of support. My daughter, Dr Emma Dux, has offered encouragement and practical advice, while my son Marcus has always been quick to offer his computer expertise. Special mention must be given to my husband Tony who has consistently provided wonderful support and encouragement. I could not have done this without him.

This book is dedicated to the memory of my parents who, as former passionate cinema goers, showed much interest in my thesis but, sadly, did not live to see its completion.

Introduction

> I really feel that the cinema, as well as being a semi-art form at its highest level, is the greatest means of communication, worldwide, that anybody has yet thought of. (Richard Attenborough, 1969)[1]

Richard Attenborough has long been recognised as a significant figure in British cinema history and film culture. While he enjoyed success in the theatre, it is in the cinema where Attenborough's career has most flourished and where his high regard for the medium, and its global implications and responsibilities, has been evident. After his screen debut in the war-time film *In Which We Serve* (Noël Coward and David Lean, 1942), Attenborough's cinema career developed through acting and later through producing and directing to become one of the industry's most renowned figures: often regarded as the 'grand old man' and 'the voice' of British cinema. Attenborough's entry into production stemmed from a desire to make films that had purpose and social relevance. His teaming with Bryan Forbes in 1959 to form Beaver Films and his later collaboration with Forbes, Basil Dearden, Michael Relph, Jack Hawkins and Guy Green, in creating Allied Film Makers (AFM), established his name as a producer. Both ventures were pivotal to Attenborough in developing his career as a director.

Attenborough's respect for the medium, as exemplified in the above quotation, was his inspiration when producing and directing *Gandhi* (1982), the film for which he is best known. The biographical portrayal of Mahatma Gandhi became a major box-office success, and gained global recognition after receiving eight Academy Awards. While *Oh! What a Lovely War* (1969) and *Shadowlands* (1993) have also been popular successes, others have been either nominated or have received national or international awards.[2] Yet, despite this success, Attenborough's films have up until now largely been neglected, receiving only limited critical attention.

The frequent televising of his films, the longevity of his career and the degree of success achieved all indicate that Attenborough's films form a significant part of British cinema culture. In 2003, Attenborough's eightieth birthday was celebrated by a series of his films at the National Film Theatre, while on television there was a concentrated showing of Attenborough's films, supplemented by a two-part *Arena* programme on his career.[3] Attenborough's influence has also been nationally recognised through his being officially honoured three times, initially as a Commander of the British Empire (CBE), then knighted and finally ennobled for his contributions.

Despite Attenborough's high public standing, however, there appears to be an almost total absence of his films from the critical historiography of British cinema. Scholars appear to be reluctant to engage with Attenborough's films, some expressing their dislike, accusing them, for example, of not being sufficiently cinematic, not pertaining to a distinctive style and for being 'too long and too much'.[4] Another criticism he refutes was proffered by an unnamed American critic who claimed that 'the problem with Attenborough's work is that he is more interested in the content than the execution'.[5] Attenborough does not accept these criticisms of his work. He resolutely maintains that he 'doesn't give a damn' as they are 'missing the point', as his films are intended for a specific purpose, either to implant a message or promote an understanding to a wide audience which the medium of cinema provides.[6] Whatever the reasoning, the continuing neglect of Attenborough's work from scholars leaves a void in film criticism.

Attenborough's films are often personal and greatly influenced by his own knowledge and love of the arts. His preference for reading biographies is reflected in the subject matter of many of his films and in his particular interest in depicting people. He claims that he is 'simply fascinated by the ways in which our lives are affected and moved and redirected in terms of other people's lives'.[7] But Attenborough's preference for biographical films may be a crucial factor in his lack of critical standing. As Steve Neale has observed, the biopic lacks critical 'esteem'. Instead, Neale claims, the biopic has become 'The target of historians and of film critics and theorists alike, it has been the butt of jokes rather more often than it has been the focus of serious analysis.'[8] Attenborough's own belief and affection for the genre has arguably been responsible for establishing the biopic within the pantheon of recent British cinema. He has adapted the genre to benefit his individual purpose. Several of Attenborough's seven biopics cannot be classed as 'pure' biographies, as they draw from other genres and are therefore not genre specific but hybrid forms making them more difficult to classify. Thus

Young Winston (1972) captures elements from the action and historical genres, *Gandhi* and *Chaplin* (1992) from the political and historical, and *Cry Freedom* (1987) the political and action film. *Shadowlands* combines the heritage, historical and romance, *In Love and War* (1996) the historical, romance and war and *Grey Owl* (1999) the historical and nature/conservation film. A similar fusion of genres can be detected in Attenborough's two war films which both offer an anti-war revisionist perspective. *Oh! What a Lovely War* merges the historical and action genres, while *A Bridge Too Far* (1977), in contrast, is a serious and vivid portrayal of war merging with the historical and action genres. *Closing the Ring* (2007), although based on a true story, merges fiction and reality within a romantic setting.

Despite his artistic background, Attenborough's films with the exception of *Oh! What a Lovely War*, cannot be described as innovative in style. Indeed, he accepts with some regret that there are limitations to his style. As he declared in 1993: 'My style is preconceived and, therefore, I think it's sometimes a bit mundane ... I sometimes wish that I had been a bit more unconventional – flamboyant almost.'[9] The convention is also due to his meticulous planning, a trait he attributes to an actor's discipline.[10] This factor also appears to contradict any claim that Attenborough can be considered an *auteur* director. Attenborough has never regarded himself as an *auteur* director, preferring to employ the collective talents of those around him to influence his direction. He explained: 'I don't use film in the way that the great *auteurs* do. I use film, the camera, to record as effectively and as perceptively as I am able what I want to say through the actors.'[11] Attenborough's films, while not noted for their individuality, nonetheless demonstrate certain individual characteristics. His use of what can be termed 'silent dialogue' where the actions and facial expression of the actors establish the depth of emotion required is in contrast to the emphasis placed on intense verbal exchange and action as favoured by many of his contemporaries. The meticulous attention that Attenborough applies to all aspects of casting and the high standard of performance that he obtains is also acknowledged as a characteristic of his films, all of which have contributed to his becoming known as the 'actors' director'.[12] In particular, Attenborough has extracted acclaimed performances from unknown cinema actors in starring roles such as Simon Ward in *Young Winston*, Ben Kingsley in *Gandhi* and Robert Downey Jr in *Chaplin*. It is the resultant performance that Jeffrey Richards has identified as an auterist perspective in Attenborough's work and one that will be further explored in this study.[13]

This study will focus predominantly on Attenborough's ten British films and will focus on three principal areas. First, by analysing production histories I will identify the effects that the variable and destabilising factors of the film industry had on Attenborough's films. By directing twelve films since the 1960s, Attenborough's lengthy directorial career has continued over four decades and into the new millennium, a feat unmatched by many contemporary directors who also began their careers in the 1960s.[14] Second, by exploring the critical and popular reception of Attenborough's films, I will be able to evaluate how he has been regarded as a director by critics and whether this has been significant to his films being considered non-cinematic. Third, by analysing the thematic and stylistic features of Attenborough's films I will demonstrate their position in the wider context of British cinema. Using these criteria I hope to demonstrate that Attenborough is a significant director in the British cinema, whose influential role in the British film industry deserves proper recognition.

Notes

1 *Films and Filming*, 15:9 (June 1969), p. 8.
2 The films include *Oh! What a Lovely War*, *Young Winston*, *A Bridge Too Far*, *A Chorus Line*, *Chaplin* and *Shadowlands*.
3 *Arena*, BBC2, broadcast 24 and 25 August 2003.
4 This was brought home to me forcefully by the response to my paper at the British Screens Now conference at Manchester Metropolitan University, 11–13 September 2006. The consensus seemed to be that Attenborough's films were 'bloated' and 'too long and too much'.
5 Quoted in David Robinson, *Richard Attenborough*, London, 2003, p. 108.
6 Author's interview with Richard Attenborough, Richmond, London, 16 February 2007.
7 Andy Dougan, *The Actor's Director: Richard Attenborough Behind the Camera*, Edinburgh, 1994, p. 31.
8 Steve Neale, *Genre and Hollywood*, London, 2000, p. 60.
9 *The Times*, 14 June 1993.
10 Robinson, *Richard Attenborough*, p. 6.
11 *Ibid.*, p. 5.
12 Andy Dougan, *The Actors' Director: Richard Attenborough Behind the Camera*, Edinburgh, 1994.
13 I am very grateful to Professor Jeffrey Richards for raising this idea during my Ph.D. viva in 2009.
14 James Ivory and Ken Loach are exceptions. Both began directing in the 1960s, with their careers continuing into the new millennium.

On-screen: Attenborough as actor   1

Richard Attenborough's first appearance in the cinema, at the age of 18 in the Noël Coward and David Lean co-directed production, *In Which We Serve* (1942), was one that went almost unnoticed. The naval propaganda production which was loosely based on the bombing of HMS *Kelly* (renamed HMS *Torrin* in the film), under the command of Lord Mountbatten (played as Captain Kinross by Noël Coward), saw Attenborough playing the part of a frightened young stoker who leaves his post at a critical moment as his ship is undergoing attack. The young actor, proud of his film debut, and looking forward to seeing himself on-screen for the first time, attended the première formally attired and accompanied by his parents. His pride, however, was short-lived. When the end credits were played, the name of Richard Attenborough was missing, a production oversight, and a profound disappointment to the actor.[1] The omission was felt more acutely as the name of Juliet Mills, the baby daughter of John Mills, who played Ordinary Seaman Shorty Blake, was included for her tiny cameo role as Blake's daughter. Although Attenborough received immediate apologies from the film's producer, Anthony Havelock-Allan, nothing, he was told, could be done to rectify the situation. Even in the subsequent VHS and DVD releases of the film, Attenborough's role remains to this day uncredited. In many ways this early uncredited debut can also be seen as a metaphor for the similar lack of recognition that Attenborough was to receive as a future director, despite his notable successes.

Richard Samuel Attenborough was born on 29 August 1923 in Cambridge to Mary (née Clegg) and Frederick Attenborough. The family moved to Leicester when Frederick Attenborough became Principal of University College (later the University of Leicester). Although not academically gifted (unlike his two brothers David and John, who followed their father to the University of Cambridge), the young Richard yearned to act, an interest inherited from his mother who was actively involved with an amateur dramatic society, known as the Leicester Little Theatre. The theatre's director, Moyra Hayward, coached Attenborough for his audition for the Royal Academy of Dramatic Art (RADA). The preparation was essential, as Frederick Attenborough stipulated that Richard had to win a scholarship to attend, as the family could not afford the fees. Attenborough's determination to succeed and his ability were proved when he was awarded a Leverhulme Scholarship. To further prove his merit, Attenborough was awarded the Bancroft Silver Medal on leaving RADA in 1942.

Although Attenborough made many successful stage appearances, it was his film acting career, and particularly the associations that he made as a result, that were to be responsible for advancing his career as a filmmaker. The young stoker's part in *In Which We Serve* was secured for Attenborough, while still at RADA, by his newly acquired agent, the American-born Al Parker, who persuaded Noël Coward to cast him. The role was also to prove a valuable platform for developing several significant friendships – the beginning of a lifelong association with Coward (who later became godfather to Attenborough's son Michael), an introduction to Earl Mountbatten whose friendship and position as former Governor General of India would prove invaluable during negotiations with the Indian authorities for *Gandhi*, and with the actor John Mills, whom Attenborough later claimed as his greatest friend, and who was responsible for securing Attenborough his first role as director in *Oh! What a Lovely War* (1969).

Attenborough's acting career was significantly affected and also influenced by the Second World War. After his debut, Attenborough played only two small film roles, in *Schweik's New Adventures* (Carl Lamac, 1943) and *The Hundred Pound Window* (Brian Desmond Hurst, 1943), before being called up for service in the Royal Air Force with the intention of training as a pilot. While Attenborough's film career was interrupted by his service commitments, these breaks were also to prove beneficial. Although Attenborough did not receive his wings, he was, instead, seconded to the RAF Film Unit, which was based at Pinewood Studios. Attenborough was given one of two leading roles in the propaganda film *Journey Together* (John Boulting, 1945), based on a script by Terence Rattigan, a part-documentary drama which focused on the training and fighting experience of a bomber crew. Attenborough plays the part of David Wilton who fails the grade in his training as a pilot and becomes a navigator instead, whereas John Aynesworth (Jack Watling) succeeds. Although intended as a training film, *Journey Together* was also released commercially to enthusiastic reviews. The *News Chronicle*, for instance, considered it as 'one of the most realistic and brilliant films of the war in the air.'[2] The film also included, as a guest star, the American actor Edward G. Robinson. It was Robinson (or Eddy G. as Attenborough preferred to call him) who provided the young actor with one-to-one film acting tuition and to whom Attenborough attributes as having 'patiently taught me the act of acting for the screen.'[3]

A life-long friendship developed between Attenborough and John Boulting. Boulting's manner of directing was clearly one that Attenborough admired and one that he was keen to follow. As he later claimed: 'From him I came to understand that good directors do not shout and stamp around. The crew is an orchestra and the director is their conductor, setting the rhythm, bringing a soloist or a whole section to the fore, each at the appropriate moment, and always remaining firmly in command.'[4] *Journey Together* also enabled Attenborough to receive advice from the documentary filmmaker Humphrey Jennings, who was working in the editing suite at the studios at the same time. Jennings was a willing teacher and encouraged the enthusiastic young Attenborough to learn the cinema skills of camerawork and editing. For Attenborough, Jennings was foremost in showing 'what could be achieved with clever composition, dramatic intercutting and the judicious use of sound effects and music'.[5]

Another unexpected career opportunity came from a visit, while on leave, to the set of *A Matter of Life and Death* at Denham Studios in 1946. The film – part romance, part war, and part fantasy story – involves the story of Peter Carter (David Niven) a pilot who, incredibly, survives jumping out of a burning aircraft without a parachute. Carter's rightful place in the other world is delayed by this error, and the situation becomes further complicated by his romance with an American radio operator, June (Kim Hunter). A heavenly court has to be summoned to decide his fate, which agrees to an extension of his life on earth, helped by the strength of the Anglo-American relationship. The filmmaking partnership of Michael Powell and Emeric Pressburger had earlier provided Attenborough's new wife, Sheila Sim, with her first co-starring film role in *A Canterbury Tale* (Powell, 1944). On this occasion, however, it was Attenborough who was invited to perform a cameo role in the film, playing the credited role of an English pilot who is entering the other world after dying in the war. While it was Attenborough's only acting role for Powell, the experience left him in awe of the man, declaring him as 'easily the best' of all British directors.[6]

After demobilisation, Attenborough signed a long-term contract with the Boulting brothers, John and his twin brother Roy. It was the Boultings who were responsible for giving Attenborough his first leading role as the psychopathic teenage killer Pinkie Brown, in *Brighton Rock*

(John Boulting, 1947). A thriller made in the manner of an American gangster film, *Brighton Rock* focuses on two rival gangs who inhabited the town during the 1930s, one of which is led by Pinkie. After committing a murder, Pinkie decides to court and then to marry a young girl, Rose (Carol Marsh), to prevent her from giving evidence against him, according to the law at the time. When Pinkie fails to persuade Rose to commit suicide, his death, falling off the pier after being pursued, provides a chilling conclusion to the film. Attenborough had played the role of Pinkie in the theatre in his first major stage role, co-starring with Dulcie Gray, which had been well received. The chance for him to reprise his successful stage role was one he relished, despite the initial concerns of Graham Greene, author of the original book and co-author with Terence Rattigan of the screenplay. Greene had disliked the stage adaptation by Frank Hardy, and had asked for his own name to be removed from the credits. For the film, Greene was concerned that Attenborough would not be able to show the required evil of the character. These concerns were later echoed by the film critic, Ivan Mosley, who declared that Attenborough's performance 'is about as close to the real thing as Donald Duck is to Greta Garbo'.[7] Greene, however, found Attenborough's performance particularly pleasing, and endorsed this by sending him a copy of the novel of *Brighton Rock* which was inscribed: 'To my dear Dick, my perfect Pinky [sic]'.[8] A similar view was expressed by the *Monthly Film Bulletin*, who declared that 'Richard Attenborough, as Pinkie, is all Pinkie should be, ruthless, craven, sinister and sadistic, and he looks and lives the part.'[9]

In the post-war crime drama *Dancing with Crime* (John Paddy Carstairs, 1947), husband and wife acted together with Attenborough playing Ted Peters, a former soldier, now working as a London taxi driver, and the boyfriend of Sheila Sim's character (Joy Goodall), who unwittingly becomes involved with a criminal gang. In the comedy thriller, *London Belongs to Me* (Sidney Gilliat, 1948), based on the novel by Norman Collins, Attenborough plays Percy Boon, a motor mechanic who discovers a body in the back of a car. Although innocent of the crime, he is found guilty of murder and is sentenced to be hanged. The residents in the street where he lives gather support to help win him a reprieve. Armed with a signed petition, they march to Parliament, only to find that clemency has already been granted. *London Belongs to Me* was described by *The Times* as 'an extremely entertaining film', declaring that it 'owes its prime distinction to a performance by Mr Richard Attenborough'.[10] It also marks the actor's first encounter with films exploring issues concerning the death penalty, a theme Attenborough was to return to on several occasions. While Attenborough was suitably convincing playing a 17–year-old at the age of 23 in *Brighton Rock*, he had to become even more youthful for the Boulting's next production, *The Guinea Pig* (Roy Boulting, 1948) in which he plays a working-class schoolboy who is removed from his local state establishment and sent to a public school as part of an educational experiment. The absurd youthfulness of Attenborough's early teenage role, when the actor was 24 (which required his bald patch to be covered up) was made all the more apparent as his wife, Sheila Sim, played his house mistress. *The Times*, too, picked up on this point when it observed: 'The mind of Mr Richard Attenborough does all it can to overcome the handicap of the body and voice too old for the part.'[11] Despite an ability to play young characters, Attenborough's youthful looks were becoming a significant hindrance to his career. He recalled: 'The kind of looks I possessed as a young actor, which were greatly responsible for my initial opportunities, ultimately became something of a liability.'[12] A more adult role was found for Attenborough in one of the many cameo roles in *The Magic Box* (John Boulting, 1951), a biopic starring Robert Donat as the pioneering filmmaker William Friese-Green, which was made as a contribution to the Festival of Britain. The large stellar cast boasted several distinguished actors, including Laurence Olivier, Michael Redgrave and Renée Asherson, who would appear later under Attenborough's direction.

Attenborough's career was also suffering from the standard of films he was being offered. While the 1940s were characterised by British films that were both original in subject and displayed artistic merit, the 1950s reflected a state of uncertainty and complacency after the postwar revival and retrospectively become known as the 'doldrums era'.[13] Although more recent appraisal has considered the decade as a transition in which a struggle existed between old and developing art forms, concerns were voiced at the time.[14] Lindsay Anderson, progressive critic and filmmaker, described the cinema of the 1950s as 'snobbish, antiintelligent, emotionally inhibited, wilfully blind to the conditions and problems of the present, dedicated to an out-of-date, exhausted national ideal'.[15] While Anderson's diatribe is clearly an oversimplification, it nevertheless points to the overriding discontent that existed within British cinema at the time and the need for significant changes to be made.

The creative component in film production was a result of several factors, many of which were related to structural alterations within the industry. At the end of the Second World War, two corporations, the Rank Organisation and the Associated British Picture Corporation (ABPC), largely controlled and dominated the British cinema, overriding the presence of British Lion, a smaller company which also played a significant role in the control and creativity of the cinema. In the 1950s, Rank became the dominant force of the two majors as the largest producer-distributor-exhibitor in Britain while ABPC owned the remaining large circuit, ABC, and had control of several smaller studios. British Lion did not have its own cinemas and was therefore not vertically integrated as were Rank and ABPC. Although British Lion attempted to end the Rank–ABPC duopoly as the only serious competitor to the two major consortia, its need for additional finance and the refusal of a loan from the Finance Corporation for Industry (FCI), ended its challenge. This decision had major consequences for the cinema industry and halted plans for an increase in British production in general. It also curtailed the main support for future production in which British Lion was significantly involved. Many smaller production companies closed as a result including Gainsborough Pictures while others, including Ealing, became absorbed within the Rank Organisation.

During the 1950s, many British films were increasingly being funded by American money. The introduction of the Eady Levy in 1951 was an incentive to increase film production in Britain. Formally known as the British Film Production Fund, the levy paid a subsidy to producers and distributors based on a percentage of box-office receipts. To obtain the levy a film had to be made in Britain or a Commonwealth country with 75 per cent of the labour costs paid to British workers. Another incentive was the establishment of the National Film Finance Corporation (NFFC) which was guaranteed a five-year loan of £5 million from the government specifically for production and distribution. The founding of the NFFC in 1948 was initially intended as a short-term policy, but its extension by way of the Cinematograph Films Act of 1957 allowed it to form a significant role in the raising of film finance. During the period 1950–61 the NFFC supplied finance for 366 out of the 730 British first feature films released on the three major circuits.[16]

The decline of Attenborough's acting career was reflected in his own personal judgement. He recalled: 'I was becoming haunted by the stigma of my simpering, whining image. Then one day I read a critic who said I had become the boy-next-door-to dreariness! And suddenly I knew my career was very sick indeed.'[17] This view was reflected in the critical response to an earlier film, *Morning Departure* (Roy Baker, 1950), in which Attenborough was playing a similar role as a stoker to that of his debut performance in *In Which We Serve*. The film concerns the submarine *Trojan*, which is sunk by a floating mine and becomes stranded on the seabed. Eight of the twelve crew escape, the others wait in vain, in the hope of being rescued. While *The Times* declared that Attenborough's character Stoker Snipe, as 'most convincing', the *Monthly Film Bulletin* denounced his role as 'the least satisfying character'.[18] The release of *Morning Departure* was also topical, having closely (and uncannily) mirrored the recent collision in the Thames estuary of the British submarine HMS *Truculent* on 12 January 1950, in which sixty-four people died. The film co-starred John Mills and also featured Nigel Patrick who was to join Attenborough in *The League of Gentlemen* (Basil Dearden, 1960).

While the complexity of the subject matter of *Morning Departure* later led Attenborough to declare that he was 'not ashamed' of the film, he was, however, 'ashamed' of his next venture, *Hell Is Sold Out* (Michael Anderson, 1951). Despite the *Monthly Film Bulletin* asserting that Attenborough's 'boyish and rather comic charm is well exploited' in the film, Attenborough himself rates the film as a particularly low point in his acting career, declaring it 'a pointless thriller'.[19] Other films which shared Attenborough's distain include *The Lost People* (Bernard Knowles, 1948), which he curtly described as 'diabolical', *Gift Horse* (Compton Bennett, 1952) as 'pretty boring', and the comedy *Father's Doing Fine* (Henry Cass, 1952) as 'ludicrous'.[20]

Attenborough's low opinion of these films was also echoed by several unenthusiastic reviews from the *Monthly Film Bulletin*. *Hell Is Sold Out* was 'a curious and rather uncertain mixture of drama and farce', while Bennett's direction in *Gift Horse* had 'surface competence and accuracy, but without feeling or imagination'.[21] Similar criticism was made of *Father's Doing Fine* as an 'artificial and laboured comedy'.[22] Although several of Attenborough's acting roles did not give him acting fulfilment, they were beneficial in other ways. In *Gift Horse* Attenborough acted in a supporting role to Trevor Howard, whom he would later cast in *Gandhi*, while *Father's Doing Fine* allowed Attenborough to witness the work of the art director, Don Ashton, who was to work alongside him on *Oh! What a Lovely War* and *Young Winston*.[23]

The Ship That Died of Shame (Basil Dearden, 1955), an Ealing crime film, brought Attenborough into contact with Dearden and Michael Relph, his future associates at Allied Film Makers. It also marked the start of an important relationship with the producer Michael Balcon. Balcon, a key figure in British cinema, became a close friend and mentor and was particularly influential in Attenborough's move into production. Although the *Monthly Film Bulletin* described Attenborough as 'efficiently unlikeable as the slippery and over-confident Hoskins', the role as Hoskins was to prove a dangerous and near catastrophic one.[24] In the film, Hoskins is killed in the climactic scene, lost overboard when the ship is flooded. The scene, which was filmed without rehearsal due to heavy time constraints, resulted in Attenborough knocking his head and losing consciousness, the injuries requiring hospital admission. As a result, Attenborough was out of work for eight months and left with permanent scars. He later referred to Dearden (whom he greatly admired) as 'the director who'd so nearly killed me'.[25]

Eight O'Clock Walk (Lance Comfort, 1953) was another encounter with the crime genre. Attenborough's character Tom Banning, a taxi driver, is fooled into going to a bombsite as the result of an April Fool's trick played on him by an 8-year-old girl. After the girl is found dead, Banning is accused of murder and has to fight for his innocence. While Attenborough considered the film was 'all right', the *Monthly Film Bulletin* complained that the 'playing is as variable as the script.'[26] The capital punishment theme continued in a comic fashion in *The Dock Brief* (James Hill, 1962), a legal satire which was adapted from the novel by John Mortimer. Attenborough played the part of a convicted man, Herbert Fowle, who confesses to crime of murder, but whose verdict is overruled by the Home Office due to the incompetence of his solicitor Wilfred Morgenhall (Peter Sellers). Attenborough was nominated for a BAFTA for his efforts.[27]

Attenborough's acting career was given a further boost when he reinstated his relationship with the Boulting brothers in 1956. Unlike many of their contemporaries, the Boultings flourished in the 1950s, especially with their satirical comedies which poked fun at certain British institutions. In reviewing *Private's Progress* (John Boulting, 1956), which satirised the army, the *Monthly Film Bulletin* welcomed the 'general irreverence of the film' and considered that Attenborough, along with Terry-Thomas and Kenneth Griffith, all played 'clever character sketches'.[28] The principal characters of *Private's Progress* were reprised in the highly acclaimed *I'm All Right Jack* (1959), also directed by John Boulting, starring Ian Carmichael as Stanley Windrush, which focused on industrial relations and ridiculing both the workers and management in the process. Attenborough's original character, Private Sidney Cox, is elevated to the grander-sounding Sidney de Vere Cox, the change reflecting the higher status the character achieved in his post-war career in industry. Although *I'm All Right Jack* was condemned by the *Monthly Film Bulletin* as having a 'lamentable' treatment, 'facetious' writing and often 'self conscious' acting, *The Times* disagreed and praised the film for having 'much to recommend it', claiming that the cast 'excels itself'.[29] *I'm All Right Jack* became the second most popular film in 1959. Carmichael also starred with Attenborough in *Brothers in Law* (Roy Boulting, 1957), adapted by Henry Cecil, which focuses on the absurdities of the legal system. Both actors play junior barristers who are eager to get themselves established in the profession. The *Monthly Film Bulletin* declared the film as 'the most enjoyable British comedy for some time', with script and performance 'unusually sophisticated'.[30] The Boultings' support was to be a crucial factor, as members of the board of British Lion, in providing Attenborough with financial backing with his first film as a producer, *The Angry Silence* (Guy Green, 1960).

The Baby and the Battleship (Jay Lewis, 1956) marked the first meeting between Attenborough and Bryan Forbes, who were acting together for the first time. Attenborough was also able to witness Forbes's talents as a writer – Forbes had co-written the script with Lewis and Gilbert Hackforth Jones, as well as taking the acting role of Professor Evans. In the comedy, Attenborough played the role of Knocker White, who with his fellow sailors on leave in Naples are forced to look after a baby after it becomes separated from its mother.

Danger Within (Don Chaffey, 1959), a drama set in a Second World War Italian prisoner-of-war camp, starring Richard Todd, provided Attenborough with another opportunity to experience Forbes's writing credentials. The war theme continued in *Dunkirk* (Leslie Norman, 1958), an Ealing production, re-enacted Operation Dynamo, the plan to rescue the British forces from the beaches in France in 1940. Attenborough plays the part of John Holden, a civilian businessman who, although initially unwilling to risk his own life, changes his views and steers his craft towards France to assist in the evacuation.

Another milestone encounter in Attenborough's acting career occurred with *Sea of Sand* (Guy Green, 1958), a war film made as a tribute to the Long Range Desert Group, where the concept of Beaver Films originated and the idea for making *The Angry Silence* was initially proposed. Attenborough, Michael Craig and Green all shared their concerns about the British film industry, and with the standard of films they were being offered. These concerns were similarly felt by the *Monthly Film Bulletin* in its review of the film which, while acknowledging that the film had 'more authority than usual', declared that it fails 'to create more than the conventionally acceptable stock characters.'[31] *The Times* noted the remarks made by Guy Green who considered that in Britain: 'Don't you think that perhaps the war film is our equivalent of the American Western?', which, the newspaper noted, was 'not without its interest, and certainly we go on turning out war film as regularly as Hollywood does Westerns.'[32] Although the film received three BAFTA nominations, Attenborough, as Trooper Brody, was not included. Green also went on to direct Attenborough in *S.O.S. Pacific* (1959). Attenborough played the role of Whitey Mullen against Pier Angeli's character, Teresa. Angeli later co-starred with Attenborough in *The Angry Silence* (Green, 1960).

S.O.S. Pacific also marked a greater significance, as the first meeting of Attenborough and Diana Carter, who despite being regarded as 'the dogsbody' was also in charge of the Photographic Library at Pinewood Studios, and assisted the actor with finding some stills.[33] Carter (later Hawkins) was to become Attenborough's long-term business partner, fulfilling a variety of production and writing roles, their working relationship beginning with *The League of Gentlemen* (Dearden, 1960) with Carter acting as unit publicist for the film.[34]

Although many of the sixty-plus films Attenborough has made during his career are undistinguished, there are plenty that stand out for his noteworthy performances. One, and a personal favourite of Attenborough's, was playing the Regimental Sergeant-Major Lauderdale of the 2nd Battalion African Rifles in *Guns at Batasi* (John Guillermin, 1964). Attenborough prepared for his role thoroughly, seeking help from the legendary RSM Ronald Brittain, the archetypal Regimental Sergeant-Major, as well as training with the Coldstream Guards.[35] The reviews included some highly praiseworthy comments on his performance. For Alexander Walker, Attenborough gives 'the performance of his career', while Cecil Wilson declared that he had 'never done a better job'.[36] *Punch* commented on 'the outstanding performance' by Attenborough and claimed that 'it's a pleasure to find someone who was for so long more or less typecast emerging as a real actor'.[37] Attenborough won a BAFTA for his role.

In *10 Rillington Place* (Richard Fleischer, 1970) Attenborough gave one of his best performances as John Reginald Christie. Based on the book *Ten Rillington Place* by Ludovic Kennedy, the film explores a famous miscarriage of justice and the resultant hanging of an innocent man, Timothy Evans (John Hurt), who is wrongly convicted for murdering his wife Beryl (Judy Geeson). Attenborough regarded the role of Christie as 'the most difficult thing I have ever done in my life'.[38] The issue was especially topical as the possible return of the death penalty was being debated in Parliament at the time, and was one that Attenborough held particularly strong feelings against, being 'resolutely opposed' to its being reinstated.[39] *The Times* declared that Attenborough, 'faced with the difficult task of playing a man who was in every way but one the quintessence even of nothingness, does a superb job'.[40] Filming took place at the actual house where Christie committed his murders, which was demolished soon after the film was completed. Attenborough confessed that he found the role 'deeply disturbing, but in the long term not unrewarding'.[41]

Attenborough claims that there are about twenty films that he regrets doing.[42] Many of these can be attributed to keeping himself financially afloat while he was attempting to get his project *Gandhi* (1982) off the ground. As *Gandhi* was not initiated until 1962, he appears to include in this category such examples as *The Bliss of Miss Blossom* (Joseph McGrath, 1968), a comedy farce in which Attenborough co-starred with Shirley MacLaine, *The Magic Christian* (McGrath, 1969), a comedy starring Ringo Starr and Peter Sellers, a cameo role as Mr Tungay in *David Copperfield* (Delbert Mann, 1969), the war film *The Last Grenade* (Gordon Flemying, 1970) starring Stanley Baker and *And Then There Were None* (Peter Collinson, 1975), based on the Agatha Christie mystery novel. These are all films Attenborough singles out as being 'pretty dreadful', although his salary 'allowed me to pay off my debts, reduce my overdraft to more reasonable proportions and keep going for a further few months'.[43] Attenborough's personal dissatisfaction of participating in mediocre films is evident when he declared: 'You know what you are appearing in is second rate and that you're about tenth rate doing it.'[44]

In the 1960s, after establishing himself as a producer, Attenborough ventured into international films. He gained global recognition for his role as Roger 'Big X' Bartlett in *The Great Escape* (John Sturges, 1963), which was filmed in Bavaria, in which Attenborough was given equal billing with Steve McQueen and James Garner. *The Great Escape*, based on the book by Paul Brickhill, concerns the daring escape plans by Second World War prisoners to escape from the notorious Stalag Luft III prison in Sagan. The film marked an acting career high with Attenborough declaring that it provided 'the massive break which was to elevate my own recently abandoned acting career into a whole new dimension'.[45] The part also paved a path to Hollywood where Attenborough played roles in three films. The first was as Lew Moran, a navigator to James Stewart's pilot in *The Flight of the Phoenix* (Robert Aldrich, 1966), the second, with Steve McQueen in *The Sand Pebbles* (Robert Wise, 1966) based on the novel by Richard McKenna and set aboard a gunboat which is patrolling the a tributary of the Yangtze river in China. The third was a cameo role involving a singing and dancing routine as Albert Blossom, the ringmaster of a circus in *Doctor Dolittle* (Richard Fleischer, 1967) which starred Rex Harrison. In addition to providing Attenborough with much needed finance to sustain the costs of *Gandhi*, he was also critically acclaimed with the last two roles, gaining Golden Globe awards for both.

A number of Attenborough's acting roles achieved personal ambitions. *Brannigan* (Douglas Hiscox, 1975) offered an opportunity for Attenborough to co-star with the Hollywood actor, John Wayne. Wayne played the role of Jim Brannigan, an American police officer who is sent to England to apprehend a Chicago villain, aided by the British police. While not a notable film, it was nevertheless an enjoyable one. David Robinson in *The Times* observes that while 'the comedy comes from Brannigan's encounters with his punctilious British counterpart (Richard Attenborough): the thrills are modest and predictable enough'.[46] As well as being notable for the only film that Wayne made in England, *Brannigan* also provided Attenborough with the enviable opportunity of landing a right-handed punch at Wayne, and felling him as a result. The effect was made somewhat more probable by standing the diminutive Attenborough on a hidden box to enable him to make contact with the tall and robust figure of Wayne.[47]

A chance opportunity for Attenborough was being directed by the renowned Indian director Satyajit Ray, in *The Chess Players* (1977). Ray had invited Attenborough to play the role of General Outram while on a visit to London and Attenborough eagerly accepted. Despite the terrible conditions of filming in the excessive Indian heat in Calcutta without any air conditioning and wearing a costume of a heavy dress uniform, Attenborough relished the opportunity to witness Ray working, declaring: 'What a great privilege, excitement and joy to work in a film of one of the world's greatest directors.'[48] The film also starred Saeed Jaffrey, later to act in *Gandhi*. The film was the first that Ray had made in Hindi, and had its première at the London Film Festival.

The Human Factor (Otto Preminger, 1979), an espionage drama based on the novel by Grahame Greene, was the last film Attenborough was to act in for several years. He played the role of Colonel John Daintry, supported by a cast that included John Gielgud and Derek Jacobi. Attenborough was by now committed financially to *Gandhi* and was relying on his film salary to aid the film. Unfortunately, Preminger, who had raised the money from a number of independent sources, ran out of finance before the end of filming. Attenborough, like all the actors, was only partially remunerated for his efforts, a situation that had yet to be resolved when *Gandhi* was released in 1982.[49]

After a thirteen-year break, during which time Attenborough had dedicated himself to directing, the person who was responsible for persuading him to return to acting was Steven Spielberg in *Jurassic Park* (1993). Spielberg offered Attenborough the role of John Hammond, a grandfather and billionaire owner of Jurassic Park, an island on which a colony of living dinosaurs has been cloned. It was the third time that Spielberg had asked him to act and the opportunity for Attenborough arose at the post-production stage of *Chaplin* (1992). Spielberg was so determined to entice Attenborough back to acting that he even offered to schedule the film around Attenborough's commitments to *Chaplin*. Although Attenborough's ego was flattered, the long break from acting resulted in doubts over his confidence. While he later recalled that he 'loved the experience', he confessed he was 'frightened to death prior to my first day.'[50] It appears his fears were groundless. Ian Johnstone declared that 'two elements of the film are excellent: the dinosaurs and Dickie Attenborough. The latter plays John Hammond, nasty in the novel but now "a cross between Ross Perot and Walt Disney", according to his director.'[51] Once again, another important contact was made. The cast included the child actor Joseph Mazzello (playing Tim Murphy, Hammond's grandson), whom Attenborough would later cast in *Shadowlands* (1993) in the leading role as the young Douglas Gresham. Spielberg also seemed determined to prolong Attenborough's acting career. Although Attenborough's character was due to be killed off in the film, Spielberg decided against this and invited Attenborough to reprise his character for the sequel: *The Lost World: Jurassic Park* (1997).

The successful return to acting encouraged Attenborough to take on more and diverse roles. In Hollywood, *Miracle on 34th Street* (Les Mayfield, 1994), a remake of the 1947 film (which had starred Edmund Gwenn in the leading role), was an easy vehicle for Attenborough who played the part in his natural and very avuncular manner. Taking on the starring role of Kriss Kringle, who has to prove in a court that he is the real Santa Claus, proved to be 'enormous fun' for Attenborough, although he was disappointed in the reaction to the film.[52] He recalled: 'It was a good performance, and a very credible performance in an incredible part really. I did one or two scenes quite well. But because it was not far from my own persona of bonhomie it did not get the credit.'[53] Philip Strick claimed that 'His celebrity status and impermeable jolliness, while never quite other-worldly enough, render him the ideal Santa Claus.'[54] George Perry was also impressed, declaring that 'The crowning triumph of this remake ... is Richard Attenborough. He is so good as Santa Claus that it is as if he was born to play him.'[55]

Attenborough's earlier elevation to the peerage in 1993, as Lord Attenborough of Richmond-Upon-Thames, together with his close association with royalty, particularly Diana, Princess of Wales, made his new position particularly fitting for his next role. Attenborough was cast as Sir William Cecil, the first Lord Burghley, in *Elizabeth* (Shekhar Kapur, 1998), a biographical portrayal of the early years of the reign of Elizabeth I which starred Cate Blanchett. Philip French, in observing a likeness between Blanchett's portrayal and the princess, remarked that 'comparisons with Princess Diana are encouraged by the casting of her mentor, Richard Attenborough, as Elizabeth's wise advisor.'[56] Attenborough's return to acting in the 1990s (*A Miracle on 34th Street, Jurassic Park, The Lost World: Jurassic Park, Elizabeth and Puckoon*) in roles where he more or less played an avuncular version of himself, seem to have elevated him to a 'national treasure' status in the eyes of critics and audiences.

Attenborough's last role, despite closely resembling his working life, was not a success. *Puckoon* (Terence Ryan, 2002) is a comedy set in Ireland, based on Spike Milligan's book, in which Attenborough is cast as the writer-director (although Attenborough has never ventured into writing). Like in his debut film, Attenborough remains nameless, this time in his character's role, not as an actor. Described as 'a terrible piece of Irish whimsy', by Philip French, and citing Attenborough as 'the head of an ill-used cast', the actor is rarely seen on-screen, his voice heard from beyond the camera as he is heard directing his characters as a narrator.[57]

Despite his long and often illustrious acting career, it is behind the camera, as a filmmaker, both as a producer, but principally as a director, where Attenborough has achieved his greatest successes and also realised his highest personal fulfilment. However, without gaining a wide range of experience in the many varied roles he undertook, the important contacts which he made and the subsequent support he was to receive from these associations, his career as a filmmaker would unlikely have achieved the level of success that followed.

Notes

1. Author's meeting with Richard Attenborough, 5 June 2003, Richmond, Surrey.
2. James Chapman, *The British at War: Cinema State and Propaganda, 1939–45*, London, 1998, p. 157.
3. Richard Attenborough and Diana Hawkins, *Entirely Up to You, Darling*, London, 2008, p. 92.
4. *Ibid.*
5. *Ibid.*, p. 93.
6. Author's interview with Attenborough, 16 February 2007.
7. *Daily Express*, 9 January 1948.
8. Tom Hibbert, 'Has Also Been Known to Act', *Empire*, 67 (January 1995), p. 69.
9. *Monthly Film Bulletin*, 14:168 (December 1947), p. 171.
10. *The Times*, 12 August 1948.
11. *The Times*, 25 October 1948.
12. Attenborough, 'Our "Silence" Was Golden', *Sunday Telegraph*, 22 August 1965.
13. The term was first introduced by Raymond Durgnat, *A Mirror for England: British Movies from Austerity to Affluence*, London, 1970, p. 140, in reference to 1950s war films.
14. Sue Harper and Vincent Porter, *The British Cinema of the 1950s: The Decline of Deference*, Oxford, 2003, p. 1.
15. Lindsay Anderson, 'Get Out and Push', in Tom Maschler (ed.), *Declaration*, London, 1957, p. 157.
16. John Hill, *Sex, Class and Realism: British Cinema 1956–1963*, London, 1997, p. 41.
17. Peter Evans, 'The Growing Up of Richard Attenborough', *People*, 23 March 1969.

18 *The Times*, 24 February 1950; *Monthly Film Bulletin*, 17:194 (February/March 1950), p. 25.
19 *Monthly Film Bulletin*, 18:210 (July 1951), p. 297; Attenborough and Hawkins, *Entirely Up to You, Darling*, p. 149.
20 David Robinson, *Richard Attenborough*, London, 2003, p. 27.
21 *Monthly Film Bulletin*, 18:210 (July 1951), p. 297; 19:223 (August 1952), p. 105.
22 *Monthly Film Bulletin*, 19:225 (October 1952), p. 143.
23 *Gift Horse* has often been referred to incorrectly as 'The Gift Horse'. There is no definite article in the title of the film.
24 *Monthly Film Bulletin*, 22:257 (June 1955), p. 85.
25 Attenborough and Hawkins, *Entirely Up to You, Darling*, p. 210.
26 Robinson, *Richard Attenborough*, p. 28; *Monthly Film Bulletin*, 248:21 (March 1954), p. 39.
27 At the time BAFTA was known as the Society of Film and Television Arts (SFTA). It became known as BAFTA in 1976.
28 *Monthly Film Bulletin*, 23:267 (April 1956), p. 44.
29 *Monthly Film Bulletin*, 26:309 (October 1959), p. 133; *The Times*, 17 August 1959, p. 12.
30 *Monthly Film Bulletin*, 24:279 (April 1957), p. 42.
31 *Monthly Film Bulletin*, 25:299 (December 1958), p. 158.
32 *The Times*, 27 October 1958, p. 12.
33 Attenborough and Hawkins, *Entirely Up to You, Darling*, p. 204.
34 *Ibid.*, p. 212.
35 Attenborough, *In Search of Gandhi*, p. 116. Brittain is misspelled here as Britten.
36 *Evening Standard*, 24, September 1964; *Daily Mail*, 25 September 1964.
37 *Punch*, 17 October 1964.
38 Hibbert, 'Has Also Been Known to Act', p. 69.
39 Attenborough, *In Search of Gandhi*, p. 147.
40 *The Times*, 29 January 1971.
41 Attenborough, *In Search of Gandhi*, p. 148.
42 Hibbert, 'Has Also Been Known to Act', p. 71.
43 Robinson, *Richard Attenborough*, p. 34.
44 Hibbert, 'Has Also Been Known to Act', p. 71.
45 Attenborough and Hawkins, *Entirely Up to You, Darling*, p. 209.
46 *The Times*, 13 June 1975.
47 Author's meeting with Attenborough, 15 February, 2007.
48 N.K. Ghosh, 'A Privilege to work with Ray – Attenborough', *Screen* (India), 3 June 1977.
49 *In Search of Gandhi*, pp. 165–6.
50 Andy Dougan, *The Actors' Director: Richard Attenborough behind the Camera*, Edinburgh, 1994, p. 144.
51 *Sunday Times*, 18 July 1993.
52 Hibbert, 'Has Also Been Known to Act', p. 68.
53 Robinson, *Richard Attenborough*, p. 92.
54 *Sight and Sound*, New Series, 5:1 (January 1995), p. 50.
55 *Sunday Times*, 11 December 1994.
56 *Observer*, 4 October 1998.
57 *Observer*, 6 April, 2003.

Attenborough as producer: Beaver Films and Allied Film Makers | 2

The start of Richard Attenborough's career as a filmmaker began during the 1950s, a decade which was his most prolific as an actor but one in which the British cinema entered a period of stagnation. The sharing of his concerns with fellow actor Bryan Forbes resulted in their decision to take control over their films by forming their own production company, Beaver Films. Forbes explained: 'The need to have a professional partnership stemmed from a growing and shared dissatisfaction with the state of the film industry and our respective roles within the industry.'[1] By employing Attenborough's financial acumen and Forbes's writing ability they combined their individual talents to form a creative production team with Beaver Films and later, as part of the independent production company, Allied Film Makers (AFM).

The return to making indigenous British films was conducive to the concept of small independent companies. Several companies were set up at the time including Woodfall Films, (1958), Beaver Films (1959) and the cooperative ventures of Bryanston Films and AFM in 1959. The newly formed companies all offered their own contribution to the changing British cinema of the time. John Hill comments: 'Woodfall provided the new working-class realism, Bryanston and AFM developed the "social problem" film, Hammer [formed in 1932] offered horror, while the "new comedy" of the *Carry On* films and the Boulting brothers emerged through independent companies as well.'[2] Beaver Films is also acknowledged. Derek Threadgall describes *The Angry Silence* as 'a remarkable film for its time. It epitomises the true spirit of independent film-making in Britain and the courage and resilience of those involved with its production.'[3]

The concept of Beaver Films originated during an enforced break in the filming of *Sea of Sand* caused by a sandstorm in the Libyan desert. Attenborough, in conversation with his co-star Michael Craig, and Guy Green, the director, found that they all shared similar frustrations. He recalled: 'We were all dirty, fed-up and disenchanted with the future. I was making the film because I was broke, and I was quite determined that it would be my last appearance as an actor.'[4] Craig related the outline of a book he was writing that was based on an idea conceived by him and his brother, Richard Gregson, which he thought would offer a suitable film treatment. The story, concerning a factory worker shunned by his fellow workers by being 'sent to Coventry', was, coincidentally, similar in theme to a draft treatment Forbes had attempted, but abandoned, entitled, 'A Dangerous Game', in which a victim's suffering had pushed him to commit suicide. Attenborough and Forbes had earlier attempted to enter into production with a project entitled 'No Cover for Harry', concerning an English cameraman working with the Army Film Unit who was killed at Anzio, but it had failed to generate sufficient interest. Another project, a joint Anglo-German joint film production, focused on the sinking of the *Bismarck* but failed to attract finance from either country. The British backer's refusal was, according to Alexander Walker, based on a fear that the filmmakers might 'take a pro-German line because it was a co-production'.[5]

Attenborough was convinced that his 'personal salvation' lay in becoming a producer. The potential of Gregson's concept inspired him to persuade Forbes to reignite his interest and write a further screenplay, which developed into *The Angry Silence*.[6] Craig, who had originally planned to star in his own production, stepped down to allow Attenborough and Forbes full control of the project. Funding, however, was difficult to obtain. Attenborough eventually went to British Lion 'in despair', the board of which included the two partnerships of the Boultings, and the screenwriter/producers Frank Launder and Sidney Gilliat. While the Boultings had been influenced by the response to their own film, *I'm All Right Jack*, which explored the volatile subject of unions in a satirical manner, the board of British Lion were doubtful whether the same success could be achieved with *The Angry Silence*.[7]

Initially the board refused both the original costing of £140,000 and its revised prediction of £125,000 but agreed to support the film if the budget could be reduced to below £100,000. To prevent any cuts in the screenplay, fearing destruction of the whole concept of the story, Attenborough and Forbes agreed on a deal in which they were to receive no fee for co-producing but would be entitled to a percentage of the profits. Attenborough was offered 9 per cent and Forbes 7, with an additional £1,000 for the screenplay. Craig, Gregson, Pier Angeli (the female co-star) and Bernard Lee (in a supporting role) waived their fee in exchange for a percentage of the profits. As a consequence of these measures, the budget was reduced to £97,000, backed 70 per cent by

British Lion (the distributors) and 30 per cent by the National Film Finance Corporation (NFFC).[8]

Financial difficulties also affected the casting. Kenneth More vacillated on his agreement to play the lead role of Tom Curtis and withdrew from the film ten days prior to the start of filming, having received a better financial offer. The timing of More's refusal and the estimated cost of finding a replacement resulted in Attenborough undertaking the role himself. Forbes also took on the cameo role of a reporter. British Lion made no further stipulations for the film allowing Attenborough and Forbes full creative autonomy. The benefits that this policy provided and the significance of the freedom they were allowed were appreciated by Attenborough:

> We had absolutely no interference, whatsoever. They never asked to see the rushes. They tried to persuade us to do things on the final cut, but the decision ultimately was ours. This achieved for the first time in England a degree of freedom for the independent filmmaker that just didn't exist prior to that. And because the picture was an enormous critical success, it pioneered this way of making pictures, both in terms of freedom and of content.[9]

Plans for the new venture were kept secret for several months until a publicity notice from Shepperton Studios revealed the imminent start of filming and the launching of Beaver Films. Nevertheless, Attenborough encountered opposition due both to the film's subject matter and to his and Forbes's status as actors. He later recalled the range of objections he encountered: 'Dealing with a social subject in this way will empty the cinemas. Nobody will be interested. Anyway, who the hell are you? You're an actor; actors have no brains, etc. etc.'[10]

Filming commenced on 1 September 1959 and finished on 28 October, taking place on location in Reavell's factory in Ipswich and at Shepperton Studios. *The Angry Silence* concerns the story of a factory worker Tom Curtis (Attenborough) whose solo stand in refusing to join his colleagues in an unofficial strike, instigated by an outsider and *agent provocateur* Travers (Alfred Burke), results in his victimisation. 'The angry silence' of being 'sent to Coventry' both isolates Curtis at work and affects his family who suffer the consequences, including a brick being thrown through a window and the son Brian being tarred and feathered for being the son of a 'dirty scab'. When Curtis is involved in a hit-and-run incident by two other workers and loses an eye, his former reticent lodger Joe (Craig) takes control of the situation, admonishing the culprits and publicising the seriousness of Curtis's injury, forcing the workers to see reason.

The film was helped by a strong supporting cast which provided several strong acting performances (including a resolute one from Attenborough) and some clever editorial cuts, the most notable being in the scene where Curtis's conversation with Brian is dramatically cut to reveal him positioned in the noisy works canteen. The success of this device in the film encouraged Attenborough to use it in his own production of *Oh! What a Lovely War*.

In Britain the reviews were predominantly in favour of the film. Penelope Houston in *Sight and Sound* admired *The Angry Silence* for having 'an air of drive of energy about it enough to recharge the flat batteries of half-a dozen studio vehicles'.[11] Dilys Powell in the *Sunday Times* considered the film was 'a brave one to make and it has been bravely made'.[12] Donald Gomery in the *Daily Express* was ecstatic in his comments:

> Humbly and most sincerely I salute today the courage and, yes, the genius of Richard Attenborough and a brilliant new team of British filmmakers who have produced a story that will shock you and shame you, make you laugh but more often bring you near to tears – a topical, controversial, vitriolic masterpiece.[13]

Derek Hill in the *Tribune* provided a rare dissenting voice in his overt criticism of the film claiming that it failed to fulfil its aims: 'The film pushes up the temperature in the cinema; but once the heat is off, and the throbbing over, what emerges?'[14] Hill's criticism in the left-wing newspaper was followed by condemnation from trades unions. In South Wales, where the miners' union owned many of the cinemas, attempts were made to ban the film. Will Whitehead, the communist president of the Welsh miners' union, argued that the film 'sets out to denigrate and deride the trade union movement, especially at local level'.[15] To prevent further attempts at denigrating the film Attenborough travelled to Wales and 'begged them [the miners] to judge it [the film] on its merits' before the showing, a gesture that resulted in a standing ovation at the end of the film.[16] In Ipswich, where the film was made, four hundred union members defied a boycott and shook hands with Attenborough after the performance to mark their approval. Attenborough was also cheered after he claimed that the film 'stands up for the right of an individual to maintain his point of view and belief'.[17] A different union perspective was raised by Howard Goorney, at Wyndham's Theatre, who complained that a small part in the film was played by a non-union man to 'the disgust of many Equity members'.[18] Although ignoring Goorney's comment Attenborough defended the film in a reply letter claiming that '*The Angry Silence* does not attack trade unions, only those who would attempt to exploit them or who, by their apathy, allow them to be exploited'.[19]

Although profits were slow to materialise, by 1971 the film had 'earned £58,000 for its makers', thus justifying the faith of its backers.[20] For Attenborough the film confirmed that he enjoyed the role of producer. 'I discovered that I adored producing and planning; the administration required to call people together and solve problems.'[21] He later revealed what he and Forbes had learned as producers:

> First and foremost I have found that a producer must be a good judge of people. Why? Because he must be able to delegate his work and rely on it being done efficiently. Bryan and I have picked a first rate team to help us make our film. Each one knows his own job backwards and cared about the final overall result. If the film is a success it will be because of this enthusiasm which was never in doubt.[22]

While *The Angry Silence* tends not to be seen as belonging to the New Wave movement, it was nevertheless comparable through its realism and social commentary, which privileged the working classes. The film also added a further dimension by breaking a previously held taboo by depicting politics as seen through its exploration of the relationship between unions, workers and managers. In this respect the film represented the embodiment of independent filmmaking by taking on a courageous subject which resulted in a commercial success. Peter Hutchings also observes that 'with its mainstream director [Green], an-already established male star [Attenborough] and an imported foreign actress in the form of Pier Angeli, it can be seen as a clearer successor to *A Room at the Top* than any of the New Wave films.'[23] Critically the film was also successful. It was the first British entry at the Berlin Film Festival, where it won the International Film Critics award and also the prize awarded by the International Catholic Film Organisation.[24] The film was also noted for its uniqueness. In 1965 Attenborough declared that '*The Angry Silence* was an experiment never since repeated'. He added: 'The film industry does not like its taboos being broken. But the independent filmmaker is here to stay.'[25] For Alexander Walker, the film's importance lies in the impact it had for its producers:

> [T]he film's success in establishing its theme with such force and timeliness in a cinema that had hitherto fought shy of political involvement was much greater than the box-office could gauge. More important to its makers' future, it established Forbes and Attenborough as people to reckon with on the production side, 'artists' who could turn to films with business-like dispatch and eventual profit.[26]

Further reaction came from Michael Balcon, who praised Attenborough's first attempts at production but revealed a political difference between them. In a letter to Attenborough Balcon commented, 'how good it was to see a film with a strong point of view. The fact that the film's view is not entirely mine makes it an even better film. It is wonderfully produced and directed and individual performances are outstanding.'[27] Attenborough's reply is of particular interest as it asserts his own political position with the film and also his confusion with Balcon's views:

> I am puzzled that you disagreed with some of what I had to say. I had always believed that we saw eye to eye on such matters. Our targets were apathy, mob violence, unofficial strikes and subversion, and if they showed otherwise, then we failed. All that we wish to uphold was the right of the minority who told its own views without fear of persecution.[28]

Balcon had taken a particular interest in Attenborough and Forbes's previous attempts to enter production. In 1958 he had written to Attenborough inviting him to be considered as part of a new venture claiming that 'I consider [this] to be a very interesting scheme.'[29] The reply reflected Attenborough's keenness in the project:

> I can only say how touched I was you should consider me as a potential member of your new scheme. And I must admit I was even more thrilled when you suggested that, if I should have any new projects in which I thought you might be interested, I should not hesitate to talk to you about them.[30]

Attenborough was considered to be a serious contender for membership of the proposed cooperative, unofficially known at the time as United Productions Limited. The producer Maxwell Setton sent a list of suitable names to Balcon. By Attenborough's name he had written: 'has innumerable successes to his credit and has just entered independent production in association with Bryan Forbes, one of the foremost screenwriters in the United K'. Although the letter was written before *The Angry Silence* was released, it nevertheless reflects the high regard that Attenborough was held in at the time.[31]

While Attenborough and Forbes did not join Balcon's group (which later became Bryanston), they instead joined another cooperative, Allied Film Makers, which was established on 30 September 1959, six months after Bryanston. The two cooperatives were similar in structure but had several marked differences. Like Bryanston, AFM was formed with the principal aim of securing distribution rights for its films, which was the purpose of its link to the Rank Organisation. Bryanston, which received backing from Lloyds Bank, was similarly linked to British Lion. Walker outlined AFM's financial arrangement in detail:

AFM liaised with the Rank Organisation, which promised them a guarantee of £143,000, while the National Provincial Bank, who were Rank's financiers, guaranteed advances to AFM producers up to five times the sum, to £840,000. (Actually Rank's guarantee was in two parts: £64,000 on setting up the company and a further £79,000 when they found a fifth partner, which they never did.)[32]

The arrangement with Rank relied on a rapid turnaround. As Walker explained: 'The crucial proviso, however, was that the AFM films should be a big enough success quickly enough to keep the box-office receipts flowing back to the principal financiers who, in turn, would keep the revolving fund topped up.'[33]

There has been some confusion over the exact composition of the AFM organisation. Walker claims that Sydney Box originally conceived the idea for AFM but illness prevented him joining the scheme.[34] However, according to Attenborough, it was Jack Hawkins who instigated the idea in collaboration with Dearden who wanted to direct *The League of Gentlemen*.[35] Similar information is also given in Jack Hawkins's autobiography.[36] There is also contradictory evidence regarding the composition of the organisation and its division into partnerships. Walker asserts that five partnerships were originally planned, but Box's departure reduced this to four. 'Attenborough and Forbes; Relph and Dearden; Jack Hawkins; and Hawkins's [unnamed] brother. Guy Green later joined the Forbes-Attenborough group.'[37] Attenborough claims never to have heard of Hawkins's brother. He also asserts that Green came later, not as Walker claimed, joining 'the Forbes-Attenborough group' but as an equal partner.[38] This concurs with the announcement of the launch of the company in *The Times*, which named the six founding members as individuals.[39] *The Times* also claimed that each of the founding members (as with Bryanston) had raised £5,000 with the Rank Organisation having 'a substantial interest in the company'.[40] It also presented the objectives of the consortium as outlined by the company's statement:

> Refuting the persistent rumours that the British film industry is a dying concern, some of the top creative talent in Britain has combined to form Allied Film Makers. The company has a capital of £1m. for its programme of pictures. It is composed of people all actively involved in the creative side of film making.[41]

The £1 million that had been negotiated between AFM and John Davis of Rank allowed 'internal autonomy'. Leslie Baker was engaged as company secretary, an appointment that Forbes credits as 'being the main architect in deciding how the enterprise should be structured'.[42]

Forbes recalled that as they were a small board 'decisions had to be unanimous' but afterwards, control was then divided. He explained:

> Once the vote to give approval on script and budget had been cast, then the individuals or partnerships actually making the film had total artistic control. The finished product was then distributed by the Rank Organisation at a fee of 27½ per cent, 2½ per cent of which was returned to Allied Film Makers.'[43]

The aims of AFM were widely reported and welcomed by other newspapers. An article in the *Evening News* revealed that the group 'plan to short-circuit the influence of the money-bag boys and further make sure that the first cut from the profits comes to the chaps who make the pictures – not the fellows who handle them to the cinemas'.[44] Ivor Adams in the *Star* commented that *The League of Gentlemen* 'represents an attempt by the people who really count in the film business, the film-makers themselves, to win independence of the money bags of Wardour Street, to show that brains and ability are more important than cash'.[45]

The films made by AFM were primarily concerned with social issues. While Attenborough and Forbes demonstrated their interest in this context with *The Angry Silence*, Dearden and Relph had a longer and more established association. Their collective time at Ealing included films such as *The Blue Lamp* (1950) (juvenile delinquency) and *The Ship that Died of Shame* (post-war adjustments). All the members (with the exception of Green) combined together for *The League of Gentlemen*, after which the two production partnerships worked independently. While Dearden and Relph were responsible for *Man in the Moon* (1960), *Life for Ruth* (1962) and *Victim* (1961), Attenborough and Forbes combined for *Whistle Down the Wind* (1961) and *Séance on a Wet Afternoon* (1964) and, separate from AFM and Beaver, *The L-Shaped Room* (Forbes, 1962).

The League of Gentlemen was considered a suitable first vehicle for AFM as it combined and utilised the talents of its members: Hawkins and Attenborough acting, Forbes acting and producing, Relph producing and Dearden directing. Carl Foreman had originally commissioned the script from Forbes as a vehicle for Cary Grant who later declined the role. Foreman sold the non-credited script to Basil Dearden in 1959 who intended to produce the film with Relph. However, after discovering Forbes as the true author, and with Dearden's wish to include Attenborough as an actor in the film, it was decided to form AFM as 'a consortium of filmmakers which would distribute the films that the members made themselves, and also those produced by outside talents'.[46]

The League of Gentlemen, a comedy, concerns a group of wartime army personnel who become disillusioned and frustrated with post-war society. All the participants can be loosely classed as criminals in their past military lives, who are missing the thrills of crime in the present mood of austere society in which they live. The frustration is exemplified in the film by Norman Hyde (Hawkins) whose personal disdain becomes evident when he vents: 'I served my country well as a regular soldier and was suitably rewarded after twenty-five years by being declared redundant.' Under the proposal suggested by Hyde, the selected group are to combine forces (and expertise) to take part in a bank robbery, planned with military precision, with each participant offered the incentive of receiving the large sum of £100,000 for their efforts.

In keeping with the era, *The League of Gentlemen* followed the moral code of conventionality with the plan being thwarted by the 'good' policeman, helped by an observant boy who notes the car number plate at a moment of unguarded complacency by the 'bad' robbers, with rightful justice succeeding. In reflecting post-war apathy the film represents the disillusionment felt in the film industry at the time. It also uses itself as a vehicle to acknowledge publicly the financial help that AFM was receiving to back the film (and British cinema) by including the name of their backers in the script. Major Race (Nigel Patrick) declares, after hearing that they are to rob a bank: 'I do hope he hasn't the National Provincial in mind – they're being awfully decent to me at the moment.' The film is notable for displaying some interesting perspectives with its casting. As well as including some very well-known character actors including Roger Livesey, Nigel Patrick (whose part was originally written for Trevor Howard), Terence Alexander, Kieron Moore and Norman Bird (and an early film appearance by Oliver Reed), there was evidence of 'nepotism' by the inclusion of both Dearden's wife, Melissa Stribling, and Forbes's wife, Nanette Newman, among the actors, ostensibly to save AFM money. More significantly the film is also an indicator for the start of Hawkins's illness (diagnosed as throat cancer) that would severely curtail his acting career. During filming Hawkins suffered acute changes to his voice, and filming had to be delayed while he underwent treatment. On his return there was such a marked change in the sound of his voice that Dearden was forced to restage some of the sequences. Despite these difficulties *The League of Gentlemen* was completed on time and within its allotted budget.

The film was released at the Odeon, Marble Arch (owned by the Rank Organisation) on 7 April 1960. It was mostly well received by both critics and audiences. The *Guardian* commented that the film 'is, almost, without reserve, a delight' while for the *Daily Herald* the actors 'are very well cast'.[47] Fred Majdalany in the *Daily Mail* was ecstatic in his praise, observing it was 'so devilishly well worked out and directed (by Basil Dearden) that I would need a lot of convincing that it is not the best comedy-thriller to come up in the past decade'.[48] Dilys Powell in the *Sunday Times* greeted the film: 'Another new group: one welcomes, one applauds *The League of Gentlemen*.' Like Majdalany, Powell also noted the similarity in theme to *Seven Thieves* as 'an elaborate concerted plan to carry out a vast improbable robbery.' Although Powell commented that it was slow to start it was 'full of ingenious and enjoyable excitements once the real business begins'.[49] The *Sunday Dispatch* claimed the film was 'often exciting, mostly witty – and always wickedly, shamefully fascinating'.[50] *The Times*, acknowledging the film as the first production of AFM, was prompted to 'extend a hearty greeting to the newcomers. If their first offering begins somewhat tentatively, it gathers a good deal of momentum, is uncharitably witty and unusually well acted.'[51] David Robinson in the *Financial Times* commented on the 'censor-teasing irrelevancies, and for its occasional failure to elucidate characters and motives' but claimed that they never 'seriously impair enjoyment at the film's chosen level of unsophisticated adventure'.[52] The *Monthly Film Bulletin* praised some aspects of the film and dismissed others but had most difficulty in deciding what sort of film it was:

> As a study of a certain strata of society, then, the film lacks a strong centre and a firm point of view – one is never quite sure how seriously the parody of the officer role is intended, especially in the ambiguous, obligatorily moral ending.
>
> Judged as a thriller, it is more successful: the two big set pieces (the army camp robbery and the raid itself) are quite skilfully put together, although the former suffers from an overdose of Army humour.[53]

The League of Gentlemen was to prove a financial success for the consortium, although the filmmakers received no money until the film went into profit.[54] It cost £192,000 and by mid-1971 its profit was over £250,000.[55] The film was also critically rewarded at the eighth international cinema festival in San Sebastian where it received the Zulueta Prize for the principal actors.[56] *The Times* announced that the accolade was an 'unusual decision' as the judging committee had decided to award the prize to all 'the eight actors as a "team" in the film'. As a downside to its moral victory, the film was also reputedly studied several times by the gang who carried out the Great Train Robbery in 1963, although unlike the film, the robbers resorted to violence.[57]

Although Attenborough and Forbes had been successful with both of their initial enterprises under Beaver Films and AFM, later films failed to maintain the same degree of success. AFM's second film to be released, a comedy, *Man in the Moon* (1960) also directed by Dearden, did not directly involve Attenborough although Forbes was involved as joint scriptwriter with Relph. The spoof science-fiction film, starring Kenneth More (one of the most popular film actors at the time), Shirley-Anne Field and Michael Hordern, and containing many Ealing comedy traits, was not a success. Despite a strong publicity and advertising campaign, the film was unable to capitalise on the current interest in space travel. The £202,000 cost of *Man in the Moon* had not been recovered by mid-1971 with a shortfall of £37,000.[58]

A further division of the members occurred with the next productions. While Relph and Dearden were occupied with *Victim*, Attenborough and Forbes were producing *Whistle Down the Wind* (1961) the second production made by Beaver Films and distributed by AFM who had purchased the rights for the film. *Whistle Down the Wind* is based on a novel by Mary Hayley Bell. It stars the child actress, Hayley Mills, the daughter of Mary Hayley Bell and Attenborough's actor friend, John Mills. The film concerns the story of three children who come across an escaped prisoner who through his surprised reaction to them, 'Jesus Christ', makes them think he is the real Christ. They continue to look after him in secret, supplying him with food and drink until the authorities eventually find out and he is arrested. The film represents debuts for Attenborough as a solo producer and Forbes as a director and is also notable for launching the film career of Alan Bates who plays the escapee. Initially, Forbes was deemed too inexperienced to direct the film and Green was appointed instead. Forbes, showing his disappointment at being 'rejected' as first-choice director, then declined to write the screenplay, which was scripted by Keith Waterhouse and Willis Hall. Green, however, was offered a more lucrative project and asked to be released from his contract, his late withdrawal causing severe problems for AFM. More significantly, there was the possibility of financial ruin for Beaver as, by this time, many of the crew had been engaged and preparations made.[59] The appointment of Forbes as director appeared to be the only solution for the film to continue. The Mills family, however, protecting their daughter's interests, were still reluctant to accept Forbes and only with Attenborough's pleading and Forbes's convincing them of his ability did they relent. The separation of roles between Attenborough as producer, and Forbes as director, was the first time the pair had worked independently. In *Films and Filming*, Attenborough explained how it worked:

> I think it would be correct to say that in terms of the assembly of the production and the overall control of its working, the producer has the final say, while unquestionably on the floor in terms of the actual shooting the director is 'boss'. Nevertheless, I would emphasize that so

far we have never reached a point whereby one of us wished to go one way and the other another.[60]

The film's success quickly meant that it recouped its budget, improving on the profits of *The League of Gentlemen*.

Dearden and Relph were involved with two notable social problem films released by AFM, *Victim* (1961) which focused on concerns over homosexuality, and *Life for Ruth* (1962), which explores the ethical question of a child whose life can only be saved, following an accident, through a blood transfusion but whose father refuses on religious grounds, resulting in the child's death.[61] Of the two films, *Victim* became the more significant production for being the first film to approach the taboo subject of homosexuality after the publication of the Wolfenden Report in 1957. The report had recommended a more tolerant legal attitude and sympathetic treatment of homosexuality, which the film combines within a crime theme of blackmail. *Victim* received several complimentary reviews and was chosen as the official British entry at the Venice Film Festival. Relph claimed that by February 1962 the costs of the film, £180,000, had already been recovered in England. Walker, however, maintained that the film made only a 'slow profit' which in mid-1971 totalled £51,762.[62]

Attenborough and Forbes's next AFM production was *Séance on a Wet Afternoon* (1964). Forbes directed the film while Attenborough acted. The cost of the film was low, £139,000, due to Attenborough and Forbes both accepting small fees and percentages as they had previously done with *The Angry Silence*. The role of Billy required Attenborough to play a weak husband who aids his mentally disturbed wife, Myra (Kim Stanley), to kidnap a child. Initially their plan was for the kidnapped child to replace their stillborn son, Arthur, but later Myra decides that the child must die to perform the role of playmate for her dead son. The role was a difficult one for Attenborough (who also had to wear a prosthetic nose) opposite Stanley's unpredictable 'Method' acting technique. Nevertheless, Attenborough enjoyed the experience, claiming his performance gave him the 'most satisfaction' of all the cinematic roles he played.[63] The film gained critical praise in America where Stanley received an Oscar nomination for her role and a New York Critics Award. Attenborough won a BAFTA and Forbes a Screenwriters' Award. The film was also selected for the San Sebastian Film Festival. Commercially, *Séance on a Wet Afternoon* suffered, however, as the money generated from the film was slow to accumulate, not helped by the film being granted a restricted release in Britain by Rank. According to Walker, 'its world gross by mid-1971 was only £195,688'.[64]

The film received varied reviews. The *Monthly Film Bulletin* commented on Forbes's direction as 'excellent' and a 'genuinely superb performance' from Stanley with Attenborough 'almost as good'.[65] Peter John Dyer in *Sight and Sound* declared that Forbes was 'only moderately ruthless in cutting down the kind of technical dead-wood (shock cuts in particular) which spoils so many British movies'. For Dyer, 'The best things in the film are like this last scene, pure and quiet, sickly and chill, with Richard Attenborough's sympathetic performance as poor, asthmatic, beak-nosed, Billy providing an invaluably self-effacing counterpoint to Miss Stanley's display of psychotic frissons.'[66] *The Times* commented on the acting, praising Stanley as 'outstanding' and Attenborough as giving 'one of his best performances'. Overall it declared: 'It is an unpretentious film – no more, really, than an unusually intelligent thriller – but on its own chosen level it works, and that, these days, is above all what the British cinema needs.'[67]

Séance on a Wet Afternoon marked the final production for AFM. Its limited commercial success in conjunction with the box-office failure of *Life for Ruth* both contributed to the downfall of AFM, leaving the company between £300,000 to £400,000 in debt to Rank.[68] As Walker has observed: 'Allied Film Makers illustrated how perilously balanced a group of producer-directors was: a single expensive flop by one or more could turn them into another sort of hyphenate-producer-bankrupts.'[69] However, the company continued to function through the expertise of Leslie Baker whose financial acumen was such that the debts were repaid to Rank by the early 1970s. The death of Dearden in a car crash in 1971 formally ended the AFM partnership. The same year, Leslie Baker provided Walker with detailed financial information regarding the company:

> The total negative cost of the seven AFM films made for Rank was £1,042,157, the distributor's gross was £1,820,940 giving them a gross profit of £778,783. But the producers of the films had to carry a loss of £142,934. Moreover, after the cinemas had taken their cut, some 65 per cent overall, there was still a return of over 75 per cent on initial capital investment.[70]

The relationship of Beaver Films Limited to Allied Film Makers has not always been clear. Both Walker and Forbes state that Allied Film Makers was responsible for seven films. Neither person identifies them all although Walker provides six titles.[71] While Walker suggests that the Beaver partnership with *The Angry Silence* is linked to the company, the film itself does not include any reference to AFM.[72]

A further confusion arises with *The L-Shaped Room* which involved both Attenborough (co-producer with James Woolf) and Forbes (writer

ATTENBOROUGH AS PRODUCER 33

and director after Jack Clayton withdrew) but was not connected to either Beaver Films or AFM. Woolf, with his brother John, ran Romulus Films, which had close connections to Bryanston.[73] Attenborough was out of work at the time and was given the task of being in charge of day-to-day production. Forbes had adapted his script from the novel by Lynn Reid Banks about the problems of Jane (Leslie Caron), a single middle-class woman who finds out she is pregnant. Jane is abandoned by both her parents and boyfriend and finds a home in a dilapidated bedsit in London and, after refusing to have an abortion, decides to bring the baby up as a single parent. The subject caused immense problems with the British Board of Film Censors, which demanded 'numerous cuts'. Forbes protested against omitting the scenes, which included the term 'abortion', and it was decided to leave the final decision to the majority decision of a trial female audience who voted to keep the scene. *The L-Shaped Room* opened on 15 November 1962. The *Monthly Film Bulletin* criticised Forbes's 'rather capricious direction', while *Sight and Sound* complained about the tone of the film, which it claimed 'is emotionally self-indulgent to a degree that falsifies both the characters and the background'.[74] Dilys Powell in the *Sunday Times* claimed 'it is a film with the quality of a best-seller'. While she acknowledged the role of both Woolf and Attenborough as producers, it was Forbes whom she singled out, declaring that he 'has an understanding which can be called creative of the actor's problems'.[75] *The Times* admired 'the good-natured, indulgent tolerance of the poor to one another is admirably conveyed', while 'the comedy ... is conventional, the lines are consistently sharp and entertaining'.[76] For *Variety* it was 'a thoroughly holding and intelligent film'.[77] Forbes was later awarded the Silver Laurel award in America 'in recognition of his '"Artistic and distinguished contribution to understanding among the peoples of the world" for the film'.[78]

Séance on a Wet Afternoon was also the final production for Beaver Films. Afterwards, Forbes and Attenborough took divergent paths; Forbes to Hollywood to direct *King Rat* (1965), which Attenborough declined to act in and produce, and Attenborough to play in *Guns at Batasi* (John Guillermin, 1964). Their paths also crossed when, on Forbes's return to Britain, Attenborough left for Hollywood and spent a year in America seeking lucrative assignments to secure funding for *Gandhi*. The quest to secure *Gandhi* also proved to be a divisive factor between Forbes and Attenborough. The previous success of their relationship, with Attenborough's optimism controlled by Forbes's pessimism, did not survive the scale of the project. As Attenborough recalled:

> He did not believe, in practical terms, that it was possible to encompass some fifty, sixty or seventy years of a man's life within a reasonable

screentime and end up with anything more than an unsatisfactory, superficial piece of work.[79]

The demise of AFM was also affected by external factors. Bryanston's crucial decision not to provide backing for *Tom Jones* (Tony Richardson, 1963) was the major contributory factor in its demise in 1965. It also effectively stifled British investment leading to a production crisis in Britain between 1963 and 1964 for independent filmmakers. The commercial success of *Tom Jones*, under United Artists, resulted in a surge of American investment into British films at the expense of the more limited British money. The American financial influx that had contributed to the fall of AFM, however, was beneficial to Attenborough with *Oh! What a Lovely War* which was financed by American money from Paramount.

Attenborough's association with Beaver Films and AFM was sufficient to establish him as a leading producer of the time. For Attenborough: 'independence isn't a gift. In the companies with which I have been associated it's a privilege which I and my colleagues have bought and backed with our own earning power.'[80] In achieving independence as a producer Attenborough also gained independence as an actor and fulfilment. '[T]he last six years have given me the parts I most wanted.[81] It was Attenborough's experience as a producer, however, that was also to prove particularly beneficial in his first film as a director.

Notes

1. Bryan Forbes, *Notes for a Life*, London, 1974, p. 279.
2. John Hill, *Sex, Class and Realism: British Cinema 1956–1963*, London, 1986, p. 48.
3. Derek Threadgall, *Shepperton Studios: An Independent View*, London, 1994, p. 95.
4. Richard Attenborough, 'Our "Silence" Was Golden', *Sunday Telegraph*, 22 August 1965.
5. Alexander Walker, *Hollywood England: The British Film Industry in the 1960s*, London, 1974, p. 97.
6. Attenborough, 'Our "Silence" Was Golden'.
7. Arthur Marwick, *British Society since 1945*, 4th edn, London, 2003, pp. 129–30. Marwick asserts that the large rise in membership in the 1950s and 1960s resulted in an increase in strikes. From 1955–64 there were 2,521 strikes that involved 1,116,000 workers.
8. Some sources give a different amount. Attenborough, 'Our "Silence" Was Golden', states the final cost was £96,000 while Robinson, *Richard Attenborough*, p. 29, claims it was £92,000.
9. Curtis Lee Hanson, 'Richard Attenborough: An Actor's Actor', *Cinema* (US) 3:2 (March 1966), p. 10.
10. Brian McFarlane, *An Autobiography of British Cinema*, London, 1997, p. 35.
11. *Sight and Sound*, 29:2 (spring 1960), p. 89.
12. *Sunday Times*, 13 March 1960.

13 *Daily Express*, 11 March 1960.
14 *Tribune*, 11 March 1960.
15 *News Chronicle*, 14 April 1960.
16 Tom Hibbert, 'Has Also Been Known to Act', *Empire*, 67 (January 1995), p. 71.
17 *Daily Herald*, 16 May 1960.
18 *The Times*, 19 May 1960.
19 *The Times*, 20 May 1960.
20 Walker, *Hollywood England*, p. 101.
21 *Sunday Telegraph* (Magazine), 13 November 1983.
22 'News Shots' Beaver Films, *The Angry Silence*, microfiche, BFI, London.
23 Peter Hutchings, 'Beyond the New Wave: Realism in British Cinema, 1959–63', in Robert Murphy (ed.), *The British Cinema Book*, London, 2001, p. 148.
24 *The Times*, 6 July 1960.
25 Attenborough, 'Our "Silence" Was Golden', 22 August 1965.
26 Walker, *Hollywood England*, p. 101.
27 Michael and Aileen Balcon Collection, MEB J/1; Balcon to Attenborough, 11 March 1960, BFI.
28 *Ibid.*, Attenborough to Balcon, 12 March 1960.
29 MEB I/240, Balcon to Attenborough, 17 December 1958.
30 MEB I/240 Attenborough to Balcon, 6 January 1959.
31 *Ibid.*, Maxwell Setton to Balcon, 21 January 1959.
32 Walker, *Hollywood England*, pp. 101–3.
33 *Ibid*, p. 103.
34 Attenborough has no recollection of Box's involvement. Neither does Diana Hawkins who was in charge of publicity at Allied Film Makers. Andrew Spicer's recent study, *Sydney Box*, Manchester, 2006, p. 175, refers only to Walker's claim that Box had the original idea for AFM.
35 Author's interview with Attenborough, 16 February 2007, Richmond.
36 Jack Hawkins, *Anything for a Quiet Life: The Autobiography of Jack Hawkins*, London, 1973, p, 137.
37 Walker, *Hollywood England*, p. 102.
38 *Ibid*. Hawkins's 'unnamed brother' is not mentioned by either Forbes or Hawkins.
39 *The Times*, 3 November 1959, p. 15, names the members as: Jack Hawkins, Richard Attenborough, Bryan Forbes, Michael Relph and Guy Green; Attenborough, 'Our "Silence" Was Golden', also gives the same six names.
40 According to Walker, it was '[t]he four groups who each put up £5,000' (*Hollywood England*, p. 103).
41 *The Times*, 3 November 1959.
42 Forbes, *Notes for a Life*, pp. 291–2.
43 *Ibid.*, p. 291.
44 *Evening News*, 7 April 1960.
45 *Star*, 7 April 1960.
46 Walker, *Hollywood England*, p. 102.
47 *Guardian*, 9 April 1960; *Daily Herald*, 8 April 1960.
48 *Daily Mail*, 8 April 1960.
49 *Sunday Times*, 10 April 1960.
50 *Sunday Dispatch*, 10 April 1960.
51 *The Times*, 11 April 1960.
52 *Financial Times*, 11 April 1960.
53 *Monthly Film Bulletin*, 27:316 (May 1960), p. 65.
54 Walker claims that the National Film Finance Corporation provided 'completion guarantees for *The League of Gentlemen*'. For the other five films made by AFM the guarantees came from the Rank Organisation (*Hollywood England*, p. 103).

55 *Ibid.*
56 *The Times*, 21 July 1960.
57 The Great Train Robbery occurred on 8 August 1963 when £2.6 million in used bank notes was stolen from the Glasgow to London mail train.
58 Walker, *Hollywood England*, p. 105.
59 *Ibid.*, p. 106.
60 Attenborough, *Films and Filming*, 7:2 (September 1961), p. 9.
61 For further details, see Sally Dux, 'Allied Film Makers: Crime, Comedy and Social Concern', *Journal of British Cinema and Television*, 9:2 (April 2012), pp. 198–213.
62 *Kinematograph Weekly*, 15 February 1962, p. 8; Walker, *Hollywood England*, p. 157.
63 Quoted in Robinson, *Richard Attenborough*, p. 31.
64 Walker, *Hollywood England*, p. 247.
65 *Monthly Film Bulletin*, 31:366 (July 1964), p. 103.
66 *Sight and Sound*, 33:3 (summer 1964), p. 146.
67 *The Times*, 4 June 1964.
68 Walker, *Hollywood England*, p. 248. Precise figures for the films were provided for Walker by Leslie Baker (see pp. 103 (note) and 246–8.
69 *Ibid.*, p. 458.
70 *Ibid.*, p. 248.
71 The six named films are: *League of Gentlemen, Man in the Moon, Whistle Down the Wind, Victim, Life for Ruth* and *Séance on a Wet Afternoon*.
72 This also refers to the DVD recording of *The Angry Silence* released in 2001 by Momentum Pictures. *Whistle Down the Wind* (1961), credits the film as a Richard Attenborough and Bryan Forbes Production, and 'A Beaver Film made for Allied Film Makers'. *Séance on a Wet Afternoon* (1964) opens with the logo of AFM and also includes the Beaver Films symbol (name and logo) at the end of the film.
73 Diana Hawkins assures me that *The L-Shaped Room* had no link to Beaver Films nor to AFM. Correspondence from Hawkins received 18 January 2007.
74 *Monthly Film Bulletin*, 30:348 (January 1963), p. 3; *Sight and Sound*, 32:1 (winter 1962/63), p. 41.
75 *Sunday Times*, 18 November 1962.
76 *The Times*, 16 November 1962.
77 *Variety*, 21 November 1962.
78 *The Times*, 29 May 1964.
79 Attenborough, *In Search of Gandhi*, p. 45.
80 Attenborough, 'Our "Silence" Was Golden'.
81 *Ibid.*

New directions:
Oh! What a Lovely War (1969)

Oh! What a Lovely War is Richard Attenborough's most innovative film and one of his finest productions. The film is notable for its stylised scenes and a cast that included the elite of British theatre, giving it a significant cachet. Yet, like many of Attenborough's films *Oh! What a Lovely War* was to prove controversial. The film has no credited screenwriter, a result of disagreements during production, the repercussions of which extended well beyond the film's release. During filming unfavourable opinions were voiced by First World War historians who challenged the accuracy of the film's depiction of the conflict. At the time of release there were adverse comments through a polemical review and critique from Alan Lovell in the *Brighton Film Review*. Yet, while the film received a rather mixed critical response, it went on to win a number of national and international awards. It also achieved popular success, becoming a British cinema top-ten box-office film for 1969.

Oh! What a Lovely War is based on the musical stage play *Oh What a Lovely War!* produced by Joan Littlewood for the Theatre Workshop Company first performed in 1963.[1] The film explores the First World War in a vivid and impressionistic portrayal which is presented through a mixture of quasi-reality and fantasy. It focuses on the perspective of the ordinary soldier, as seen through the men of the Smith family, whose own lives contrast those of the generals and politicians. The women of the Smith family similarly represent the ordinary female against the very different lives experienced by the wives of the high command and elite of society. The film's narrative is woven between a framework of traditional songs of the period that were sung by the soldiers accompanied by vignette sequences, each of which focuses on a specific aspect of the war on the Western Front. While several themes are incorporated within the film, its principal concern is to demonstrate the difference between the popular image of war at the time of the conflict and the reality of the situation. To enhance its message the film employs comedy in the form of satire which links it in to the satire boom of the 1960s. The film attacks the methods by which the soldiers were lured into the conflict by the false optimism of war amid the patriotic fervour that existed in 1914. By combining several genre forms including the musical, historical, comedy and war film, the First World War is transferred to a seaside pier upon which 'the war game' is played as the young men are drawn in to the war by the words of the narrator/'chorus': 'Take your places for the ever popular War Game – complete with songs, battles and a few jokes.' The unusual concept and innovative style of the film provided an opportunity for Attenborough to make his mark as a new director and to challenge the conventional label with which he had been previously associated as an actor and producer. *Oh! What a Lovely War* is unique in using a non-realist approach to the First World War, a style that had recently been seen in the Second World War anti-war film, *How I Won the War* (Richard Lester, 1967). It also draws from the mood of anti-authority and anti-militarism from two other recent films: the First World War portrayal, *King and Country* (Joseph Losey,1964), and *The Charge of the Light Brigade* (Tony Richardson, 1969) based on the Crimean War of 1854–56.

The original stage production of *Oh What a Lovely War!* was first performed at the Theatre Royal, Stratford East, on 19 March 1963. The play heralded an innovative approach to dramatising the First World War using a Brechtian style which reflected a Marxist interpretation of society as a vehicle for 'rational didacticism', stimulating audiences to respond to the version of the truth as depicted on the stage. Alex Danchev considered it was 'the most memorable stage treatment of the Great War since *Journey's End* (1928)'.[2] Through its particular interpretation of the war, *Oh What a Lovely War!* attracted much controversy, due to its content, its overt socialist overtones, and disagreements over its authorship.

The idea for the play had originated from a radio musical documentary entitled *The Long Long Trail: Soldiers' Songs of the First World War*, which was devised by the jazz musician and radio producer Charles Chilton. The programme resulted from Chilton's failed attempt, in 1958, to locate his father's grave at the site of the Battle of Arras. Instead, Chilton found only his father's name inscribed in small letters on a stone memorial. As he later recalled: 'What could possibly have happened to a man that rendered his burial impossible? What horror could have taken place that rendered the burial of 35,942 men impossible and all in one relatively small area?'[3] Chilton's response was to turn the songs sung by the soldiers into a form that could convey their experiences. The resultant hour-long show was transmitted in December 1961.[4] Gerry Raffles, manager of the Theatre Workshop Company, envisaged the songs as a basis for a stage production that he considered was ideally suited to the company's unstructured approach. Several writers, including Gwyn Thomas and Ted Allan, were invited to submit scripts but all were rejected. The rejection of Allan's script caused legal problems for Theatre Workshop after it was dismissed for excluding the songs which Chilton considered were fundamental to his concept.[5] Allan, however, challenged his rejection in the High Court, accusing the production of being 'a deliberate attempt to steal his play'.[6] The dispute was eventually settled in an out-of-court settlement in 1964 with Allan being allowed authorship of the original title.[7] The confusion over the authorship still continues. In the recent DVD release of the film, Allan's name is given incorrectly as the play's author.[8]

Chilton was responsible for coordinating the script, while Littlewood was in charge of the production. Littlewood conceived the idea of the actors being presented as a Pierrot troop, called 'The Merry Roosters', the Pierrot show representing the most popular form of seaside entertainment at the time of the war. She also provided the innovative idea of assembling a large screen behind the actors on which were projected slide photographs of images of the war, and a 'ticker-tape' mechanism, positioned over the stage, which ran instant newsflashes of war casualties. Military guidance was given from the historian and future Labour MP, Raymond Fletcher. Another influential source was Alan Clark's study *The Donkeys*, published in 1961. Clark attributed the title of his book to General Hoffmann, a German, whom Clark claimed had described the British soldiers as lions who were led by incompetent generals, the donkeys. While the authenticity of Clark's attribution has since been questioned, his idea nevertheless influenced future studies and provided the play with its primary focus.[9] As John Ramsden argues, Clark 'fastened round the necks of Douglas Haig and his fellow-generals an instantly remembered and apparently-authentic insult which decades of scholarship have so far failed to budge from the popular mind.'[10] The historian, A.J.P. Taylor, whose study, *The First World War*, published in 1963, was dedicated to Littlewood, gave the production additional historical integrity when he publicly praised the play in his valedictory lecture in Oxford, declaring:

> Oh what a lovely war [sic] is one of the most remarkable theatrical successes in London, and does what the historians have failed to do. No doubt it owes a great deal of success to the skill of the producer, Miss Littlewood. But it does combine popular feelings about the war with a striking demonstration of what the war was about.[11]

To make the play accessible to a wider audience, it was transferred to Wyndham's Theatre in the West End on 20 June 1963. After six months it moved to Paris and then toured in Europe. A move to America was less successful. Goorney suggests that the lack of popular appeal was due to the play's focus on the early years of the war which was prior to American involvement, and therefore of less interest.[12] Derek Paget, however, detected a generational shift of opinion, noting that the play was 'much performed on the American college circuit' which suggests that the play was more accessible for a younger and more progressive generation.[13]

Oh! What a Lovely War was not an obvious choice for Attenborough's debut as a director. The success of the play did not guarantee a similar response as the film needed to attract a different type of audience. As Mark Connelly has observed: 'The vast majority of British cinema-goers were not regular attenders of the theatre.'[14] There was also the difficulty of transferring the style of the play with its stage-based concept to the more open dimensions of the cinema. The loosely bound and fragmented narrative also made it difficult to restructure the play as a cohesive film. It was for these reasons that the actor, John Mills (who originally intended to direct the film), and the production team of Len Deighton and Brian Duffy decided that an untried director unhindered by previous experiences would be preferable. Mills had been impressed by the imaginative approach Attenborough had demonstrated as co-producer of *Whistle Down the Wind*, while Deighton and Duffy had worked with Attenborough when they co-produced *Only When I Larf* (Basil Dearden, 1968). Attenborough also possessed the necessary musical ability for the production which he had recently demonstrated in *Doctor Dolittle*. It was also an opportunity for Attenborough to make use of his knowledge of art with paintings by Cézanne and Monet influencing the composition of scenes.

Despite Attenborough's previous insistence that the only film he wanted to direct was *Gandhi*, the publicity that the project had generated had attracted other offers, all of which he had so far declined. Moreover, the longevity and intensity of Attenborough's involvement with *Gandhi* had also proved detrimental to his reputation. David Castell claimed that 'there were those around him who began to fear for the continuing validity of his professional judgement.'[15] *Oh! What a Lovely War* was therefore an opportunity to prove his credibility as a director and help towards restoring his reputation. While it also offered a suitable vehicle to explore his particular interests concerned with human interaction, he also believed passionately in the subject of the First World War. In *The Times* Attenborough declared that he was totally outraged by the conflict, outraged by suffering, injustice and the trampling down of the rights of the individual – 'tolerance, compassion, they matter very much to me'.[16]

Oh! What a Lovely War was well suited to the climate of the 1960s which reflected a mood of optimism and change as a reaction to the 'doldrums era' of the 1950s. Sarah Street describes the 1960s as 'an exciting period for British cinema', while Robert Murphy claims that, '[t]aken as a whole, the 1960s saw a greater number of significant and exciting films made in Britain than at any time before or since'.[17] Although realism was still regarded as the dominant critical discourse, the era was receptive to new ideas. These came from the French New Wave and from the arrival of foreign directors making films in Britain, who brought an auteurist perspective to British cinema including Michelangelo Antonioni (*Blow Up*, 1966), Joseph Losey (*The Servant*, 1963, *Accident*, 1967), François Truffaut (*Fahrenheit 451*, 1966) and Franco Zeffirelli (*Romeo and Juliet*, 1968). Finance for British films in the 1960s still principally came from America. After 1967, however, the situation changed when American audiences developed a renewed interest for their own indigenous topics and, simultaneously, British films began to be less profitable. Several box-office disappointments contributed to this drop, including *Far from the Madding Crowd* (John Schlesinger 1967), *The Charge of the Light Brigade* and *Goodbye Mr Chips* (Herbert Ross, 1969).

The 1960s represented a time of rapid political, social and cultural change in Britain. New codes of behaviour were challenging old traditions in society as authority was being questioned by a new openness as depicted through the advent of the 'Swinging Sixties' and an emerging youth culture as depicted in films such as *Alfie* (Lewis Gilbert, 1966) and *Darling* (John Schlesinger, 1965). The 1960s also saw the triggering of a satire explosion which was seen as an effective tool in attacking the ruling elite. *Oh What a Lovely War!* became part of this explosion due to its vehemently anti-establishment outlook. A letter to the Lord Chamberlain in 1963 called attention to 'the dangerously anti-British propaganda embodied in the play'.[18] Anger was also expressed in John Osborne's play *Look Back in Anger* at the Royal Court in 1956, emerging through the play's hero, Jimmy Porter, who represented the 'Angry Young Men'. Satire also came to prominence at the Edinburgh Festival in August 1960, with the revue *Beyond the Fringe*. The show's principal writer and presenter, Peter Cook, also went on to found the magazine *Private Eye* in 1961, which provided a satirical overview of contemporary politics and events. On television, *That Was the Week that Was* (*TW3*), first broadcast on 24 November 1962, broke new ground by adopting a similar policy to *Private Eye*, but in a live show attacking people in powerful positions in society. Politically, satire proved an effective tool when, in 1963, both *TW3* and *Private Eye* contributed to publicising the 'Profumo Affair', the former by featuring the relationship of Christine Keeler and John Profumo and the latter by a cartoon on its front cover which accelerated the decline of the Conservative government.[19] While *TW3* came to an end in December 1963, the closure of *Beyond the Fringe* in 1964 marked a significant change in the way satire was perceived. Humphrey Carpenter observes that '[t]he style of humour was now moving away from the would-be-satirical towards the surrealism that would eventually come to boil in *Monty Python's Flying Circus*', a television show which was launched in October 1969.[20] The changing face of satire had a significant effect on *Oh! What a Lovely War*. In the late 1960s, war and religion were still deemed sensitive subjects. Even as late as 1979, the film *Monty Python's Life of Brian* (Terry Jones) received many complaints due to parodying the perceived absurdities of religious belief.

The theme of war was still prevalent in British society in the 1960s. The British Army was still involved in conflicts abroad, while the Vietnam War, which had begun in 1965, was vividly portrayed through the media, particularly on television. The continuing Cold War had resulted in heightened tensions in 1961 with the building of the Berlin Wall and more acutely in 1962 with the Cuban Missile Crisis. A renewed interest in the First World War had resulted in over three hundred books being published during the 1960s. The scholarly books offered an alternative interpretation from the official histories published soon after the end of the war and challenged the role of the generals, particularly that of Field-Marshal Sir Douglas Haig. This surge had been influenced by the new availability of private papers including the published version of Haig's war diary, which allowed individual interpretations of the war to be compared to the official versions. The Public Records Act of 1967 was particularly significant, as it reduced from fifty to thirty years the time of release of government papers. There was also a rekindling of interest in the works of the war poets and writers whose publications in the 1920s had introduced the futility and waste of human life. Authors such as Robert Graves whose book *Goodbye to All That* appeared in Penguin in 1960 and Erich Maria Remarque, whose work *All Quiet on the Western Front* had previously been filmed in 1930 (Lewis Milestone), were reissued in book form.

On television, *The Great War* was broadcast in 1964 to mark the fiftieth anniversary of the start of the war. The programme, comprising twenty-six episodes, was unexpectedly popular with 'some eight million people on average' viewing each episode, bringing the conflict into the home and making it accessible for family viewing.[21] Although the series was controversial in employing reconstructions in addition to genuine archive footage, its pioneering method of portraying personal interviews from veteran soldiers allowed the opinions of 'forgotten voices' to be heard. However, while the series was intended to promote the views of its historical adviser and co-writer, John Terraine, and his pro-Haig perspective, it inadvertently produced an anti-war perspective. As Danchev explained, 'the message the series actually communicated was as unexpected as the scale of its success. It was the utter futility of the war.'[22] To add an element of light relief, the BBC had purchased the rights for *Oh What a Lovely War!* with the intention, although not carried out, of broadcasting it 'as a sort of warm-up act'.[23]

In the cinema, the subject of the First World War had only been marginally represented during the 1960s. Prior to *Oh! What a Lovely War* there were only four British productions, all very different in content and style: *Lawrence of Arabia* (David Lean, 1962), a biographical and epic portrayal, *King and Country* concerning the trial and execution of a private soldier, *Doctor Zhivago* (Lean, 1965), a depiction of the conflict in Russia and *The Blue Max* (John Guillermin, 1966), which provides a German perspective of the war.[24] The interest generated by the huge audiences was also a significant factor in deciding to transform *Oh What a Lovely War!* to film. Although initially Littlewood was not in favour, questioning the film's relevance to cinema and proclaiming its uniqueness to theatre, she changed her mind in June 1967 and agreed to sell the film rights to Deighton, who had been encouraged to purchase them by A.J.P. Taylor.[25] Deighton and Duffy set up a new company, Accord Productions, in collaboration with Mills for the production.

Attenborough was initially wary of the project and of his ability to direct it, admitting that he suffered from personal doubts concerning his 'intellectual inadequacy' for the position. In the *Guardian* Attenborough revealed how he overcame the problem:

> I came to realise that to communicate, which is what directing is all about, it doesn't necessarily help to be an intellectual; there's a direct, instinctive, simple way of getting through to people. And you must get through to them. There's no point in caring desperately about a statement you want to make if no one's listening.[26]

David Lean's earlier warning to him had also influenced Attenborough's concerns. Lean, who had co-directed Attenborough in *In Which We Serve*, had advocated a policy of patience and gaining a particular affiliation with a film by impressing upon him not to direct 'until you find a subject that so absorbs you that you feel that there is no further point in living unless you direct it'.[27] Crucial to Lean's advice was the standard and concept of the script, which provided the final catalyst for Attenborough to accept. For Attenborough, Deighton and Duffy had, in his view:

> [C]onceived a brilliant form by which to transfer it to cinema, that of changing a pierrot show – a charade – into a format which still permitted the feeling of make-believe whilst, at the same time, allowing for the reality which the camera creates and, consequently demands.[28]

Attenborough's experience as a producer was also put to effective use. The first task he was given was to obtain the finance, which he viewed with some trepidation, claiming: 'Raising money for independent production was difficult at the time. But a musical was even more difficult.'[29] The production team decided to consult George H. Ornstein, head of production for Paramount in London, who was renowned for backing films that 'did not necessarily fall within the accepted pattern'.[30] Ornstein arranged for Attenborough to meet Charles Bludhorn, head of Gulf and Western, a non-filmic corporation, which had recently acquired Paramount.[31] To help his cause and to provide an indication of the proposed concept, Attenborough gave a one-man performance of a short rendition of the script to Bludhorn and to his chief executive, Martin Davies. The singing-and-dancing routine was sufficient to convince them of its viability. As Attenborough recalled:

> I realised it would be fatal to let him read the script: it was very complex, hard to visualise. Instead I decided to act it out for him. For an hour and a half I gave him scenes, bits of dialogue, sang some of the songs: I described the action. At the end he was almost in tears and he said I could go right ahead.[32]

Bludhorn, however, laid down certain stipulations: he insisted that neither Attenborough nor the filmmakers should be paid for their roles; instead they were to benefit from the profits. He also demanded that Attenborough obtain five star names for the film, a stipulation that he exceeded by attracting fourteen 'stars'. The first was Laurence Olivier who was keen to support Attenborough as he was an advocate of 'actor-managers', maintaining that actors made the best directors. Olivier's endorsement of Attenborough encouraged others to follow with each actor agreeing to appear for minimum Equity rates. This fee, although later modified, was based on a time basis related purely to the number of days on which they were required. Moreover, the prestigious cast ensured that the film maintained a degree of theatrical kudos.[33] Four of the six theatrical knights of the time – Olivier (Sir John French), John Gielgud (Count Berchtold), Ralph Richardson (Sir Edward Grey) and Michael Redgrave (Sir Henry Wilson) were included – while John

Clements (General von Moltke) received his knighthood during production. The star names were chosen for the cameo roles of prominent figures of the campaign, thereby contributing to the elevated status of their characters. John Mills was rewarded with the role of Haig for recommending Attenborough as director.

The principal roles were given to relatively unknown names. While unfamiliar faces emphasised the image of the ordinary soldier, the policy appears similar to the one that Thorold Dickinson had adopted with *Next of Kin* (1942), which Jeffrey Richards observes was to 'make the impact of the story greater'.[34] It also helped to reduce costs as 'unknown' actors were paid lower fees which, for Attenborough, allowed sufficient funds to be maintained for screen effects. The budget for the film was relatively modest, publicised as £1,465,000 by *Today's Cinema* and $3 million by *Filmfacts*.[35] In comparison, *Battle of Britain* (Guy Hamilton, 1969) was estimated to have cost $12 million.

Deighton had positioned the war on a seaside pier with the action moving further towards the sea as the conflict progressed. He also devised the use of a helter-skelter from which Haig and his officers could view the war's progress. The origin of other ideas is less clear. Paget argues that the concept of the 'universal soldier' in the film, named Smith, was one of Allan's original ideas which he had introduced into his rejected script for Theatre Workshop.[36] Deighton appears to have adapted this or a similar concept for the Smith family. Attenborough also added his own creative input, most notably the red poppy as a symbolic indicator of death.[37] He also attempted to add a corrective to the play, as he considered that it ignored the contribution of the officer class. Despite the inclusion of some extra scenes, Attenborough still considered the point was not adequately emphasised: 'I think we may be criticised for not stressing sufficiently that the losses and suffering weren't simply confined to the working classes. And I regret that.'[38]

The film applies a variety of devices to enhance its anti-military message. In the dramatic and poignant title sequence a stylised series of images, devised by Raymond Hawkey, provide a brief pictorial synopsis of the film. The images initially depict vibrant colour but this gradually diminishes as it moves from scenes of civilian normality: a coronation mug, a dainty teaset, uniforms, to weaponry (the daily life of a soldier), which becomes more bleak as the war takes hold, an unlaced boot, a gas mask, before the greater horrors of war are exposed – a grenade, barbed wire, ending with a startling image of a skull as the tempo and tone of the music change. The sequence is accompanied by military band music reflecting the mood of the pictures, diminishing in mood and tempo as the situation deteriorates. At the start of the film the Smith family are sold tickets to 'The War Game', by Haig in which the Smith men participate in the sideshows and entertainments drawing them in various ways into war. Harry (Colin Farrell) is lured by the seductive tones of a music hall artist (Maggie Smith), and is 'captured' by the recruiting officer; Jack (Paul Shelley) is tempted by the shooting, while Bertie (Corin Redgrave), 'the only officer in the family', goes optimistically off to war on a model train happily singing 'Goodbye-ee'.

Oh! What a Lovely War has been described as 'a film of great moments rather than a great film'.[39] These 'great moments' are best demonstrated in the film's style which include some dramatic scenes which aimed to equate the film with the innovative techniques and influence of the *auteur*. One occurrence is when Jack Smith is miraculously transported to war, from a shooting stall in England to France by the camera rotating 180 degrees in a continuous movement.[40] This allows Jack, originally dressed in civilian clothes, to be changed by the end of the shot (by a quick costume change) into army uniform. Attenborough later explained his reasoning:

> The normal way to achieve this effect would have been simply to cut away or dissolve. But, by staying with the shot, we took the audience with us, persuading them unconsciously to swallow the fantasy. They then readily accepted that the style of the film was going to take them seamlessly from fantasy to reality and reality to fantasy.[41]

Another example is Attenborough's employment of dramatic cuts to change locations within a sequence. This is evident in the scene when a model railway disappears towards the end of the pier but by the process of a cut is transferred to Waterloo Station. A similar method is used in a puppet show depicting the 'Army Français'. The soldiers mount real horses but sit down on roundabout models. The sequence ends with a war scene portraying a defeated French troop amid a field of corpses. Both scenes use the technique and devices of intellectual montage in order to create meaning through the juxtaposition of images. Another scene, focusing on injured soldiers returning to England shows remarkable similarity with a similar scene in *In Which We Serve*. Both films use a camera which pans down the line of servicemen where no words are spoken, with the quiet sound of a military band playing off-screen. This was the first occasion that Attenborough employed 'silent dialogue' to create an effect of emotional oblivion, the empty faces devoid of any expression. When the music increases in volume, it allows the soldiers to be immediately released from their war experiences, and they march away, singing.

The stark message of the film, the poignancy and futility of war, comes to a climax in the final and most memorable sequence. The scene, consciously reminiscent of Monet's painting, *Poppy field*, required the use of a helicopter and 15,000 white crosses all individually drilled into position.[42] To the words of Jerome Kern's song 'And When They Ask Us', the female relatives of the dead soldiers dance among the graves as the camera pulls back leaving the numerous crosses disappearing into unrecognisable dots on the landscape as the figures disappear before the film ends abruptly with a black screen. Philip French referred to it leaving 'a feeling of impenetrable sadness, of unassuagable [sic] grief'.[43] The scene also returns the film to Chilton's original concept and is analogous to his own father's memorial, containing thousands of names. The ending was changed from the original stage version which concluded the play with an attempted mutiny by the French soldiers who on threat of being shot for revolt follow their officer like lambs to the slaughter. A deliberate ploy to appeal to American audiences was to introduce the scene of the American entry into the war. The colourful and striking scene contrasts the cheering crowds which welcome the American presence. Haig's authority is seen to diminish by the symbolic act of an American soldier turning a world map towards him and placing his hand upon it, taking over control. A different change was instigated for contractual reasons. An early draft of the screenplay dated 14 March 1968 has the title 'Oh What a Lovely War' without an exclamation mark. This was added later to prevent possible legal difficulties regarding Allan's claim to the title. [44]

Attenborough's film is unique in its portrayal of the First World War for setting out the historical context. As Michael Paris observes:

> *Oh! What a Lovely War* was the first British film to even mention the causes of the War – a family squabble between the crowned heads of Europe, it suggests, into which the British government were drawn by self interest and imperial ambition.[45]

The sequence depicting the causes is also notable for including most of the elite cast who offer glimpses of the significance of their characters by promoting their eccentric and other prominent attributes. The causes are presented in a highly stylised manner where the crowned and political heads of Europe are gathered together in a non-realistic setting on the pier to discuss and change their own national allegiances. Thus Sir Edward Grey, the British Foreign Secretary, voices his country's concerns: 'The lights will go out all over Europe. They will not be lit again in our lifetime.' Grey's presence in the film, instead of King George V, was explained by Attenborough: 'The Tsar and the Kaiser were actively engaged in the political situation which led to the war. Our Royal Family didn't have any political power and weren't involved in the negotiations.'[46] Thus Grey is in discussion with Kaiser Wilhelm (Kenneth More), President Poincare (Ian Holm), Count Berchtold, (Gielgud), General von Moltke (Clements) and Tsar Nicholas (Paul Daneman). The Emperor Franz Josef (Jack Hawkins) had a non-speaking role. Although a recent operation had left Hawkins voiceless, Attenborough cast him in the role for 'his great personality and stature' which were used 'to register the significance of there being no alternative but for emperor to sign the declaration of war'.[47] A different but notable performance occurred during rehearsal. Laurence Olivier, playing Field Marshal Sir John French, gave Attenborough some much valued support as a director when he announced:

> You really mustn't let me go over the top [...] you have a particular style that you have chosen and you must make certain that I fit into it. Just tell me what you want and I will try and come up with it for you.[48]

This gesture, spoken in front of the entire crew, Attenborough acknowledged as one of 'enormous generosity and kindness' and reflected an attitude which he also experienced from the rest of the cast.

The decisive event of the war, the assassination of Archduke Franz Ferdinand and his wife, is re-enacted as a photograph of the gathering, the click of the camera symbolising the fatal gunshot. The scene also establishes the meaning and symbolic use of the poppy as a symbol of impending death. This is first demonstrated when the Archduke and his wife are each presented with one by the Poppyman (Joe Melia) before their demise. Alan Burton observes that this particular use of the poppy 'subverts' its meaning from its present-day one of commemorating death to one of 'anticipation and expectation of death'.[49] The Poppyman thus adopts different guises (a photographer, model train driver, soldier), throughout the film which allows him to give poppies to unsuspecting victims. Another lasting symbol of the film is the use of a cricket scoreboard to relay the numbers of casualties, thus emphasising the war game theme of the film. The name of the battle (match), date, the number of casualties (wickets) and the amount of ground gained (runs) are displayed. Although it was widely believed that the statistical impact was far greater in the play through the ticker-tape reel against the image of authentic photographs of the time, the cricket board is a stark reminder of how the impact of historical statistics can be forgotten as easily as those of a game.

The anti-war and particularly anti-military perspective the film follows is intensified through the themed strands of class and religion that dominate the film. The pacifist position is presented by the Suffragette, Sylvia Pankhurst (Vanessa Redgrave), whose gender and authoritative stance results in her being harangued by her audience. Her feminist stand is mocked and jostled, 'what's your old man having for dinner tonight', while the evidence she offers of the wastage of human life is refuted by the masses. Class is evident in attacking the upper members of society for being unaware of and ignoring the actual conditions of war. This is particularly well shown in the film's representation of the Christmas season which is demonstrated in three different ways. The officers' party shows a room decorated with streamers and paper chains as Haig and his entourage dance and frolic to celebrate. The socialites, Eleanor (Susannah York) and Stephen (Dirk Bogarde), are distanced from the war and show no understanding of it but are pleased to pronounce on their individual efforts. Stephen refuses to drink German wine for the duration of the war, while Eleanor instructs her staff to 'knit mittens or something'. In contrast, out of the trenches in No Man's Land the lower officers and soldiers of both sides meet for the Christmas Day Truce of 1914, forming instant friendships with their German counterparts. This pointedly suggests to the audience that it is the generals and high command who become the real enemy, not the German soldiers. This tripartite view of the different classes has resonances with the Christmas celebrations in *In Which We Serve*, which makes a clear demarcation between the social classes. In *Oh! What a Lovely War* the upper classes appear to infiltrate all three variants, the 'them and us' dichotomy firmly situated between those fighting the war and those who are in relative safety away from the lines.

Religion is another key theme and shown to have influence over Haig's military decisions. He prays for victory before the Americans come while Nurse Betty pleads for peace. Haig is also seen praying and congratulating himself claiming that the Battle of Passchendaele which resulted in 244,897 deaths is 'a great success'. Religion is also central to one of the most moving scenes of the film, the open-air church service where the insignificant offerings relayed by the Chaplain (Gerald Sim) are woefully out of touch with the reality of the situation. The concessions announced that Catholics can eat flesh on a Friday, Protestants can fight on the Sabbath and Jews can eat pork in the trenches are all insulting to the soldiers facing the likely prospect of imminent death. The pomposity of his statements is reflected by the soldiers' responses with the coarse version of the hymns which are far more meaningful and relevant to their lives than the official versions. The scene caused accusations of the play being anti-religious in 1963. A letter to the Lord Chamberlain complained that the play was 'an all-out attack upon our Christian faith, including a blasphemous burlesque of a church service with a mockery of prayer and faith'.[50] By 1969, the freer society and the loss of moral high ground meant that the filmmakers received fewer anti-religious complaints.

Filming began on 27 March 1968 and was completed by 24 August. The locations were all centred in and around Brighton. In addition to the two piers, the ruins of Bayham Abbey, near Tunbridge Wells, provided the site for the church service, while a 25–acre municipal rubbish tip was transformed into battlefield trenches on the Western Front.

An extract of the film was shown at the opening of the British Film Institute's new venue, the Brighton Film Theatre, in front of a VIP audience on 23 February 1969 as a gesture of appreciation to the town. On television, a programme entitled *The Ragtime Infantry*, on the making of the film, resulted in notable complaints.[51] The then Lord Haig wrote to *The Times* complaining that Kenneth More (as the Kaiser) had 'left me with the impression that his view was that the First World War was fought unnecessarily – and he gave no indication of there having been any purpose or ideal behind our resistance to Germany's armed aggression'.[52] Haig's concerns were voiced before the film was released but based on the assumption that it was 'similar to the stage version'. Less significant was the concern of Sir John French's son who complained about a matter of dress protocol. He claimed that a photograph, taken in rehearsal, showed Olivier 'in shirt and braces' playing his father. Although Attenborough had written to reassure French that in the scene when filmed, correct attire would be worn, nonetheless letters from him on the subject persisted.[53]

The post-production period was marked by further controversy, the most notable being Deighton's insistence on removing his name from the credits. *Variety* revealed that there had been 'a difference of opinion as to Attenborough's interpretation of the film, which Deighton believes should have been tougher'.[54] Attenborough denied this implication asserting: 'The difference of opinion was purely contractual and was not in any way to do with the artistic conception of the film.'[55] This opinion was later modified:

> [O]ne of the abiding sadnesses of *Oh! What a Lovely War* was that Len Deighton absented himself. He'd had a disagreement and he never confronted me with it so I don't really know what in fact it was all about. But he had this sort of blood-brother partner called Brian Duffy and they ended up having a terrible falling out. I don't quite know what the cause of it was, it may have even been what I was doing, I just don't know. But Len certainly wanted no part of it and indeed took his name off it.[56]

The matter concerning Deighton's position was still an issue in 1984. A letter from Brian Duffy to Shelia Whitaker, the programming director for the National Film Theatre (during Attenborough's term as Chairman) took umbrage that 'the screen writer credit (uncredited) is attributed to Len Deighton'. Duffy claimed:

> The transportation from stage play into filmic terms was conceived and devised by me. The narrative ideas of the family and the pier were part of this concept as was the final sequence.
> As to Len Deighton's involvement, the British Screenwriters Guild stated that he had no claims to a writer's credit and he withdrew his name.[57]

Duffy's argument was a surprise to Attenborough who had no knowledge of the letter at the time it was sent.[58] Moreover, while Attenborough had always credited Duffy as a contributor to the film, the actual concept he always considered to be the work of Deighton.

> [T]he manner in which it was transferred to the screen was not mine. I embellished it but it was a brilliant idea of Len's and I very much regret that he was not part of it. I think in a way he might have reined me back a bit. I am an emotional character and that tends to take me over sometimes and I think perhaps if Len had stayed on board he might have been a corrective.[59]

The letter also confirms Attenborough's suggestion that a dispute had arisen between Duffy and Deighton. More recently Deighton has added to this version. On a television programme broadcast in 2006, entitled, *The Truth about Len Deighton*, he recalled the difficulties during production. Deighton, in his capacity as producer and scriptwriter, had requested that Attenborough should 'respect every line' of his script. With hindsight Deighton was more sympathetic to Attenborough's predicament at the time commenting 'I think I was a bit insensitive to how claustrophobic he probably felt about this situation' and voiced his disappointment over his impulsive action, which he described as 'a very stupid and infantile thing to do'.[60] Deighton's departure resulted in Attenborough taking the credit as co-producer of the film with Duffy.

There were also contentious issues relating to the film's historical accuracy. Correlli Barnett, a major contributor to the *The Great War*, criticised the film in the *Observer*. Barnett's views were based on his assumption that *Oh! What a Lovely War* was 'a film supposed to be a serious statement about British involvement in the Great War'. He denounced the film for making the generals 'scapegoats' and for the absence of the wartime premier, David Lloyd George, which he claimed 'omits the man in charge of the whole business – the generals' boss'.[61] Attenborough hotly disputed Barnett's criticism that the film laid the blame of the horrors of the war on the 'generals' incompetence', claiming that this had been 'refuted by a number of national critics' and quoted from

Ian Christie's review in the *Daily Express* who asserted that the blame for the war 'is not laid solely at the door of the military establishment'. For Attenborough, Barnett's view was 'somewhat lacking in objective judgement'.[62]

Despite employing a stylised format, *Oh! What a Lovely War* nevertheless asserts its claim firmly to historical authenticity with a caption that appears immediately after the opening credits, stating: 'The principal statements made by the historical characters in this film are based on documentary evidence and the words of the songs are those sung by the troops during the First World War.' Attenborough claimed: 'there is very little in this film that wasn't actually said during those four years'.[63] While the published stage play included an impressive number of references that point to the play's observance and desire for historical authenticity, one element of the film was intentionally altered. The lines read from Rupert Brooke's poem 'The Soldier' challenge the film's authenticity by shifting the authorship from Brooke, an officer, to Jack, a fictional private. As Jack embodies the common soldier, the transfer can be seen to speak the words for all soldiers of whatever rank. A more certain reference applies to the scene where Haig is filmed praying on his knees and asking: 'Please God let there be victory before the Americans arrive.' John Terraine in his study, *Douglas Haig: The Educated Soldier*, claimed that the 'sense of working under a Divine Providence never left him'.[64] Although the words attributed to Haig in the film may not be exact, they are very similar, 'I ask thee for victory Lord before the Americans arrive.' Another incident when the King was thrown from Haig's horse on 28 October 1915 is also recorded. While the words are not identical the impression the film portrays is that Haig's own reputation appears more important to him than the lives of soldiers.

> At the waving of hats, the mare threw up her head, the king seemed to clutch the reins very firmly and pulled the mare backwards. The ground was very wet and the grass slippery, so that the mare's hind legs slipped from underneath her [...] It was a most unfortunate accident.[65]

Before the film was premièred the *Sunday Telegraph* proclaimed: '[F]ew productions have excited so much interest and controversy. It is boldly original and very possibly the most powerful pacifist statement since *All Quiet on the Western Front*.'[66] Some controversy came from official sources. The Chairman of the United Nations Association (UNA) wished to benefit from the première for *Oh! What a Lovely War* and accordingly asked the Secretary of State for Foreign Affairs to inform Paramount of 'the importance' Britain attaches to the UNA. While the UNA could gain £15,000, concerns were raised to the publicity handouts of the film and its satirical elements. Although accusations of 'make[ing] fun of the Establishment and the military commanders', were expressed there was acknowledgement that it contained 'a most powerful implicit [sic] for the avoidance of war'. There was also unease with the political links to the film from its original associations. Littlewood and Theatre Workshop were claimed to be 'closely associated with the Communist party' and the play itself had 'strong anti-war propaganda from a near-Marxist viewpoint'.[67] A letter from the Secretary of State, Michael Stewart, attacked the film for its anti-war message which he asserted was 'in conflict with what the supporters of the United Nations believe'.[68] The letter, with many words underlined, continued:

> We have to avoid a situation in which the most humane and civilised people, in all nations, are so repelled by the evils of war that they resolve never to use force in any circumstances: for this would hand over the government of the world to those who have no such scruples. It is this *error* which 'Oh What a Lovely War!' seems to me to promote.[69]

The letter also expressed the Foreign Secretary's personal views of the film and demonstrated the depth of feeling that the film was able to produce:

> 'Oh' presents the First World War as a bloodthirsty farce engineered by a small number of stupid or wicked people at the expense of innocent mankind. If we accept this facile explanation we shall get no-where with peace-keeping. In fact, that war was a tragedy which occurred because mankind as a whole had not to construct a political framework suitable to the 20th century. To present this tragedy as a farce and a subject for mockery will cause great distress to many people: it is also a profoundly misleading presentation, in that it diverts people's attention from the real effort, both of mind and heart, that is needed if the objects of the United Nations are to be achieved and the scourge of war banished from the earth.

The letters are, however, revealing in expressing the Foreign Office's view that film could influence public opinion and in particular to the degree of sensitivity that communism still held in 1969. However, the concerns were unfounded as the United Nations Association was 'unable' to secure the première.

The film opened on Thursday 10 April 1969 at the Paramount Cinema in Piccadilly, London. Precise box-office figures were not regularly published in the trade press at this time, but *Kinematograph Weekly* included the film as one of its 'Box-office Winners of 1969' under the category of 'Top Ten General Releases'. It was also credited with winning the category of 'Best musical satire'.[70]

As an adaptation of a prestigious stage play it was inevitable that many reviewers would compare the film to the original play and judge it accordingly. Those who had not seen the play were also provided with an opportunity to see a revival of it at its original venue at the Theatre Royal. Michael Billington's review commented that the new production 'catches something of the flavour and spirit' of the original.[71] In the quality press there was a consensus in favour of the film. Dilys Powell acknowledged Attenborough's 'skill and sympathy as a director of acting', but saved her greatest praise for the impact of the film, claiming: 'the impression you are left with is of a fantasia, beautiful, dreadful, heart breaking, on history: history re-interpreted through the songs of those it massacred.'[72] David Robinson, too, asserted his liking for Attenborough's film by claiming that he 'has done rather more that the apparently impossible. He has not only translated *Oh! What a Lovely War* from the stage; but made it seem to belong pre-eminently to the cinema.'[73]

Critics who had not seen the play included Margaret Hinxman, who found the film 'exhilarating', claiming that Attenborough's portrayal of simple human emotion 'turns an enormously talented film into a deeply significant one', and Ernest Betts, who harshly renamed the film 'Oh! What a Lovely Bore!', castigating it for not being 'a movie at all but a series of acts'.[74] In contrast, Kenneth Allsop, in the *Observer*, was less impressed with the film than the play, despite his assertion that a film 'shouldn't be compared with the stage, or whatever, original: a work of art or entertainment has its own *is*-ness [sic]'. He revealed that while he was 'impaled' by Littlewood's production, he was critical of the film for being 'too romantically nostalgic'.[75]

Other critics who favoured the film included John Russell Taylor in *The Times*, who claimed the film was 'an almost complete triumph, showing an imaginative range and a large number of individual skills'.[76] *The Times* also noted the film's significance in an editorial entitled 'A Spectacular Triumph'. It applauded Attenborough's film as 'a tribute, above all, to the taste and good sense of those involved in the film's making'.[77] The *Daily Telegraph* described the film as a 'remarkably intricate and accomplished piece of work'.[78] While the *Guardian* praised the film as 'a considerable achievement', the *Morning Star* found Attenborough's version a 'singularly non-involving film' which 'challenges nothing'.[79] In the popular press, the *Sun* praised Attenborough for his 'stunning debut', while Ian Christie in the *Daily Express*, called the film 'a work of art – a masterpiece of insight and interpretation – beautifully put together by Richard Attenborough'.[80] For Alexander Walker in the *Evening Standard*, Attenborough has 'made one of the most moving and memorable films I've ever seen'.[81]

While the film journals offered similarly varied opinions, the occasion of the première resulted in the journal *Cinema*, an intellectual publication based at the University of Cambridge, to include 'an obituary' to British cinema written by the left-wing writer, Tom Nairn.[82] The article, edged with a black rectangular border, was stark in its message, under its heading:

10 April 1969
Deceased at the Paramount, Piccadilly, London W 1,
THE BRITISH CINEMA

Although Nairn reproached Attenborough for the way his adaptation had removed most of the leftist view from the original, thus allowing the middle classes to 'indulge their nostalgia with a good conscience', his principal attack was aimed at the critics. Quoting from those who offered suitable funereal comments, including Powell ('I could not restrain my tears') Hinxman ('stunned moments of grief') and Walker (who 'wrestled with a lump in his throat'). Nairn explained his reasoning:

> How fitting that 'British Cinema' should commit suicide in this last paroxysm of cinematic Britishry, [sic] mourned by the mass blubbering of the critics! The event was long overdue. Once the corpse is out of the way, we must hope that it will be a bit easier to make decent films in Britain.

A similar criticism was presented by Alan Lovell in the *Brighton Film Review*. Lovell's disdain for the film was clear, claiming that *Oh! What a Lovely War* is 'such an unintelligent dull film'. His dismissal of the film also needs to be seen in the context of Lovell's general views of British cinema at the time and his particular well-known dislike of theatrical adaptations. The review came after his landmark seminar paper to the British Film Institute 'British cinema: the unknown cinema', which was delivered in March 1969, just prior to the release of *Oh! What a Lovely War*.[83] In the unpublished paper Lovell complained of the lack of *auteur* directors, as there were none 'for whom a prima facie case could be made out for their interest and representative quality'.[84] Lovell's view was also influenced by his opinion that the war and historical films had 'little intrinsic interest'.[85] This opinion had also been evident in his review. For Lovell: 'Like the incoherent structure and the blurring of attitudes, these deficiencies work to make the film a smudged, indistinct copy of the stage original.'[86]

Other specialist film journals were less critical. The *Monthly Film Bulletin* considered the film as 'a mammoth pageant, intelligently assembled and with a few moments of real inspiration but without the cumulative effect essential to this sort of theatrical display'.[87] *Screen* claimed that the film's most remarkable achievement is that it is 'a successful British *musical*', and claimed that it succeeds because 'the music gives the film its form'.[88] *Sight and Sound* was fulsome in its praise, regarding Attenborough's first film as 'little short of a triumph and one that reflects credit on everyone concerned'.[89]

The film opened in America at the Paris Theatre, New York, cut by twelve minutes, on 3 October, six months after it was shown as the closing feature of the 7th New York Film Festival. The *Evening News* reported that '[a] jubilant Richard Attenborough woke up today to find himself the toast of New York' after his film 'captured ecstatic reviews and two standing ovations from last night's film festival audience'.[90] Included in the article were excerpts from some of the other critics: Judith Crist in *New York Magazine* ('It is not merely at this point the best film of 1969 but an outstanding film for all time'), *McCall's* ('If you see no other film this year, you must see this one. It's brilliant') and the *New York Post* ('A masterpiece that will endure as long as nations have wars'). It also included a word of caution from the *New York Times:* 'Much is brilliant, superb – but it overwhelms its material with a surfeit of good intentions'.

Variety had described the film, viewed in its full length in Britain, as 'dedicated, exhilarating, shrewd, mocking, funny, emotional, witty, poignant and technically brilliant'. In America, however, Vincent Canby was more critical, claiming that its 'elephantine physical proportions and often brilliant all-star cast simply overwhelm the material.[91] Other unfavourable reviews included Pauline Kael in the *New Yorker* who complained that the film 'lapses back into blandness' and *Newsweek*, which suggested that the film 'is an all-too-easy and obvious dismissal of the English upper crust as hopeless boobs'.[92] In contrast, the *Saturday Review* called the film 'a bold, venturesome, and wholly commendable project', while the *Los Angeles Times* regarded the film as a 'beautifully imaginative, unorthodox, uncompromising, emotionally powerful piece of cinema'.[93]

Oh! What Lovely War was chosen as Britain's entry in two international film festivals: Mar Del Plata in the Argentine and also, in a noncompetitive basis, at the Osaka festival in Japan as part of World Fair. At the Society of Film and Television Arts Awards of 1969 (now BAFTA), where Attenborough was chairman 1969–70, it won five categories including Best Supporting Actor (Olivier), and Best Cinematography (Turpin). The film also won the United Nations Award.

Oh! What a Lovely War can be linked to several cycles of films that were prevalent during the 1960s. As part of the anti-war cycle which had seen a revival in popularity in the cinema in the decade, it challenged conventional views of the representation of war. The convention had also been seen in *How I Won the War* which relates the story of a British platoon in North Africa who is assigned a mission behind enemy lines to set up a cricket match in order to impress a visiting American VIP. The film, famous for casting John Lennon as Private Gripweed, explores class differences between men and officers employing a mixture of comedy, parody and surrealism. Another link can be seen with *The Charge of the Light Brigade*, a colourful costume drama which re-enacts the event in the Battle of Balaclava in the Crimean War – another event regarded as a military disaster by many military historians. The film questions the role of the officer class by exposing the violence, sexuality and corruption that existed, thus paving the way for the satirical approach that *Oh! What a Lovely War* developed. Both films also demonstrate similarities by including three of the same actors (Gielgud, Corin and Vanessa Redgrave), and both shared difficulties between their director and screenwriter.

As a film representation of the First World War *Oh! What a Lovely War* can be seen as part of a long series of films that began in the 1920s. Early reconstructions of the conflict, as depicted by British Instructional Films, including the battlefield films *Ypres* (1925) and *Mons* (1926), represented the official view. The 1930s provided a more direct link with the fictional depictions of *Journey's End* (James Whale, 1930) and *All Quiet on the Western Front*, which both conveyed an anti-war perspective. The timing and consequences of the Second World War (1939–45) had a significant impact on how the former conflict was viewed while also creating a forced hiatus in filming the earlier conflict. The distance of time and the generally accepted greater justification for the Second World War added a new perspective to viewing the Great War. Thus while the cinema had celebrated British victory in the Second World War during the 1950s, the 1960s created a cultural space in which the former conflict could be reassessed. Only two other films of the decade look at the British perspective. *Lawrence of Arabia*, an epic portrayal of T.E. Lawrence starring Peter O'Toole and based on Lawrence's autobiography, depicts a British officer in a distant part of the conflict. The film opens with Lawrence's death in 1935 in a motor cycle accident and then applies a flashback technique to explore his character through the Desert Revolt. Lawrence's pro-killing statement: 'No prisoners!' can be seen as an anti-war perspective, promoting the idea that 'war can also bring out their worst qualities as well'.[94]

It is through the subject matter with the emphasis on the plight of the ordinary soldier that *King and Country* is closer to *Oh! What a Lovely War*. Both also share a stage origin, with *King and Country* adapted from

John Wilson's play, *Hamp*, and both featuring Dirk Bogarde in the cast. Joseph Losey also explores a similar class-based theme to show the contempt for the ordinary soldiers willing to serve 'King and Country' but who receive no support from the higher command for the horrors they experience and are summarily executed if they fail in their duty. The film questions the responsibilities of the officer class who fail to show any concern for soldiers who have fought bravely for their country but then fall victims to shell-shock. Hamp (Tom Courtenay) represents the plight of the ordinary soldier for all the hundreds executed for failing in their duty. *King and Country* also shares a complex narrative structure with *Oh! What a Lovely War* by attempting to show a distinction between the higher officers and the lower officers. Thus Haig can be compared with Captain Midgely (James Villiers) in his non-yielding stance at the Court Martial, and in their collective lack of compassion. Hargreaves, as the voice of conscience, by sharing his doubts of Hamp's guilt, can be compared to the role of Haig's first aide (Edward Fox) who warns of the slaughter that will result from the general's tactics.

Despite its critical and popular success, Attenborough was highly critical of his first film as director particularly in the film's message of futility. As he explained:

> I have to admit that in the final analysis it was not as good a film as the play; in the play there was an astringency which the film lacked. It was not my intention, that's what's so aggravating, but in the end result it was not as powerful in those terms.[95]

Oh! What a Lovely War, nevertheless, demonstrates Attenborough's strong passion for his subject and an ability to put over a strong anti-war message with a clear and uncompromising perspective. Moreover, the role of directing was clearly an experience that Attenborough enjoyed and one with which he wished to continue: 'Unequivocally, I'd like to go on directing. But the subject has to be right for me.'[96] His next directorial venture with *Young Winston* (1972), however, was destined to be a very different experience.

Notes

1 The stage play, *Oh What a Lovely War!* is distinguishable from its filmic adaptation, *Oh! What a Lovely War*, by the different positioning of the exclamation mark.
2 Alex Danchev, 'Bunking and Debunking: The Controversies of the 1960s', in Brian Bond (ed.), *The First World War and Military History*, Oxford, 1991, p. 264.
3 Quoted in Mary Blume, '"Lovely War" Remembered in Brighton', *International Herald Tribune*, 15 May 1968.
4 *The Long Long Trail* was transmitted on 27 December 1961. It was repeated on 21

February and 11 November 1962. Information obtained from author's correspondence with Charles Chilton, 24 November 2003.
5 Author's interview with Chilton, 9 March, 2004, London; correspondence with Murray Melvin, archivist at Theatre Royal, 4 November 2003. Both Philip French, *Sight and Sound*, 38:2 (spring 1969), p. 93 and David Robinson, *Richard Attenborough*, London, 2003, p. 38 attribute the play to Allan.
6 Quoted in *The Times*, 18 May 1963, p. 12. The application was refused by the High Court judge who stated that he was satisfied that it was Littlewood's own work.
7 Ted Allan's name is cited in all theatre productions for suggesting the title.
8 DVD *Oh! What a Lovely War*, Paramount Pictures, 2006, EU111865.
9 John Ramsden, 'The Great War: The Making of the Series', *Historical Journal of Film, Radio and Television*, 22:1 (2002), pp. 7–8. Ramsden argues that the phrase was actually applied to the French army of 1870.
10 Ibid., p. 7.
11 *The Times*, 31 May 1963.
12 Howard Goorney, *The Theatre Workshop Story*, London, p. 157.
13 Derek Paget, *True Stories? Documentary Drama on Radio, Screen and Stage*, Manchester, 1990, pp. 76–7.
14 Mark Connelly, *The Charge of the Light Brigade*, London, 2003, p. 8.
15 David Castell, *Richard Attenborough: A Pictorial Biography*, London, 1984, p. 17.
16 Quoted in Benedict Nightingale, 'Richard Attenborough and His Methods', *The Times*, 8 January 1968.
17 Sarah Street, *British National Cinema*, London, 1997, p. 81; Robert Murphy, *1960s British Cinema*, London, 1992, p. 278.
18 Captain H.C.B. Pipon to Lord Chamberlain. Lord Chamberlain's Correspondence Files, 3308/1963.
19 The Profumo Affair involved the Conservative minister, John Profumo, who resigned in 1963 for lying to Parliament about his affair with a prostitute, Christine Keeler. It was later the subject of the film, *Scandal* (Michael Caton-Jones, 1989).
20 Carpenter, *That Was Satire That Was: The Satire Boom of the 1960s*, London, 2000, p. 301.
21 Danchev, 'Bunking and Debunking', p. 279.
22 Ibid., p. 281.
23 Ramsden, 'The Great War: The Making of the Series', pp. 10 and 13.
24 I consider *Doctor Zhivago* as a British film as it is included in Denis Gifford, *The British Film Catalogue*, London, 2000, p. 1039.
25 Edward Milward-Oliver, *The Len Deighton Companion*, London, 1988, p. 216.
26 Quoted in Lee Langley, 'Up and Attenborough', *Guardian*, 29 March 1969.
27 'Attenborough, Why I Became a Director', *Action* (US) 5:1 (Jan./Feb. 1970), p. 15.
28 Ibid., pp. 15–16.
29 Attenborough, quoted on DVD *Oh! What a Lovely War*.
30 Attenborough, 'Oh! What a Lovely Way to Start', *Today's Cinema*, 9 April 1969, p. 8.
31 Charles Bludhorn's name is spelled Bluhdorn by other commentators. Attenborough has used the former spelling in *In Search of Gandhi*, London, 1982, which I have continued.
32 Quoted in Langley, 'Up and Attenborough'.
33 DVD, *Oh! What a Lovely War*.
34 Jeffrey Richards, *Thorold Dickinson and the British Cinema*, Folkestone, 1997, p. 84.
35 *Today's Cinema*, 26 February 1969, p. 14; *Filmfacts*, 12:17 (1969), p. 386. The DVD of *Oh! What a Lovely War* gives the amount as $3.25 million.

36 Paget, 'Oh What a Lovely War and the token tradition of documentary theatre: an investigation into the origins, manifestations and influence of documentary theatre in the UK'. Unpublished Ph.D. thesis, 1988, Manchester University, SM D7781, British Library, London.
37 Author's interview with Attenborough, Richmond, Surrey, 16 February 2007.
38 Quoted in Margaret Hinxman, 'A Lovely War for British films', *Sunday Telegraph*, 6 April 1969.
39 James, Chapman, *Past and Present: National Identity and the British Historical Film*, London, 2005, p. 252.
40 Other commentators have suggested it is a 360 degree shot. Attenborough and I, together, calculated it to be 180 degrees.
41 Quoted in David Robinson, *Richard Attenborough*, London, p. 42.
42 Andy Dougan, *The Actors' Director: Richard Attenborough behind the Camera*, Edinburgh, 1994, p. 26.
43 *Sight and Sound*, 38:2 (spring 1969), p. 94.
44 *Oh What a Lovely War* (script) Ann Skinner Collection (Box 4) BFI, London.
45 Michael Paris, 'Enduring Heroes', in Paris (ed.), *The First World War and Popular Culture*, Edinburgh, 1999, p. 68.
46 Quoted in Hinxman, 'A Lovely War for British Films'.
47 DVD, *Oh! What a Lovely War*.
48 Quoted in Attenborough, 'Why I Became a Director', p. 16.
49 Alan Burton, 'The Great War in British Film', in Claire Monk and Amy Sargeant (eds), *British Historical Cinema*, London, 2002, p. 39.
50 Kenneth D. Belden to the Lord Chamberlain, Lord Chamberlain's Correspondence Files, 3308/1963.
51 The programme was initially broadcast on BBC1 on 26 December 1968 and repeated on BBC2, prior to the film's release on 8 April 1969.
52 *The Times*, 3 January 1969.
53 Quoted in Hinxman, 'A Lovely War for British Films'.
54 *Variety*, 19 March 1969.
55 Quoted in Hinxman, 'A Lovely War for British Films'.
56 Dougan, *The Actors' Director*, p. 19.
57 Brian Duffy to Sheila Whitaker, dated 21 August 1984. *Oh! What a Lovely War* microfiche, BFI, London.
58 Author's interview with Attenborough, 16 February 2007.
59 Dougan, *The Actors' Director*, p. 19.
60 Quoted on *The Truth about Len Deighton*, BBC4, 7 January 2006.
61 *Observer*, 20 April 1969.
62 *Observer*, 27 April 1969.
63 Quoted in Blume, '"Lovely War" Remembered in Brighton'.
64 John Terraine, *Douglas Haig: The Educated Soldier*, London, 1963, p. 173.
65 Robert Blake (ed.), *The Private Papers of Sir Douglas Haig 1914–1919*, London, 1952, p. 110.
66 Hinxman, 'A Lovely War for British Films'.
67 National Archives (NA) FCO 26/188, J. Peck to D.J. Maitland, 1 Jan. 1969–31 December 1969. (The letter is dated incorrectly as 1968.)
68 (NA) FCO 26/188, Michael Stewart to Humphrey Berkeley, dated 5 Feb. 1969.
69 *Ibid.* (emphases in original).
70 *Kinematograph Weekly*, 20 December 1969, p. 8.
71 *The Times*, 20 October 1969, p. 12.
72 *Sunday Times*, 13 April 1969.
73 *Financial Times*, 11 April 1969.
74 *Sunday Telegraph*, 13 April 1969; *People*, 13 April 1969.

75 *Observer*, 13 April 1969.
76 *The Times*, 10 April 1969.
77 *The Times*, 26 April 1969.
78 *Daily Telegraph*, 11 April 1969.
79 *Guardian*, 9 April 1969; *Morning Star*, 9 April 1969.
80 *Sun*, 9 April 1969; *Daily Express*, 9 April 1969.
81 *Evening Standard*, 10 April 1969.
82 *Cinema* (UK), 3 June 1969, p. 15.
83 Alan Lovell, 'The British cinema: the unknown cinema', seminar paper, BFI, 13 March 1969.
84 *Ibid.*, p. 5.
85 *Ibid.*, p. 6.
86 *Brighton Film Review*, 17 (February 1970), p. 20.
87 *Monthly Film Bulletin*, 36:424 (May 1969), p. 94.
88 *Screen*, 10:3 (May/June 1969), p. 84.
89 *Sight and Sound*, 38:2 (spring 1969), p. 93.
90 *Evening News*, 3 October 1969.
91 *Variety*, 16 April and 3 October 1969.
92 *New Yorker*, 11 October, 1969; *Newsweek*, 13 October 1969.
93 *Saturday Review*, 4 October 1969; *Los Angeles Times*, 6 November 1969.
94 Paris, 'Enduring Heroes', p. 66.
95 Dougan, *The Actors' Director*, p. 19.
96 *Films and Filming*, 15:9 (June 1969), p. 8.

Anglo-American alliances: *Young Winston* (1972), *A Bridge Too Far* (1977) and *Magic* (1978)

4

In the 1970s Richard Attenborough consolidated his move into directing by completing three films, all different in style and subject. Two were British productions: *Young Winston*, a portrayal of Winston Churchill's early life, and *A Bridge Too Far*, a re-enactment of the Battle of Arnhem, a significant Allied defeat of the Second World War. Both films are notable for their high production values, stellar casts and complex narratives. They also demonstrate Attenborough's development as a director both in his skilful control of epic sequences and his subtle approach to human interaction. The third film, *Magic* (1978), a contemporary thriller, is distinct by being both a fictional story, significantly smaller in scale, and the first of only two films Attenborough made in America.

The critical success of *Oh! What a Lovely War* had highlighted Attenborough as a promising director. His name was linked with a group of new directors, Stephen Frears, Ken Russell, Nicolas Roeg and Ken Loach, whom Andrew Higson considered to have distinguished themselves by producing films in the 1960s that were 'intelligent, sophisticated, intellectually demanding and strongly cinematic'.[1] In order to build on his early success Attenborough took particular care in choosing his next project, rejecting several before accepting Carl Foreman's offer to direct *Young Winston*, and later Joseph E. Levine's *A Bridge Too Far*.

Both Foreman and Levine were powerful and highly influential figures who engaged Attenborough to direct films they had planned themselves. Both were American and owned their own production companies, Foreman with Open Road and Levine who headed Joseph E. Levine Presents. Both producers were attracted by the innovative style and critical success of *Oh! What a Lovely War*. Both producers were also influenced by Attenborough's connections with the Establishment, which included his friendship with Earl Mountbatten, who was supporting him in negotiations for *Gandhi*. Attenborough's treatment by the two producers, however, was very different: the extent of directorial control he was permitted raises questions regarding the agency of the two films. *Young Winston*, he later declared, was 'not a happy experience', with Foreman's stronger position as writer and producer allowing Attenborough no 'creative autonomy'.² In *A Bridge Too Far*, Levine gave Attenborough greater latitude and more creative freedom, constrained only by the budget. However, Attenborough was unwilling to jeopardise his relationship with Levine by doing anything that might endanger the future production of *Gandhi*.

Both films were given substantial budgets: *Young Winston* was supported by Columbia to the extent of $6,500,000 while *A Bridge Too Far* cost $25,000,000. The sums, however, were at variance with the dramatic decline of American investment in British films in the early 1970s. The total amount invested had dropped from £20.9 million in 1969 to £14 million in 1972 before reaching the lowest point in 1974 of £2.9 million with a further drop in 1979 to £6 million.³ The decade ended with 50 per cent less American investment than it had done at the beginning.

Although the total number of British films increased in the early 1970s, they were mainly low-budgeted genre films for home consumption as Hollywood studios in England had curtailed their overseas involvement in favour of more indigenous productions. The repercussions in England had a severe effect resulting in the closure of MGM's Borehamwood Studios in 1970 and a reduced workforce at others including Pinewood, Shepperton and Elstree.⁴ As a result production changed from the subsidiaries of major American companies to independent companies of which both Open Road and Joseph E. Levine Presents were representative. While the Hollywood majors still retained control over distribution, the 'big-budget' film dominated 1970s film culture. Both *Young Winston* and *A Bridge Too Far* were integral to this culture. However, whereas the major companies, including Columbia, provided the finance, controlled the distribution and retained overall control of the films, Levine's situation was different. As a man of substantial means he acted as the bank himself, requiring United Artists for distribution only. Columbia's close association with Shepperton Studios was also significant. *Young Winston* required several interior scenes that involved expensive and detailed set constructions, including a replica House of Commons.

Young Winston was Attenborough's first biopic, a genre that would dominate his directorial career. The film is more correctly identified as a partial biopic as the film concerns a defined period of Churchill's life, his childhood from the age of 7, when he entered boarding preparatory school, to his reaching maturity at the age of 27, an event marked by his maiden speech to the House of Commons on 13 May 1901. The film mixes traditional cinematic styles of crowd-filled action-packed epic scenes contrasting with slow-tempo intimate portrayals. It uses a non-linear narrative, employing devices such as flashbacks, repetition and out-of-context face-to-face interviews, the latter, introducing a contemporary mechanism into a period piece, bridging the modern with the old while allowing intimate feelings to be openly expressed. Churchill's life and premiership were sufficiently recent to be recalled by many of the population including Attenborough, who expressed his admiration of Churchill by declaring: 'I believe that his stature, the respect in which he was held and his phenomenal courage and his ability to speak to the nation, saved, I genuinely believe, the world's democracy.'[5]

Young Winston can be considered as part of the middle-brow film culture of the 1970s. It also conformed to the demand for traditional historical films which had pervaded the early 1970s but whose popularity did not survive beyond the middle of the decade. Prominent examples include *The Iron Duke* (Victor Saville, 1934), *Henry V* (Laurence Olivier, 1944) and *Lawrence of Arabia* (David Lean, 1962). *Young Winston* was also part of the 1970s cycle of historical biopics which have been claimed to have 'exemplified the persistence of traditional filmmaking practices', such as *Anne of the Thousand Days* (Charles Jarrott, 1969, released in Britain in 1970), *Cromwell* (Ken Hughes, 1970) and *Lady Caroline Lamb* (Robert Bolt, 1972).[6] The films have all been noted for 'their cultural and aesthetic conservatism: respectable, literate, wordy scripts and a sober visual style of sensitive colour cinematography', all characteristics that would become central to Attenborough's œuvre.[7]

Young Winston can also be classed as an 'end of empire' portrayal by its inclusion of specific historical events pertaining to the loss of imperial power. The film portrays Churchill as a cavalry officer, a Second Lieutenant, acting as a war correspondent with the Malakand Field Force in India, and his role in the Sudan expedition of 1898, where he took part in what the film describes as the last ever cavalry charge. It also includes Churchill's experiences in South Africa, working as a reporter covering the Boer War, where he was captured and imprisoned before making a daring escape, returning to England as a hero. Churchill's early political life is explored, leading to his election as Member of Parliament for Oldham, following in the footsteps of his late father, Lord Randolph Churchill, the former Chancellor of the Exchequer. The question of historical accuracy in *Young Winston* was important for Attenborough who considered the manner and representation of history as a 'massive responsibility' as 'knowledge is in that movie and there it stands for future generations'.[8] This responsibility appears to have been successful. David Castell supports this notion by maintaining that *Young Winston* 'crystallised Attenborough's singular gift for examining the impact of recent history upon the people who live in its wake'.[9]

Although a non-fictional piece *Young Winston* also embraces characteristics of the adventure film with its exploration of Churchill's heroism and patriotism in his courage during an ambush and his subsequent escape from imprisonment. The 'adventure' correlation is also perpetuated by Churchill's claim that he saw his own life as an adventure film based on the heroism and courageous tales in the '*Boy's Own* tradition' as depicted in the *Boy's Own Paper*, founded in 1879.[10] The adventure film was also represented by Foreman's earlier production, *The Guns of Navarone* (J. Lee Thompson, 1961).

Young Winston can also be regarded as a forerunner of the 'heritage film', a critical term that applied to a particular cycle of British historical films dominant during the 1980s and 1990s. While *Chariots of Fire* (Hugh Hudson, 1981) has often been recognised with beginning this cycle, which later became closely associated with Merchant–Ivory productions such as *A Room with a View* (James Ivory, 1986) and *Howards End* (Ivory, 1992), *Young Winston* shares the same principal characteristics. Sarah Street identifies the qualities that characterise the cycle as 'precise and loving photography of sites of national heritage ... a focus on male rivalry and bonding, and a nostalgic view of the past', all of which are evident in the film.[11] It also presents a particular image of 'Britishness', particularly Englishness, which was later to become a profitable and exportable commodity to America.

The origins of *Young Winston* can be traced back to 1941 when Sir Winston Churchill sold the rights to his autobiography *My Early Life* to Alexander Korda.[12] In the 1950s the rights were purchased by Paramount Pictures which included a proviso that Churchill was entitled to view the script before the film was accepted for production.[13] Bryan Forbes, Attenborough's then production partner, produced a script in 1963 entitled 'The Young Mr Churchill', which, although gaining Churchill's approval, was rejected by Paramount. The script was donated to the British Film Institute by Forbes in 1985 with a memorandum enclosed, revealing his personal views:

> This was commissioned by Paramount, but they subsequently sold the script to Columbia who acquired it for Carl Foreman. Mr. Foreman wrote his own script and offered this to me to direct. In the circumstances I declined and of course the film was eventually directed by Sir Richard Attenborough. I have a great liking for this still-born child which I think contains some of my best writing on a difficult subject.[14]

Forbes's ill feeling is understandable as his script also begins around the time of Churchill's birth but, as he indicated in a foreword, he limits his treatment between 'Lord Randolph's maiden speech to the House in 1874 and Sir Winston's speech in 1901'.[15] As Foreman's script also includes Lord Randolph's speech and ends at the time of Winston's speech, the similarities to Forbes's script are easily identified.

Foreman believed that as a foreigner he would not be acceptable to direct a film on a British subject of such magnitude. He was, nevertheless, acceptable to Churchill as a writer, despite being 'a black-listed left-wing American writer who had been accused of being a subversive influence in Hollywood'.[16] Foreman had originally come to England in 1952, after being victimised by the anti-communist witch-hunt. He was employed at Shepperton by Alexander Korda, who had previously engaged Churchill in the 1930s to write six political short films and a script for the 1935 Silver Jubilee.[17] In 1958 Foreman formed Open Road Films under the umbrella of Columbia and produced three films: *The Key* (Carol Reed, 1958), *The Mouse that Roared* (Jack Arnold, 1959) and *The Guns of Navarone*. Directing *The Victors* (1963), which he also wrote and produced, gave Foreman greater control and much creative satisfaction, but the film was a critical and financial failure. As a result, Columbia banned Foreman from directing until he had repaid his monetary debt.

In 1961 Churchill's secretary Anthony Montague Brown, informed Foreman that Churchill had admired *The Guns of Navarone*, which Foreman had also written, and wanted to discuss the possibility of making his own life into a film. Churchill had noted that *The Guns of Navarone* was 'one of the most prosperous war films ever made' and that Foreman as an American 'will be in a position to pay him [Churchill] a great deal of money'.[18] Foreman had previously purchased the film rights to Churchill's autobiography, *My Early Life* and his study *The World Crisis*, at Churchill's request.[19] No financial details were divulged, at Churchill's request, but the amount was substantially more than had been agreed with Paramount as Columbia had bought outright control of Churchill's works.[20] However, Columbia's initial enthusiasm for the film waned after a less than enthusiastic popular response to the company's documentary feature film on Churchill, *The Finest Hours* (Peter Baylis, 1964), based on Churchill's war memoirs, *The Second World War*. Although the film was critically well received, gaining an Academy Award nomination, it failed commercially. Columbia agreed to continue with the project only after Foreman offered to write a screenplay for 'nothing' and to use his own money as a 'buffer' against extra costs.

Attenborough's involvement with *Young Winston* came after Foreman had completed a draft script and secured the necessary funding. Both

Attenborough and Foreman had been one of several signatories to a letter to The Times in 1971, headed by Lindsay Anderson, complaining about the newly elected Conservative government's plan to disregard a loan of £5 million to the National Film Finance Corporation, as had been agreed in the 1970 Films Act.[21] For Young Winston, it was Attenborough's British nationality and directorial qualities that were pivotal to Foreman's requirements:

> I had felt all along that it was essential to have an Englishman to make the film, and as it deals with the early days of his life, it was also necessary to find a director with the right sensitivity. A soon as I saw Oh! What a Lovely War I knew that Dickie was my man.[22]

Foreman offered Attenborough both the position of director and also as actor for the role of Lord Randolph Churchill. Attenborough rejected the latter. As he later explained:

> One of the principal requirements of a director is that of objectivity. This must apply, not only to the film as a whole but also in assessing each individual moment and scene as one progresses through the shooting and editing period. Consequently, if such perspective is, in any way, impaired by a counter-involvement as total as playing one of the three principal characters, it would, I felt, jeopardize one's ultimate judgement. This, I was sure, was a risk which, if I were completely honest, I should not take.[23]

The working relationship between Attenborough and Foreman was a crucial factor in Young Winston. There were early signs that this was not going to be easy. In 1968 Foreman had declared that he took 'no pleasure in being a producer' and commented that directing is 'where the fun is'.[24] Moreover, J. Lee Thompson, who directed The Guns of Navarone and MacKenna's Gold (1969), which Foreman produced, had found him a 'very complex person, and very desirous of directing himself'.[25] Both Attenborough and Foreman shared similar obsessions with their chosen film projects, Foreman with Young Winston and Attenborough with Gandhi. Both men refused to yield to the various difficulties that plagued both projects. As Barry Norman observed:

> Foreman can be very persuasive. But then so, too, can Attenborough. Indeed, another thing that makes the combination of the pair of them so interesting is that they are, each of them, men of great guile and charm, equally bent on and accustomed to getting their own way.[26]

The Times provided a chronology of the production of Young Winston, ostensibly written by Attenborough, which indicates that Foreman soon exerted his influence. Attenborough revealed that Foreman would return scripts 'rewritten, often with further innovations of which we had not even talked'.[27] While Foreman's control over the script was helped by his being President of the Writers' Guild of Great Britain at the time, difficulties also occurred with casting.[28] Whereas Foreman approved of Attenborough's choice of Anne Bancroft to play Churchill's mother, Jennie, Lady Randolph, and Robert Shaw as Lord Randolph Churchill, the role of Churchill caused a bitter dispute. Attenborough's choice was Simon Ward, who was an experienced theatre actor but relatively unknown in cinema; however Foreman was initially unconvinced of his suitability. Attenborough persisted and later described the feat as winning 'my first and most vital battle'.[29] The part of the younger Churchill required two child actors, Russell Lewis and Michael Audreson, while a non-actor, Sanders Watney, was chosen for a non-speaking role of the elderly Sir Winston.

Young Winston had a budget of $6.5 million (£2.5 million). It was filmed on location in Morocco, which represented both Sudan and India, and in South Wales which stood in for South Africa. In England, permission for filming was granted at Blenheim Palace, Harrow, and at Windsor Race Track but not at the House of Commons. *Variety* reported that 'Officials did not stop him [Foreman] filming in the House of Commons but precedent did'. Permission was granted, however, to 'shoot plates and footage for front projection'.[30]

What is particularly notable in *Young Winston* is its pictorial style. Attenborough's intention was for its appearance to resemble early copies of the *Illustrated London News* and *The Sphere* and achieve 'the quality of the painter Vermeer'. Gerry Turpin, the cinematographer, had been experimenting three months before filming began with a new process, known as Colorflex, using effects to mute the high colour tones by means of a series of filters.[31] This format was also helpful to the audience as different filters distinguished the different locations. A red overlay was used for India and a brown one for England thus allowing the audience to be easily transported between the two countries as the scenes cut back and forth.

In contrast to the period pictorial style, *Young Winston* also employs contemporary devices. These included three face-to-camera interview sequences, instigated by Foreman, which deviated from the expected narrative structure of biographical and historical representations. The manner and style were also contrary to the conduct of behaviour of the period. Foreman explained his reasoning for the sequences:

> [I]t occurred to me that today's audience had grown up with the television interview as a part of their general viewing [...] The idea intrigued me very much. It would give me the opportunity to expose character and advance the story at the same time.[32]

The interviews allow the coexistence of a contemporary form of interrogation within the film's historical setting, thus providing a method by which the three principal characters are able to express their feelings and emotions to an off-screen interrogator. Foreman's claim that he was 'concerned with cruelty of that kind' pushed Gordon Gow to suggest to him that they might stem from Foreman's own experience of interrogation during the McCarthy era and thus act as a form of catharsis, which Foreman indicated might be correct.[33] The sequences caused much tension between Foreman and Attenborough. Although Foreman claimed that Attenborough 'came round and became very enthusiastic', about them, this claim appears untrue, as Attenborough later maintained 'I just didn't think it worked at all and I felt ill at ease with it.'[34] He further explained:

> It was almost impossible to set up circumstances under which they might be asked. So, rather having lost the battle and rather nervous nevertheless of it, I accepted the technique which Carl had devised and settled for the fact that we would shoot it very blatantly, rather like television.[35]

The interviews were reminiscent of the BBC television programme *Face to Face*, that ran from 1959 to 1962, in which the interviewee was subjected to a probing style of questioning by the presenter, John Freeman, aided by close-up and intrusive camera focus. In *Young Winston*, each of the three actors gave individual cameo roles that expose their character's private lives fully to the audience as well as to the hidden interviewer. The first interview, conducted with Lord Randolph, consists of a series of questions, mainly political, that are answered with assurance. The second, and most contentious, is with Lady Randolph. This involves harsh allegations being put to her: being a neglectful mother, having a romantic 'link' with royalty, and that she and Lord Randolph had a 'pro-forma marriage', with divorce a possibility. The aggressive manner of the interviewer forces Lady Randolph to rush away clearly upset. The third interview is with Winston and occurs after his triumphs in the army and his participation in the Battle of Omdurman. Although Winston receives several penetrating questions, including the accusation that he was 'detested' in the army, he answers with confidence, turning the interview around so that he asserts himself thus demonstrating his abilities as a future leader.

Another unusual device in the film is a fantasy dream sequence in which Lord Randolph appears before his elderly son, who is sleeping in front of an unfinished watercolour he is painting. Annoyingly, Churchill does not inform his father of his political successes, instead he allows him to depart still thinking of his son as a failure. Although the dream is based on an event which is recorded in Churchill's book, *The Dream*, the scene was only included in the British version of the film which also incorporated other additional scenes, adding twelve minutes to the film.[36] The scenes were excluded from the American version, because Attenborough claimed, 'without a very familiar knowledge of that period they stick out like sore thumbs'.[37]

By including innovative devices and applying a flashback technique *Young Winston* departs from the conventional film format and dovetails into films which Higson considers 'eschewed the narrative linearity of the classical film, and which shifted towards the narrational complexity, the fragmentation of time, space and action and the psychological realism of modernist fiction and European art cinema'.[38] *Young Winston* also included some notable camera techniques. Original photographs of Churchill astride his grey horse are 'copied' and replicated into Ward's Churchill changing from static to moving images. For Lord Randolph's funeral scene, filmed at Blenheim Palace, one camera was mounted on a long crane and remained static allowing a single shot for the whole scene beginning with the carriages entering the gates and sweeping round to zoom in on Winston's face before he escorts his mother up the steps into the Palace. The film also contrasts fast action scenes such as the one depicting the Battle of Omdurman which portrays some vicious fighting sequences between the British and the Dervishes, with a more intense scene depicting Churchill's first maiden speech in the House of Commons. This was shot in a long take, though there are some containing shots to show the reaction of fellow Conservative members, Churchill's liberal friend, David Lloyd George (Anthony Hopkins), and his mother in the gallery. To add historical authenticity to the film, newsreel footage is also included depicting Churchill waving triumphantly from the balcony of Buckingham Palace, standing between the King and Queen to receive the nation's applause after the victory of the Second World War. The national theme is also projected in the music which plays a powerful part in the film. Alfred Ralston's original score integrated several of Edward Elgar's well-known compositions, highlighting the English feel to the film that the camera created.

During the six months of filming Foreman publicly declared a cordial relationship commenting that Attenborough is 'doing a wonderful job'. He also added: 'It's tempting for me to tell him what to do, because I've made more epics than he has. But there's no point in my engaging someone and then sitting in his shoulder all the time.'[39] Attenborough also spoke warmly of Foreman's script remarking that it had 'effectively spread Winston's escapes as correspondent and subaltern throughout the tale, making it a fascinating adventure yarn'.[40] Privately, however, the two disagreed on a number of issues including the filming of alternative versions of several scenes. Although Attenborough insisted that he was involved in the editing process to maintain directorial control, Foreman's dominance took precedence to the extent that he persuaded Attenborough to recut the film to his own satisfaction.[41]

Young Winston opened in London on 20 July 1972 with a joint première at the Odeon, Leicester Square and at the Leicester Square Theatre. The principal star guest was Churchill's widow, Baroness Spencer Churchill, while the leaders of the three main political parties, Edward Heath, Harold Wilson and Jeremy Thorpe, were all present. The following day, *The Times* revealed that accounts in *My Early Life* had been challenged by the discovery of a copy of the book that had been critically annotated by General Hubert Gough, who was also present at the battle of Ladysmith. Gough accused Churchill's account of having 'disregard' for the truth, refuting his claims as 'Bunk. Pure fabrication.'[42] The article stimulated a number of letters including one from Gough's nephew, Colonel Frederick Gough, who supported the opinion that the annotations were genuine through the distinctive handwriting and 'pungency of the remarks'.[43] Although *The Times* gave no date of when the annotated copy was discovered, John Ramsden claims it was found in 1971. Ramsden was somewhat unfairly critical of *Young Winston* for taking 'no account' of the discovery and complained that *The Times* 'saw no need to refer to them when reviewing the film'.[44]

The reception in Britain was mixed. Praiseworthy reviews included *Cinema/TV Today* which called the film 'moving, enlightening, witty and exciting', and *Films and Filming* which considered that Attenborough and Foreman had been 'refreshingly radical in their treatment'.[45] Less enthusiastic was the *Monthly Film Bulletin*, which argued that the film displays 'a continually varying perspective on the subject', and Penelope Houston in *Sight and Sound* who commented that the film is 'on the whole a gingerly production'.[46] Newspapers which were more vociferous in their praise included the *Daily Mail* considering the film 'a handsome, living portrait of a giant in the making', while *The Times* praised the 'sober but sensitive directorial hand of Richard Attenborough'.[47] For Patrick Gibbs in the *Daily Telegraph*, 'Fact is not followed slavishly but the spirit of the story, and the personality of the central character, are captured, I would say completely.'[48] Reviews which were more discerning included the *Observer* which claimed the film suffered from 'excess length and hagiography', while the *Guardian* declared *Young Winston* 'an honourable film' but considered it 'an impossible task', questioning, 'how do you film something that's a cross between *Boy's Own Paper* and holy writ?'[49]

After a New York première on 11 October *Young Winston* also received varied critical response in America. *The New York Times* denounced the film as 'a big balsa-wood monument', while *Village Voice* declared that the 'lingering impression [of the film] is that of a visit to Mme. Tussaud's waxworks'.[50] *Variety*, however, reported *Young Winston* as a 'brilliant artistic achievement and a fascinating, highly enjoyable film'.[51] For Pauline Kael in the *New Yorker, Young Winston* was 'inoffensively relaxing' with Attenborough's handling 'splendidly done'.[52]

Young Winston made a total net profit of just under £160,000 in the nine-week run at the Odeon, Leicester Square.[53] In America the film was given exclusive runs in both New York and Los Angeles, opening at the Beverly Theatre in Beverly Hills at a special beneficiary on 12 November. Despite Columbia's boast that *Young Winston* was 'one of the most highly-praised and successful British films to be shown in the United States', the film failed to recoup its costs.[54] *Young Winston* gained more critical success by being chosen to inaugurate the 1972 Hollywood Film Festival, and by gaining three nominations for Academy Awards: Best Screenplay, Best Art Direction and Best Costume Design. It won none, however.

Young Winston is a better film than it was given credit with the three leading actors, Robert Shaw, Anne Bancroft and Simon Ward, all giving first-rate performances. Ward's, in particular, resulted in a triumphant embodiment of Churchill, both in appearance and in voice. The film also demonstrates its skill in contrasting the intimate biographical portrayal of three people with the spectacular epic sequences, which added both pace and excitement to the narrative.

For Attenborough, the experience with *Young Winston* was not a positive one. This was partly due to his personal regret in not agreeing to play Lord Randolph, later claiming that 'I would love to have done it but I didn't think I was really up to it', but principally due to the excessive control that Foreman exerted.[55] As he later commented: 'The experience of working with Carl Foreman on *Young Winston* strengthened my resolve to be my own boss if possible.'[56]

Attenborough's quest for more creative autonomy was better achieved with his next film. Based on the book by Cornelius Ryan, *A Bridge Too Far* continued the war theme that had been a central focus of both *Oh! What a Lovely War* and *Young Winston*. The depiction of war in *A Bridge Too Far* was, however, more explicit in the film's attempt to create a realistic representation of the battle. It was heralded at the time, albeit with some exaggeration, as the most expensive film ever made, supported by a budget of $25 million (£15 million) which resulted from its high production values and a cast of fourteen major stars.[57] Due to Joseph E. Levine's commercial skill and his much heralded statement that the film would be in profit before its release, *A Bridge Too Far* appeared destined for guaranteed commercial success.[58] Yet, for all its bold assertions, *A Bridge Too Far* failed in the critical American market and became more renowned for the contentious issues that surrounded it than for the actual film itself.

The Battle of Arnhem took place from 17–28 September 1944. The ambitious plan, code-named 'Operation Market Garden', devised by Field-Marshal Sir Bernard Montgomery and sanctioned by General Dwight D. Eisenhower, involved a massive Allied air and land assault sending 35,000 airborne troops (the Market) into Holland to lay 'a carpet' that would capture and hold the five key bridges across the Rhine.[59] Once held, the land forces (the Garden) would speedily advance along the 64-mile corridor by linking up with each airborne division on route to Arnhem. It was estimated that the land forces of General Horrocks's British XXX Corps would take two days to reach the Anglo-Polish 1st Airborne Corps at Arnhem, after linking with the American 101st Airborne Division in Eindhoven and the American 82nd in Nijmegen. The combined armies were to march to the Ruhr, the industrial heartland of Germany, which, once under Allied control, was anticipated to end the war by Christmas. Although Montgomery claimed that the operation was '90 per cent successful', the overall result was a military failure, not capturing the final and most significant bridge at Arnhem. The operation ended in a humiliating defeat, which resulted in over 13,226 British and 3,550 American casualties. Many Dutch civilians were also either killed or injured. After the operation was abandoned, 2,163 British and 160 Polish troops were hastily withdrawn to safety.[60]

A Bridge Too Far is an important though critically neglected film in the history of the war genre. It was the last in a cycle of big-budget, international productions which re-enacted major battles or campaigns of the Second World War that were prevalent during the 1960s and early 1970s. The cycle, which had begun with *The Longest Day* (Andrew Marton, Ken Annakin, Bernhard Wicki, 1962), also included *Battle of the Bulge* (Annakin, 1965), *Battle of Britain* (Guy Hamilton, 1969), *Tora! Tora! Tora!* (Richard Fleischer, 1970) and *Midway* (Jack Smight, 1976). *A Bridge Too Far* is unusual as, unlike the others in the cycle which feature victorious campaigns, the film re-enacts a military failure.[61] The campaign had been recently seen by television audiences, after it was included as part of the twenty-six-part documentary series, *The World at War*, first broadcast in 1973.[62]

A Bridge Too Far was devised by Levine, who had taken a keen interest in the research on the Battle of Arnhem by his friend, Cornelius Ryan, an Irish-born historian and former *Daily Telegraph* war correspondent. Ryan had previously written both the book and the screenplay for *The Longest Day*. He employed a similar methodological approach to *A Bridge Too Far*, basing his research on personal accounts from participants of the campaign, consisting of over a thousand interviews from both sides with all accounts verified by at least two sources. The title was taken from the sentence uttered by Lieutenant-General Frederick Browning – 'But Sir, I think we might be going a bridge too far'- to Montgomery on 10 September 1944, as a warning that he considered the enterprise might be too ambitious.[63] Although Ryan was suffering from terminal cancer, he completed the book and survived to see it published in September 1974. The book was an immediate success in America and in Britain and was also translated into several languages for worldwide distribution. The greatest impact was felt in America. As Levine commented: 'In Europe everyone knows about the battle. In America no one knows about it because General Eisenhower swept it under the carpet.'[64] This view is reiterated by the historian Stephen E. Ambrose:

> [Arnhem Bridge] was better known in the British Isles than in the United States until 1974 when Cornelius Ryan published *A Bridge Too Far*. With that book, the exploits of Colonel John Frost and his paratroopers on the Arnhem Bridge received their proper due on both sides of the Atlantic.[65]

Levine purchased the film rights to the book from Ryan's widow for $800,000. His conviction that the film was so important pushed him to donate a large sum of his own money for the project so that it could be made with the best actors, equipment and crew. As he declared: 'the story of the heroes of Arnhem deserves to be recorded on film for posterity to see'.[66]

The completion of *Young Winston* had allowed Attenborough to refocus his efforts on *Gandhi* and in 1974 he revived talks with Warner Bros. After a meeting in Los Angeles in February 1975 with the company, Attenborough was invited by Levine, who had been impressed with *Oh! What a Lovely War*, to direct *A Bridge Too Far*. Levine told him to '[f]orget that B-picture of yours [*Gandhi*]. This is the big one'.[67] After Warner Bros. pulled out of the deal Attenborough accepted Levine's offer, on two conditions. First, that the film would be registered as British, and, second, that Levine would guarantee to finance *Gandhi* after *A Bridge Too Far* was completed.

A Bridge Too Far was claimed by Levine to be the 493rd film he had either produced or imported.[68] Levine was a legendary producer in Hollywood, and almost unique for working as a solo businessman. His motto: 'You can fool all the people all of the time if the advertising is right and the budget is big enough' was the basis to his working ethos.[69] Levine's breakthrough came through marketing the Italian film *Hercules* (Pietro Francisci, 1959), which he had bought for $125,000 before spending a further $1.5 million in promoting it, resulting with a box-office return of over $10 million.[70] In 1967 he sold his company, Embassy, to the Avco-Corporation for $40 million, with Levine becoming president of the board. In 1973 Levine left Avco-Embassy, ostensibly to retire, but later formed his own company, Joseph E. Levine Presents, for the benefit of *A Bridge Too Far*. Although Levine had become the most famous and the most successful independent film producer, he was 'an enormously antiestablishment figure' which had not made him popular in Hollywood.[71] The decision to produce *A Bridge Too Far* was a personal and prized project for Levine in a similar way that *Young Winston* was for Foreman.

Levine had approached Attenborough before engaging William Goldman, a fellow American Jew, known as Hollywood's 'hottest screenwriter' who was signed to the project in June 1975. Levine's desire was to have a British director to balance an American scriptwriter. As Goldman recalled:

> Mr Levine had insisted all along that, since it was an Allied operation, the writer should be of a different nationality from the director. If he had two Americans, say, then the British aspect of the drama might have been slighted – or vice-versa.[72]

Goldman had made his name with films such as *Butch Cassidy and the Sundance Kid* (George Roy Hill, 1969) and *All the President's Men* (Alan J. Pakula, 1976), both of which won him Academy Awards. On their first meeting Attenborough considered they had an 'immediate *rapport*', whereas Goldman remarked that it was 'dreadful'.[73] All initial reticence, however, disappeared in the good working relationship that developed with Goldman producing, in Attenborough's words, 'an exceptional script, which more than any other single contribution to the team effort made *A Bridge Too Far* work as a movie'.[74]

While viewing the documentary film *Theirs Is the Glory* (Brian Desmond Hurst, 1946), which reconstructed the battle a year after the event, was beneficial to Goldman, his main difficulty was integrating perspectives from the American, British, Dutch, German and Polish sides. Several significant incidents had to be omitted, including the events surrounding the five Victoria Crosses awarded. A more significant omission was the High Command from all sides. The original intention was to include both General Eisenhower and Field-Marshal Montgomery, but their inclusion was later abandoned as Montgomery was still alive until a month before filming began.[75]

Attenborough had previously contributed (uncredited) to the commentary of *The True Glory* (Carol Reed and Garson Kanin, 1945), a Ministry of Information/Office of War Information film. This Anglo-American collaboration in a documentary form focused on the last year of the war and also included the Battle of Arnhem. The conflict was told through actuality footage shot by service cameramen, where Attenborough and other actors, including Peter Ustinov and Celia Johnson, contributed to the narration.[76] The task of bringing the event to a modern audience appealed to Attenborough's interest in the battle:

> I'm fascinated by the way Arnhem encapsulated within a period of ten days the whole of war from the rows between Patton, Eisenhower and Montgomery to the character of the men who made the landing. There is the cruel disaster of it all: the British, dogged, unquestioning and incredibly brave: the Americans, uninhibited, full of bravura and unmatchable courage.[77]

The production succeeded in gaining the cooperation of the Allied nations involved in the conflict. Official help came from the defence departments of Britain, America, the Netherlands, Belgium and Denmark. Attenborough's previous production experience, particularly his negotiating skills, were put to effective use by Levine. Attenborough initially discussed the film project with the British Prime Minister, Harold Wilson, before seeking official approval. The letter to Roy Mason, Secretary of State for Defence, reveals the degree of national significance that Attenborough attached to the film:

> I really do believe it is to be a picture of very considerable importance as far as the Country is concerned, both from the point of view of reintroducing major dollar financing and in recording for world viewing one of the greatest military actions in our history.[78]

Wilson gave his official support to Attenborough via a letter to Mason, from J.D. Groves, Chief of Public Relations to the Ministry of Defence (MOD), which 'expresses the hope that the MOD will give its "full co-operation" to the venture'. In reply the Foreign and Commonwealth Office (FCO) 'saw no political difficulty about [the film] provided the Dutch are content'. Levine had already obtained the support of Prince Bernhard of the Netherlands. The Prince, who was Commander-in Chief of the Netherlands Forces and headed the Dutch resistance organisation during the conflict, promised the help of the Dutch army. Support also came from the Ministry of Defence who agreed to provide troops from 16 Parachute Brigade.[79] The MOD recognised that there was 'considerable PR value in making the film as authentic as possible', but added a proviso that '[s]ervice participations would be withheld unless the Min of Def has approved the shooting script for the Production', thereby maintaining significant control.

The film's budget was important both for the film and for the British film industry. At its initial estimation at $15 million Attenborough claimed that it is 'probably the biggest single sum of money to have come into the industry since David Lean made *Ryan's Daughter* [1970]'.[80] By August 1975, the budget had escalated to over $20 million.[81] Levine became personally responsible for $22 million of the eventual $25 million budget for the film, more than twice the cost of the original operation. Two million dollars came from Levine's own pocket to instigate the film with the rest of the money coming from bank loans for which Levine was personally liable, granted on the basis of his financial and business records. The majority of the film's budget went on the cast, which was claimed to be the 'most costly cast in movie history'.[82] The requirement to have a stellar cast with a top name was incorporated into the distribution deals that Levine had negotiated which enabled him, as an independent producer, to pre-sell his films. Fourteen star names were signed up. This number was fewer than in *The Longest Day*, which included forty-two star names, but the stars in *A Bridge Too Far* were all considered 'A' list. However, the policy of stars representing important historical figures had previously caused concerns. As Ambrose argues: '*The Longest Day* is the bane of American historians of D-Day, because, ever since, to the average audience, one must identify the men one is talking about not by their names but by the actors who played them in this movie.'[83] The recognition factor was used in *A Bridge Too Far* as a device to enable the audience to be able to identify historical characters quickly. This is particularly applicable where characters are seen in fleeting moments or when several are depicted together, as is seen in the initial briefing session. The scene shows Dirk Bogarde (Browning) addressing a small group allowing brief glimpses of the actors. It then focuses on their faces, first Ryan O'Neal, who is named by Browning as General Gavin, followed by Sean Connery, identified as Major-General Robert 'Roy' Urquhart, Paul Maxwell as General Maxwell Taylor and, finally, Gene Hackman as the Polish General Sosabowski. In his review of the film, Vincent Canby acknowledged that cameo roles were 'as necessary to narrative coherence – as the screenplay'.[84] Attenborough's perception was slightly different, claiming that stars 'have to make an impact instantly. The men they are portraying are big men with big personalities. The same must be true of the actors portraying them.[85]

Screen International reported in February 1977 that Levine had 'completed deals with virtually every country in the world' which means that 'he should get all his money back – no matter what the critics say'.[86]

The foreign deals were more important to Levine than the American ones as he predicted the film would be better received away from the country. His claim that '*Bridge* will already be in a profit position by the time it opens in the US on June 15 1977' was until then, unique. The mechanisms were explained in *Variety*:

> The deals are structured on step-payment basis with all the money to be in before production is completed. That makes Levine's deals significantly different from other foreign distribution selloff arrangements, the producer emphasizes, since under the latter, full payment is made when a final print is delivered.[87]

By April 1976 Levine had signed deals with several countries including Japan, Holland, Belgium, Italy and Hong Kong. He had also been offered $12 million by a major distributor (unnamed) for the United States and Canada.[88]

British stars were paid varying amounts but mostly less than the American stars. Bogarde was first offered $80,000 and refused but accepted when his fee was raised to $100,000.[89] Audrey Hepburn, Robert De Niro and Steve McQueen were all rejected for their high pay demands. Although Levine claimed that he never offered McQueen a role, Attenborough has since confirmed that he offered him the role of Major Julian Cook.[90] Levine considered that fourteen stars were too many to pay on a percentage basis so they were all signed on an increased salary basis. The top Hollywood actors, Hackman, James Caan, Elliott Gould and O'Neal, were all paid $1 million dollars each, but Robert Redford, as the top 'A' star, was paid $2 million dollars. Redford was also on a different contract to the others known as a 'four and one' in which he was paid for four weeks' work, but if required would do an additional one for free. The fee also included specific clauses, one of which 'included any personal suffering endured having his hair cut ... to approximately the style of a U.S. Army major in 1944'.[91] Although he succeeded in evading the hair stipulation, Attenborough pointed out 'I suppose physically Redford had the most difficult part' crossing the river 'just as the men had done during the actual battle'.[92] While Redford's enhanced pay angered the other actors, to Levine he was crucial to the distribution deals. The Japanese distributor, Fuji Eiga, offered Levine an extra £1 million if Redford was in the cast. Although some critics argued that Levine was setting a dangerous precedent for the future with his method of payment, Levine himself was unrepentant. In *Screen International* he declared:

> My opinion is an actor has the right to anything he can get. The reason I paid Redford and some of the others so much is that they are used to

having an interest. But there are fourteen stars, and I couldn't afford to give one a share without the others, so nobody has a piece of the picture.[93]

Connery's salary was also raised to Hollywood levels after he learned of Redford's fee, and he renegotiated his contract.[94] Connery was Attenborough's first choice to play Urquhart, the largest part in the film. Although Connery turned the part down twice, he was persuaded by the screenplay that the film would be 'more of an antiwar statement that [sic] a glamorisation of war'.[95]

Attenborough engaged many actors with whom he had previously worked including Laurence Olivier (Dr Spaander), Dirk Bogarde, Anthony Hopkins (Colonel John Frost) and Edward Fox (Lieutenant-General Brian Horrocks). The important female role of Kate ter Horst, the Dutch heroine whose house was used for the injured soldiers, was played by Liv Ullmann. A large group of a hundred actors was chosen for the non-speaking roles of soldiers. These 'soldiers', hailed as 'Attenborough's Private Army', were selected to portray the 'Red Devils' as realistic soldiers for close-up scenes. They all had to undergo special Commando-type training, learning how to march, fire a variety of weapons and 'to think and act like crack troops'.[96]

Locations were kept as close as possible to the original battlegrounds in Holland, including the towns of Eindhoven, Grave, Nijmegen and the drop zones around Arnhem. The city of Arnhem which had been destroyed in the battle and now had a modern bridge was substituted by Deventer which had a similar bridge to the original one at Arnhem. Prince Bernhard used his influence to secure permission for the use of the bridge for seven days during May and June 1976 for one hour each time. To compensate for the nuisance, the film company built alternative roads to provide an eight-mile detour and had to arrange ferries to take traffic across the river.

Filming began on Monday 26 April 1976, before Goldman had finished writing the script, a fact that he claimed was 'the only time that a picture was in production *before* a first draft screenplay ... was seen by anyone'.[97] While the weather dictated that filming had to be completed by October 1976, the greatest time constraint was imposed by Levine who had set the opening date of the film, 15 June 1977, due to his distribution deals. This and Levine's personal financial involvement put enormous pressure on the whole production. Goldman recalls how this affected his writing but also noted the effect it had on the team, having 'never seen a crew work as hard'.[98]

A number of military experts were appointed, separated into advisers and consultants. The advisers were Arnhem veterans, one British, Colonel John Waddy, and one American, Colonel Frank Gregg. The two men saw their roles in different terms. Gregg, who had been at Arnhem with the 101st Airborne Division, was concerned with characterisation. He voiced objections to the role of Bobby Stout (Elliot Gould), protesting at his zealous manner of 'bossing the building of a Bailey Bridge by British troops'. By contrast, Waddy saw his role as 'technical rather than political' – checking troops to see if they were properly attired and their salutes correctly executed.[99] The military consultants (four British, one American) were all characters portrayed in the film. Their role was to provide a greater degree of accuracy, particularly in the areas in which they had participated in the original event. The British were represented by four veterans: Major-General 'Roy' Urquhart, Major-General John Frost, Brigadier 'Joe' Vandeleur and Lieutenant-General Sir Brian Horrocks. The Americans had only one representative, General James Gavin, who had also acted as an adviser on *The Longest Day*. Julian Cook (now Colonel) offered his services as a consultant to Levine but his request was ignored. A similar offer from General Sir John Hackett was refused. Although Cook felt offended by his treatment by Levine, Attenborough and Terence Clegg (production manager) claimed that too many experts was counterproductive, interfering rather than enhancing the production.[100]

Attenborough admitted that he might have been tempted to photograph the film in monochrome instead of colour.[101] While this would have linked the film more closely to *The Longest Day*, monochrome films had become so rare by the 1970s that there was concern that it could have a detrimental effect at the box office. Instead, the filmmakers decided to 'bleed out most of the colour' for much of the film resulting in a visual style of muted colours normally associated with war. One exception is the scene at Eindhoven, where the paratroops received a large welcome from the Dutch people waving brightly coloured flags which contrasted with the muted shades of the soldiers' uniforms. Black-and-white footage is also used in the opening sequence in a montage of actuality footage which is narrated by ter Horst. The voice-over acts as a warning to the audience that the anticipated success of the operation was not to happen: 'The plan, like so many plans in so many wars before it, was meant to end the fighting by Christmas and bring the boys back home.' While ter Horst speaks in English, the German characters all speak in their own language, employing subtitles to aid translation, thus following the precedent adopted by *The Longest Day*.

A Bridge Too Far is a serious anti-war film but uses several humorous interludes to enhance its entertainment value. The use of humour is varied and subtle and evident in the banter between fellow soldiers, and rivalry between Allies. The change from optimism to despair felt in the film is also reflected in John Addison's powerful music which was influenced by the composer's personal experiences as he served with the ground forces at Arnhem in the tank regiment. Addison had volunteered himself as director of music for the film in order to honour his fallen comrades.[102] To enhance the reality of the situation, Attenborough and Addison decided that no music was to be played during the battle sequences, with only the sounds of war detectable.

A Bridge Too Far benefited from the experience of award-winning cinematographer Geoffrey Unsworth, who had the unenviable task of having to film in a variety of weather conditions, coping with the varying light changes and with the difficulty of matching up all the discrepancies within sequences. The main difficulty, however, was the parachute drop. The sequence was impossible to rehearse due to the unpredictable factors involved including the weather, number and position of aircraft flying, and parachutists dropping. A number of expert cameramen with knowledge of documentary filming were employed, using a variety of cameras – fixed, action and ground – to achieve the impact of the mass drop. Accounts are misleading about the actual number of days' filming the drop involved. *Photoplay* quoted Attenborough saying that four days were involved, while in Dougan's account, he recalls only two.[103] What is not disputed is that the sequence was repeated at Attenborough's request. Although the weather conditions were favourable for the first filming, the lighting was below the standard that Attenborough desired. Attenborough had to request permission from Levine to spend the extra money (around $75,000) required. After much persuasion, Levine agreed. All the material that is in the film came from the repeat filming.[104]

Another concern was the pressure imposed on the film schedule which included a six-week period that involved many of the stars. The cooperation of all the actors was also paramount to keeping within the time-frame. While Attenborough reported at the time that '[t]here were no star temperaments' he later admitted that one actor 'thought it was a great romp – didn't take it too seriously' and caused irritation to the other actors.[105] Although he did not publicly name the actor, Attenborough later confided it was O'Neal.[106] Iain Johnstone, who was present on the set, was also critical of O'Neal's attitude, claiming he had made no attempt to meet Gavin, his character, and was guilty of 'laughing his head off and ruining the end of an already ruinously expensive shot'.[107]

The only actor who had been part of the Arnhem campaign was Bogarde who had assisted with the evacuation of Urquhart's troops. Before filming, Attenborough had written to Bogarde to explain the character of Browning, who despite his 'urbane sophistication' was a caring person and if Bogarde could bring that to his portrayal 'it will result in a man, not only of considerable stature, but, indeed, of real flesh and blood'.[108] Bogarde had met Browning in Normandy finding him 'very charming and very much liked'.[109] This contradicts the impression he gives in John Coldstream's biography, where he is quoted as saying that he considered the character as '[r]ather a prick, I think'.[110] Commenting upon his performance he declared that he hoped that 'I have made him Brave, Courageous, Wise and a Gentleman'.[111]

The issue of historical authenticity was considered particularly important. The problems of portraying an accurate representation of the past are well recognised. As Jeffrey Richards observes: 'It is a commonplace that cinema cannot deal accurately with history. The dictates of the drama and the constraints of running time combine to ensure that the history in films is almost never authentic.'[112] Goldman later commented that he had 'never been involved in a project where authenticity was more sought after and achieved'.[113] Archival footage was studied before key scenes were shot and Goldman's script was sent to key personnel including Frost, Urquhart and Horrocks for their comments as well as General Anthony Farrah-Hockley, historian to the Parachute Regiment.

Despite the desire for accuracy, Goldman was also forced to make alterations that differed from the original campaign. This included changing the names of some of the characters. Major Digby Tatham-Warter, Lieutenant-Colonel Frost's second-in-command, described in Ryan's book as an eccentric who carried a furled umbrella, had his name changed to Carlisle (Christopher Good), a move which was done 'to prevent legal implications' as the character dies of his injuries although Tatham-Warter survived. A significant death in the film was deemed necessary as, according to Goldman, 'you can't have an antiwar movie where all the leads live'.[114] Another name change is that of Major Brian Urquhart who was changed to Fuller (to avoid confusion with Roy Urquhart). Fuller is the intelligence officer who presents Browning with photographic evidence of the German tank presence in Arnhem. Urquhart's evidence, which if acted upon could have prevented the catastrophe, is ignored. While Browning dismisses Fuller's evidence, his brusque tone and quick retort make it appear that Browning is under pressure from his superiors not to jeopardise the mission. Major-General Ian Gill, at the time a major in XXX Corp and an escort commander under Horrocks, later acknowledged that 'they all knew about the intelligence reports', a fact that is hinted at in the film by Horrocks's comments to Vandeleur: 'this isn't going to be the pushover that everybody seems to think it is'.[115] Goldman also had found sufficient evidence to corroborate these observations which are depicted in the film.

The quest to retain historical authenticity also resulted in audience disbelief, despite written evidence to the contrary. The scene after Eddie Dohun (Caan) has rescued his captain to take him to the medical centre shows him holding a gun to the head of a surgeon, demanding that he examines his seriously injured captain who is near to death. The surgeon complies and despite all probabilities, successfully removes a bullet from the captain's head. The event is recorded in Ryan's book (with Eddy named Charles). Dohun's recollections are poignant as he informed Ryan that 'I don't know to this day if I would have shot that medic or not.'[116] However, according to Goldman, this was one of many aspects of the film that the Americans would not believe; instead they saw it as 'another piece of phony Hollywood theatrics'.[117] A similar disbelief was with the portrayal of James Gavin by O'Neal. Although Gavin had the distinction of being the youngest general in the American army, in *The Longest Day* he had been played by Robert Ryan, who was considerably older than Gavin was at the time. This older perception of the character led to the general dislike of O'Neal in the same role although he was only two years younger that Gavin had been in 1944.

A theme linked to historical accuracy was also evident in Anglo-American relations. *A Bridge Too Far* can be said to have reactivated the rivalry between the two nations. Despite a gap of over thirty years from the actual event, the film demonstrated that relationships between the two countries could still be strained in relation to the exactness of their roles. The theme of rivalry had been identified before in the Anglo-American documentary film *The True Glory*. James Chapman argues that there appears to have been 'a deliberate policy in Washington to use the film to emphasise the American contribution to the European war'.[118] The foregrounding of the American presence is also evident in *The Longest Day* and was an issue in *A Bridge Too Far*.

The most contentious sequence in the film involved the demarcation of the Anglo-American roles in the capture of the bridge at Nijmegen. This included the scene that formed a key action sequence, the crossing of the Waal River, in which Cook (Redford) is seen encouraging his men across the fast flowing river in canvas boats, while under German fire. The event, the first successful daylight river crossing in US military, was only partially re-enacted in the film. Goldman was forced to exclude the second wave of the crossing from the script as he could not have Redford in both. As a cinematic rule, Goldman insisted 'the star must be in the center of the action'. Goldman recalled his frustrations:

> I tried as hard as I knew to use the second wave, but I failed. The single most heroic action of the war, and I couldn't figure out how to include it. The moral I guess is this: Truth is terrific, reality is even better, but believability is best of all.[119]

The crossing is followed by a serious argument between Cook and an unnamed British major (John Stride). The British refuse to continue to advance to Arnhem as they have 'their orders' and they would be left like 'sitting ducks'. Cook, having led his men over the Waal River, losing many in the process, admonishes the British officer for refusing to attack and denounces the British attitude 'just sitting there and drinking tea'. The scene illustrates the stereotypical differences between the two nations, American 'gung-ho' contrasted with British reserve. Horrocks's account of Gavin's reaction was publicised in *The Times* just prior to the film's release.

> Gavin told me afterwards that he and his men of his Division felt bitterly disappointed that we had not sent a task force straight for Arnhem Bridge, after the capture, intact, of the two Nijmegen bridges. In fact, at the time, he felt that the British had let them down badly.[120]

The decision to stop XXX tank corps was much denounced by the Americans. Captain Carrington recalled their fury, claiming that Horrocks had not kept his word, and stating that 'everyman in airborne was against XXX corps at time.'[121] On the film set, Colonel Waddy, an Arnhem paratrooper veteran, informed Richard P. Levine (co-producer) that 'the capture of the road bridge at Nijmegen had been notably a British operation' with the Americans capturing the nearby railway bridge.[122] Levine's reply was dismissive, 'The facts Jahn [sic] would be more difficult and more expensive.' He added 'Doing it this way means an awful lot to the box-office.'[123] For Attenborough, however, the attempt at maintaining an Anglo-American balance was a priority for the film, declaring: 'We have been immensely careful about documentary reality, and there's no major event or dialogue sequence which is not fully authentic. The Americans are certainly not given any more credit in the film than they have a right to.'[124]

Filming ended on 6 October, after 133 days, with Attenborough claiming it was 'finished under budget and 12 hours ahead of the schedule'.[125] The film had also survived the difficulties of the 'Million Dollar Hour', a phrase coined by Goldman describing a critical period on 3 October 1976, the last day that both the bridge at Nijmegen and the river traffic could be closed.[126] Further pressure was added with Redford's contract terminating the following Wednesday. Failure to complete the shooting of the crucial scene would have resulted in an excess payment which would have put the film beyond its budget with the 'overage' (Redford's salary) costing $125,000 per day. After post-production at Twickenham Studios, the film was distributed by United Artists who abandoned their current emblem and used the one from 1945 to conform to the period of the film.

A *Bridge Too Far* opened in America on its intended date on 15 June 1977 at the Rivoli Theatre in New York. Premières were also held in Boston and Washington. In Britain the film's Royal Première in London at the Leicester Square Theatre on 23 June was in the presence of the Duchess of Kent, who was accompanied by Earl Mountbatten of Burma. Mountbatten's grandson, Norton Knatchbull, had been employed as the film's location manager. The film opened the following day at the same cinema and, also at the Odeon Leicester Square. On the day of opening a television programme was broadcast, entitled *The Arnhem Report*, written and narrated by Iain Johnstone. The LWT programme was a two-part documentary telling the story of the battle, through its participants and also the story of the film heralded as 'the most expensive film ever made' and seen 'through the eyes of the stars, with spectacular action from the film'.[127]

The film was better received by the public than by the critics. On its release it reached the number one position taking £25,014 at the Leicester Square Theatre and £17,834 at the Odeon, Marble Arch in its first week, bettering, in both venues, the previous highs of the year.[128] *Screen International* announced it as its fifth most successful film in Britain in 1977.[129] *A Bridge Too Far* did well commercially on a global basis but was not as well received in America, despite a strong beginning with a five-day gross of $4,233,616 in 448 cinemas. The film's final box-office receipt was $20.4 million.[130]

American reviews of *A Bridge Too Far* were varied, many reflecting the controversial nature of the subject. Several critics commented unfavourably on its length, the number of stars and its extravagant scale. The *New York Times* called it 'massive, shapeless, often unexpectedly moving, confusing, sad, vivid and very, very long'.[131] Penelope Gilliat, the British critic of the *New Yorker*, found herself 'angered and harrowed by a film that can make something like A Night of a Thousand Stars at the London Palladium of such an unforgettable military tragedy'.[132] Those which praised the film included *Newsweek* which declared it 'an absorbing, well-crafted, honourable movie' and the *Hollywood Reporter* which applauded Goldman's screenplay and Attenborough's direction which 'effectively capitalizes on the human element of the script creating numerous poignant moments, without losing sight of the overall scope of the battle'.[133]

In Britain, the newspapers expressed equally diverse opinions. The *Daily Express* offered conflicting views with Ian Christie praising the film as 'a military defeat turned in a cinematic triumph', while Douglas Orgill attacked it for being 'a caricature of history' which made him feel 'nationally resentful'.[134] The *Daily Telegraph* complained that the film's final impression was 'so muddled' and depictions of senior British officers 'so curious' that it could 'only assume that something other was being attempted than a clear account of the battle'.[135] Reviewers who praised the film included *The Times*'s Philip French who considered it was 'better written, acted and directed than *The Longest Day* and *The Battle of the Bulge*, [sic] less pretentious than the bogus *Bridge on the River Kwai*, and matched only by *Patton*, which is psychologically more interesting but has inferior battle sequences'. For French the battle scene at Arnhem Bridge 'is among the best re-created movie combat footage I have ever seen'.[136]

In the Netherlands, many of the critics highlighted the portrayal of the Dutch in the film. *De Waarheid*, a communist daily, praised its 'realistic impression of the small acts of resistance'.[137] *Gooi en Eemlander*, a provincial newspaper, admired 'the skill' of Goldman and Attenborough's 'sometimes stunning direction' but pointed out that 'the terrible consequences for the civilian population are almost completely ignored'.[138] *Trouw*, a Protestant Christian daily, considered that it is 'nearly impossible to follow the events' and complained about the 'incomprehensible Dutch of Ullmann'.[139] *Twentsche Courant*, similarly complained about 'the ridiculous way in which Liv Ullmann babbles a few unintelligible Dutch texts in her role of a Dutch resistance woman'.[140]

Another significant feature of the response to *A Bridge Too Far* was the controversy that erupted in the correspondence pages of *The Times*. The criticisms of the film were concerned with different aspects of historical accuracy. Colonel Graeme Warrack, focusing his attack on the medical services, was dismayed that it implied 'that the officers and other ranks of the RAMC were a spent force', and asked: 'Where do truth and poetic licence part?'[141] Lieutenant-General Sir Alexander Hood complained that the medical portrayal was a 'dreadful misrepresentation', asking: 'What can be done to counteract such gross libels? Surely the Ministry of Defence should take appropriate steps to correct errors which can only be very damaging to the morale of the Army and the Medical Services.'[142] Hood's letter was challenged by Professor Lipmann Kessel as being 'such a travesty of the truth that it cannot remain unchallenged'. While Kessel accepted that 'some details may be altered, the *spirit* of the medical services in the British 1st A/B Div was accurately portrayed'.[143] The film's policy of changing names of principal personnel concerned the Reverend Michael Saward, who asked: 'Why do the Attenboroughs of this world play God with men's hard earned reputations?'[144]

The majority of the criticism, however, was concerned with the characterisation of General Browning and his role in the operation. The letters appeared to act as a forum to preserve Browning's reputation, especially the contributions from military and former military sources, whose aim appeared to be to exonerate him of all blame for errors made either at the time, or, as depicted in the film. General John Hackett, who had served under Urquhart at Arnhem, argued that the portrayal of Browning 'is both untruthful and unkind', being 'the outstanding blot on an otherwise generally fair picture'.[45] Major Alastair Tower, Browning's son-in-law, did not refer to the film but wanted 'to set the record straight' and proceeded to provide a glowing character appraisal of Browning. Tower asserted that Browning 'had the quality of superb leadership' and had 'established magnificent cooperation and team spirit between air and land forces'.[46] Colonel Frederick Gough, whose uncle questioned Churchill's account in *My Early Life*, attacked Attenborough for ignoring the 'serious criticisms' outlined by General Hackett's letter. Gough appeared to agree with Hackett that Attenborough had 'assumed a right to trample on people's feelings and to play ducks and drakes with historical facts in order to dish up an extravaganza fit for the American massed cinema market'. For Gough, 'great offence has already been caused, and that [Attenborough's] silence had made matters much worse.'[47] This last point provoked Attenborough to reply, although he was careful to point out that as the letters were written to the editor of the newspaper and not directly to him, he was not obliged to answer himself. Nevertheless, he acknowledged that 'offence has been caused', but was keen to assert that the 'intentions of those involved in the making of the film were honourable'.[48] The most persistent critic of the portrayal of Browning, however, was his widow, Dame Daphne du Maurier. Du Maurier had voiced her concerns in March as to how Browning would be portrayed. While she considered Bogarde 'an intriguing choice and I suppose not too bad a decision' to play him, she was intent on seeing the script to prevent any 'mickey-taking' occurring.[49] This included the removal of a scene depicting Browning about to take off in his glider which she denounced as sounding 'frightfully stupid'. Du Maurier's main objection, however, referred to the film's most crucial line:

> [M]y husband said to Monty 'Don't you think we're going a bridge too far?' In the film this is cut out completely and Dirk Bogarde only says it after the battle in a stony-faced way. I can't remember what I actually said to Attenborough but I think I said: 'Put it back to the beginning.'[50]

Attenborough recalled that he agreed to an important change in Bogarde's [Browning's] final dialogue with Urquhart in order to demonstrate Browning's position:

> Instead of Bogarde declaring flatly that Arnhem was a bridge too far, the phrase 'I've always thought...' was inserted. Elsewhere in the script Bogarde makes a number of references to 'Monty says...' or 'Monty thinks...' to indicate he is acting under orders.[151]

Du Maurier appeared to have approved of the change, as on 14 April 1976, just prior to filming, she wrote to Attenborough, claiming 'I truly appreciate the immense trouble you have taken with the script and the Boy's part in it.'[152] Her views changed after being contacted by Barry Powell from the *News of the World* who had seen an early preview of the film. Powell considered that Browning was depicted as 'an aloof officer, deliberately ignoring solid evidence of a crack Panzer division build-up at Arnhem'. Du Maurier's reaction was to attack the film, commenting: 'They were just looking for a fall guy. I knew it would happen', and asserted that Ryan's book 'never portrayed my husband in this vicious way'.[153] The *Daily Mail* revealed that du Maurier had no intention of seeing the film and had written to Mountbatten, her friend, to ask him (after seeing the première) to inform her if the film 'is as harmful to her husband's reputation as is suggested'.[154] Significantly, both the *News of the World* and the *Daily Mail* publicised the union of the two families; Browning's daughter, Tessa had married David Montgomery, the son of the field marshal, in 1970, thus providing an united force against the film.

Du Maurier's views were further expressed in October when the *Sunday Times* declared the film had 'stirred deeply protective memories among veterans of the campaign'.[155] The author, Peter Dunn, also revealed that the Queen Mother had 'expressed approval' of 'the indignant letters written to *The Times* 'defending "Boy's" good name', and that Mountbatten had enjoyed the film but wrote to her 'regretting the public quarrel over her husband's reputation'. While Mountbatten's careful assessment of the film took into account his support for Attenborough to make *Gandhi*, Dunn was also overtly critical of Browning's portrayal claiming 'it is not so much what Bogarde says so much as the way he says it' and that he 'interpreted the role badly'.[156] The attack provoked another response from Attenborough who did his best to defend Bogarde:

> It was my decision to cast him in that part since I felt that, although not bearing any physical resemblance to General Browning, he most certainly had the qualities, experience and skill to be able to depict a character as complex as the one required. The characterisation eventually arrived at was as a result of discussions between us but, finally of course, what appears on-screen is the responsibility of the director.[157]

Another concern that neither the correspondence to *The Times* nor the articles address is that the furore over Bogarde's portrayal might have been related to rumours concerning the actor's sexuality. Bogarde's previous association with several homosexual roles, including *Victim* (Basil Dearden, 1961), *The Servant* (Joseph Losey, 1963) and *Death in Venice* (Luchino Visconti, 1971), had strengthened public suspicion of his sexuality. Although Browning's sexuality is not questioned in the film, various claims to his appearance as 'smart', 'beautifully turned out' and 'effete' were made that could imply either homosexual or bisexual leanings. Moreover, despite being married and the father of her three children, du Maurier also felt the need to stress: 'Whatever Moper [Browning] was, he certainly *wasn't* a homo!'[158] Browning became known as 'Boy' to distinguish him from his father who was also an Army officer when Browning joined up in 1916. The nickname, however, persisted, probably relating to his not being particularly masculine, with Browning later referred to in the Army as 'a pretty boy' and 'not a man's man'.[159] Whether the attacks on the film also were intended to camouflage any homosexual/bisexual insinuations against Browning (homosexuality being strictly prohibited in the Armed Forces), it might well explain the vehemence of the Army reaction to disassociate Browning from Bogarde's portrayal. The controversial response to his portrayal induced Bogarde to accuse Attenborough of 'both a personal betrayal and of "treachery"' by presenting the character based on Boy Browning in an untrue light, knowing full well that it was untrue'.[160] He wrote to Attenborough accusing him of ruining 'any possible recognition that I might receive nationally. And I shall never forgive you for that.'[161] The letter was still fresh in Attenborough's mind in 2003. He recalled that Bogarde had denounced him for 'putting him in this difficult role' but commented that it was the potential loss of a knighthood that concerned Bogarde most.[162]

A Bridge Too Far can be regarded as one of Attenborough's finest films. While the film received much criticism over its length and confused narrative, it nevertheless provides an accurate representation of the battle, as based on Ryan's account. The film was nominated for eight BAFTAs, yet failed to win any. More recently the film·has been viewed more favourably, coming seventh in the Channel 4's 100 Greatest War Films in 2005.[163]

Levine was delighted with the film, publicly praising Attenborough in a full-page letter in *Variety*: 'Dear Dickie, I want you to know, and I want the world to know, of the total admiration I have for you as a director, and the extreme affection I feel for you as a human being.'[164] In return, Attenborough announced that he never wanted to work for any other producer than Levine.[165] It was this happy experience of working with Levine and Goldman that persuaded Attenborough to embark on *Magic*, the second Joseph E. Levine Presents production. *Magic*, an intimate thriller, also represented Attenborough's first Hollywood venture as a director.

Levine purchased the rights while *A Bridge Too Far* was being edited. Goldman had completed the novel on which *Magic* was based in the autumn of 1976. The novel was written with the American actress Ann-Margret in mind, whose real name, Margaret-Ann, was changed to the shortened form of Peggy Ann. *Magic* relates the tale of a ventriloquist whose mind is dominated by the actions and commands of his own dummy. The concept was not new to cinema, having been originally introduced in *The Great Gabbo* (James Cruze, 1929), but was most notable in an episode of a portmanteau film, *Dead of Night* (1945), an Ealing production which focuses on five separate events concerned with the supernatural. The sequence, 'The Ventriloquist's Dummy', which starred Michael Redgrave and was directed by Alberto Cavalcanti, focused on a dummy who takes control of his ventriloquist's mind. In 1963, another film, *The Devil Doll* (Lindsay Shonteff), applied hypnotic qualities to the ventriloquist act in order to direct the dummy to evil deeds. While both films can be seen to have their original themes reworked in *Magic*, the supernatural and hypnotic elements are both replaced by the advancing psychosis of the ventriloquist. *Magic* focuses more on the human mind as it delves deeply into the inner turmoil of a man verging on the cusp of insanity.

Despite Levine's apparent keenness for Attenborough to direct *Magic*, it was only after Norman Jewison, the original appointee, and Levine quarrelled, that he was offered the position. Attenborough only agreed on the condition, volunteered by Levine, that *Gandhi* would definitely follow. The condition appeared secure as during filming, Levine bought back the rights to *Gandhi* from Avco-Embassy for $100,000 and agreed to engage John Briley, Attenborough's choice, as scriptwriter for the film. With his prized project now appearing secure, Attenborough rose to the challenge, maintaining that: 'The thriller requires a director to be more sure than any other kind of film.'[166]

Casting was once again considered by Attenborough of utmost importance. As with *Young Winston*, Attenborough firmly asserted his directorial control by insisting that Hopkins should play the leading role of Corky Withers, going against Levine's own wishes for a major star. Although Levine reluctantly agreed to Attenborough's demand, he later declared: 'I knew the minute we signed Anthony Hopkins for this picture that advance sales were dead.'[167] A different type of persuasion was required with the leading actress in the film, with Ann-Margret, who had recently co-starred in *Carnal Knowledge* (Mike Nichols, 1971) with Jack Nicholson. Unlike her normal sophisticated roles, Ann-Margret was required to change her appearance and 'deglamourise herself', by performing without make-up and wearing unflattering clothes, which Attenborough claimed made her feel 'vulnerable'.[168] However, the greatest acting challenge was for Hopkins who, with his limited experience, faced the most difficult role of his career so far. In addition to the demands of portraying a psychopathic character, Hopkins also had to handle the dexterities of card tricks and the intricacies of ventriloquism, in what Attenborough claimed was 'probably as difficult as anything one can recall in the cinema'.[169]

Although *Magic* was Attenborough's first attempt at directing a thriller he had experience with the genre as an actor, most notably in *Séance on a Wet Afternoon* (Bryan Forbes, 1964). In addition, Attenborough's role as John Reginald Christie in *10 Rillington Place* (Richard Fleischer, 1971) had allowed him to explore the mind of a murderer which Corky Withers (Hopkins) becomes in *Magic*. The small principal cast of four (plus the dummy, Fats), made the interplay of the relationships particularly crucial to the film. Corky is a magician and a psychologically unstable person who becomes further disturbed by the prospect of undergoing an employment medical examination. He escapes to the Catskill Mountains where he rekindles a relationship with Peggy Ann Snow. Fat's corrupted character slowly takes over from Corky's former inhibited self. When Corky's agent, Ben Green (Burgess Meredith), locates him Corky murders Green after being 'told to' by Fats. Fats also orders Corky to kill Peggy Ann's husband, Duke (Ed Lauter), when he becomes suspicious of her and Corky's relationship. The climatic ending occurs when Fats commands Corky to kill Peggy Ann. Corky fails to do this, and instead, kills himself.

In contrast to *A Bridge Too Far*, *Magic* had a small budget of $5 million. While there were no logistical concerns that dominated *A Bridge Too Far*, continuous poor weather resulted in filming in the Catskill Mountains having to take place in rain. Production began in January 1978, taking place in New York and in the Catskill Mountains, and ended in March. The film opened in America in November 1978 and in Britain, two months later, in January 1979. Levine also kept to his rule of not securing distributers until the film was completed, on this occasion with 20th Century-Fox. He also persuaded Goldman to sign a three-film contract to write three original screenplays.

Similarly to *A Bridge Too Far*, *Magic* is filmed throughout in muted colours, to enhance the murky situation of the story which is supported by atmospheric music from the score of Jerry Goldsmith. The settings contrast oppressive internal scenes to ones depicting sweeping landscapes, where Corky seeks to reclaim his former relationship with Peggy Ann. One of the most notable scenes involves Peggy Ann provoking Corky into showing her a card trick. Corky instructs Peggy Ann to select a card and hold it close to her. In order to be able to read her mind and identify the card, Corky needs to be convinced that Peggy Ann really loves him. While the trick succeeds, Peggy Ann becomes fearful of the negative and dangerous side of Corky's character. The scene marks a pivotal point in the film where Corky's mental state turns towards the psychotic, the tension gradually building up through the clever employment of distorted camera angles and cross-cut editing.

While many of the reviews were unfavourable, the most contentious issue concerned Goldman's script, both for being too contrived but mostly for its similarity to *Dead of Night*. The *Scotsman* declared that Attenborough had 'duplicated, but perhaps not surpassed Cavalcanti's chilling film'.[170] The *Evening News* considered the concept of the ventriloquist dominated by his dummy as 'over familiar since it first chilled us in *Dead of Night*.[171] Philip French in the *Observer* was critical of the script for 'revealing nothing.' He also was disparaging with Hopkins's acting for being 'crazy too soon and too obviously'.[172] Those who applauded the film included the *Sunday Telegraph* who praised Attenborough's direction as 'a moving study of human relationships' and *Films and Filming* which called *Magic* a 'thriller *par excellence*'.[173] The *Monthly Film Bulletin* could only refer to the film as 'a dreary little melodrama'.[174]

The worst reviews for the film came from America where criticisms were rife. Pauline Kael in the *New Yorker* regarded *Magic* as 'an atrocious-looking movie', declaring Hopkins as 'bewilderingly miscast'.[175] *Variety* described it as 'an occasionally absorbing character study that never fulfils its promise as a suspense chiller, despite an extraordinary performance by Anthony Hopkins.'[176] *Films in Review* focused its attack on Attenborough's direction, calling it 'so leaden that the odd moments of astute editing or interesting camera movements seem almost accidental'.[177] Attenborough was forced to recognise that *Magic* was difficult for Hopkins to produce a good performance because he was playing against a dummy, and not a fellow actor. He also acknowledged that the film lacked emotional chemistry, claiming that 'Tony was not really at ease with Ann-Margret.'[178] Hopkins also admitted his own lack of confidence in the role: 'There were times when I felt incapable of coping with all the eerie contradictions of the character.'[179]

Despite the predominantly critical assault on the film, *Magic* was more popularly acclaimed, and grossed just under $12 million, double its costs. The financial success also proved that Attenborough had become a bankable director. He also gained personal financial gain by being on a percentage pay of the films gross, unlike in *A Bridge Too Far*, the actors were not on the same scheme, the smaller cast paid for their roles.[180] *Magic* was nominated for several awards, including a BAFTA and a Golden Globe for Hopkins.

Notwithstanding its commercial success, the film's adverse critical judgement, however, resulted in *Magic* becoming one of Attenborough's least acclaimed films. It was also considered at variance with Attenborough's œuvre. In 1984, David Castell declared *Magic* as 'clearly the odd film out, with very few characters, a small and claustrophobic setting'.[181] Attenborough, however, asserts the opposite view claiming that 'though *Magic* may at first seem to fall outside my genre, it is actually typical of it. It is about [...] a game of creating characters and interweaving them and allowing them to react on each other.[182] While *Magic* can be seen to be following the intimate portrayal that Attenborough explored so adeptly in *Young Winston*, the results were less successful. Attenborough later confessed that he would not have directed *Magic* if it wasn't for Levine's promise to support *Gandhi*.[183] Pandering to Levine was obviously his prime motivation in directing a film, in which it appears he was unable to fully engage his mind, courtesy of Levine's promise, more focused on *Gandhi*. Moreover, *Magic* also remains Attenborough's only foray into the thriller, a genre which clearly fascinated him, but one in which he appeared ill at ease in directing.

Notes

1. Andrew Higson, 'Renewing British Cinema in the 1970s', in Bart Moore-Gilbert (ed.), *The Arts in the 1970s: Cultural Closure?*, London, 1994, p. 217.
2. Author's meeting with Attenborough, 15 February 2007, Richmond, Surrey.
3. Margaret Dickinson and Sarah Street, *Cinema and State: the Film Industry and the British Government 1927–1984*, London, 1985, p. 240.
4. Ibid.
5. Attenborough quoted on DVD, *Young Winston*, Columbia Pictures, 2006, VFD 02542.
6. James Chapman, *Past and Present: National Identity and the British Historical Film*, London, 2005, p. 10.
7. Ibid., p. 255.
8. 'Reflections of a Director', *Young Winston*, DVD.
9. David Castell, *Richard Attenborough: A Pictorial Film Biography*, London, 1984, p. 22.
10. Carl Foreman quoted in Tom Hutchinson, 'How "the Lion" Tamed Mr Foreman', *Sunday Telegraph*, 11 April 1971.
11. Sarah Street, *British National Cinema*, London, 1997, p. 103.
12. Information obtained from James Chapman; John Ramsden, *Man of the Century:*

Winston Churchill and His Legend since 1945, London, 2003, p. 204, claims Churchill signed a deal in 1941, although he doesn't specify with whom.
13 *Sunday Telegraph*, 11 April 1971.
14 Script, S11697 'The Young Mr Churchill', 10 February 1963, BFI, London.
15 *Ibid.*; Churchill was not actually knighted until 1953.
16 *Listener*, 3 August 1972.
17 D. J. Wenden and K.R.M. Short, 'Winston S. Churchill: Film Fan', *Historical Journal of Film, Radio and Television*, 11:3 (1991), p. 199.
18 Hutchinson, 'How "the Lion" Tamed Mr Foreman', *Listener*, 3 August 1972.
19 *The Times*, 6 December 1963.
20 Hutchinson, 'How "the Lion" Tamed Mr Foreman'.
21 *The Times*, 5 August 1971. See also Sian Barber, 'Government Aid and Film Legislation: "An Elastoplast to Stop a Haemorrhage"', in Sue Porter and Justin Smith (eds), *British Film Culture in the 1970s: The Boundaries of Pleasure*, Edinburgh, 2012, pp. 12–13.
22 *Films Illustrated*, 2:13 (July 1972), p. 12.
23 Richard Attenborough, 'The Birth of Young Winston', *The Times*, 8 July 1972.
24 Quoted in Mary Blume, 'A Tycoon Who Got His Job through HUAC', *International Herald Tribune*, 5 April 1968.
25 Quoted in Steve Chibnall, *J. Lee Thompson*, Manchester, 2000, p. 260.
26 Press Book, *Young Winston*, microfiche, BFI, London.
27 Attenborough, 'The Birth of Young Winston'. Attenborough denied writing the article himself. Author's meeting with Attenborough, 15 June 2003.
28 Sue Harper, 'History and Representation: The Case of 1970s British Cinema', in James Chapman, Mark Glancy and Harper (eds), *The New Film History: Sources, Methods, Approaches*, Basingstoke, 2007, p. 31.
29 David Robinson, *Richard Attenborough*, London, 2003, p. 45.
30 *Variety*, 1 December 1971.
31 David Lewin, 'He Fought to Be Free', *Cinema/TV Today*, 22 July 1972, p. 25.
32 Gordon Gow, 'Interrogation', *Films and Filming*, 18:11 (August 1972), p. 15.
33 *Ibid.*, pp. 15–16.
34 *Ibid.*, p. 15; James Powers, 'Richard Attenborough Seminar', *Dialogue on Film* (February 1973), p. 9.
35 *Ibid.*, p. 10.
36 Winston Churchill, *The Dream*, Cambridge, 1987. It was first published as an article in the *Daily Telegraph*, 30 January 1966.
37 Powers, 'Richard Attenborough Seminar', p. 4.
38 Higson, 'Renewing British Cinema in the 1970s' p. 228.
39 Quoted in *Evening News*, 13 July 1972.
40 *Guardian*, 30 October 1971.
41 Andy Dougan, *The Actors' Director: Richard Attenborough Behind the Camera*, Edinburgh, 1994, p. 34.
42 *The Times*, 21 July 1972.
43 *The Times*, 29 July 1972.
44 Ramsden, *Man of the Century*, p. 205. I can find no account of the discovery in *The Times* digital archive of the discovery in 1971 (including for Ramsden's endnote, 21 July 1971). The only article in *The Times* I have discovered was published on 21 July 1972.
45 *Cinema/TV Today*, 29 July 1972, p. 24; *Films and Filming*, 19:1 (October 1972), p. 49.
46 *Monthly Film Bulletin*, 39:464 (September 1972), p. 198; *Sight and Sound*, 1:4 (autumn 1972), p. 232.
47 *Daily Mail*, 19 July 1972; *The Times*, 19 July 1972.

48 *Daily Telegraph*, 19 July 1972.
49 *Observer*, 30 July 1972; *Guardian*, 19 July 1972.
50 *New York Times*, 11 October 1972; *Village Voice*, 23 November 1972.
51 *Variety*, 26 July, 1972.
52 Quoted in *Filmfacts*, 15:14 (1972), p. 310.
53 *Cinema/TV Today*, 23 September 1972, p. 2.
54 *Young Winston*, microfiche.
55 Quoted in Dougan, *The Actors' Director*, p. 33.
56 *Ibid.*, p. 36.
57 Dougan, *The Actors' Director*, p. 58, gives the amount as $23.5 million. *Cleopatra* (1963) is also said to have cost more than $25 million.
58 *Variety*, 21 April 1976.
59 The number of bridges varies in different publications. I have taken the same number as Cornelius Ryan, *A Bridge Too Far*, Hertfordshire, 1999, p. 66.
60 *Battlefront: Operation Market Garden*, Public Record Office, Richmond, 2000, p. 7.
61 *Tora! Tora! Tora!* did not portray a victory but the event changed the direction of the war in favour of the Allies.
62 *The World at War* was first broadcast on 31 October 1973 on ITV by Thames Television.
63 Ryan, *A Bridge Too Far*, p. 67.
64 *Screen International*, 25 June 1977, p. 20.
65 Stephen E. Ambrose, *Pegasus Bridge: 6 June 1944*, London, 1984, p. xi.
66 *Screen International*, 4 September 1976, p. 25.
67 Quoted in John Higgins, 'Richard Attenborough's Quest for an Indian Grail', *The Times*, 24 July 1975, p. 13.
68 Victor Davis, 'How the Bridge at Arnhem Came to Be Paved with Gold', *Daily Express*, 7 February 1977.
69 John Walker (ed.), *Halliwell's Who's Who in the Movies*, 2nd edn, London, 2001, p. 268.
70 Peter Dunn, 'The Last Movie Mogul', *Sunday Times* (Magazine), 5 February 1978, pp. 43 and 45.
71 William Goldman, *Adventures in the Screen Trade*, London, 1983, p. 277.
72 *Screen International*, 2 July 1977, p. 11.
73 Attenborough, *In Search of Gandhi*, p. 158; Goldman, *Adventures in the Screen Trade*, p. 279.
74 Attenborough, *In Search of Gandhi*, p. 158.
75 *A Bridge Too Far*, microfiche.
76 Attenborough provided several 'voices' including a cockney, a Leicester accent and either a Scottish or Welsh voice, he couldn't remember which one. Author's interview with Attenborough, 16 June 2003.
77 Quoted in Higgins, 'Richard Attenborough's quest for an Indian Grail'.
78 Attenborough to Mason, 17 September 1975, National Archives, London, DEFE 68/85.
79 Terms of Agreement signed by Abraham and Attenborough, 29 July 1976, DEFE 24/974 1976, 19 Mar.–29 July 1976.
80 Quoted in Higgins, 'Richard Attenborough's Quest for an Indian Grail'.
81 Attenborough to Wilson, 6 August 1975, DEFE 68/85.
82 Davis, 'How the Bridge at Arnhem Came to Be Paved with Gold'.
83 Stephen E. Ambrose, '*The Longest Day* (1962): "Blockbuster" History', *Historical Journal of Film, Radio and Television*, 14:4 (1994), p. 422.
84 *New York Times*, 16 June 1977.
85 *Film Review*, 27:7 (July 1977), p. 8.
86 *Screen International*, 26 February 1977, p. 19.

87 *Variety*, 21 April 1976.
88 *Ibid.*
89 John Coldstream, *Dirk Bogarde*, London, 2004, p. 506.
90 *Filmfacts*, 20:9 (1977), p. 194; Author's interview with Richard Attenborough and Terence Clegg 16 June, 2003. According to Clegg it was 'typical of Joe [Levine] to deny something he never wanted'.
91 Davis, 'How the Bridge at Arnhem Came to Be Paved with Gold'.
92 Quoted in Roy Pickard, 'Attenborough's Battles', *Photoplay*, 28:7 (1977), p. 45.
93 *Screen International*, 25 June 1977, p. 20.
94 Andrew Yule, *Sean Connery: Neither Shaken Nor Stirred*, London, 1994, p. 203.
95 Iain Johnstone, *The Arnhem Report*, London, 1977, p. 34.
96 Production Notes, *A Bridge Too Far*, microfiche, BFI, London.
97 Goldman, *Adventures in the Screen Trade*, p. 274. Goldman also states (p.282) that 'the first draft was finished by November 1975'.
98 *Ibid.*, p. 280.
99 Quoted in Peter Dunn, 'The Second Battle of Arnhem', *Sunday Times*, 23 October 1977.
100 Author's interview with Attenborough and Clegg, 16 June 2003.
101 *American Cinematographer*, 58:4 (April 1977), p. 288.
102 Andrew Keech, 'John Addison, *A Bridge Too Far*', *Music from the Movies*, 24 (summer 1999), p. 32.
103 Pickard, 'Attenborough's Battles', p. 32; Dougan, *The Actors' Director*, p. 62.
104 Dougan, *The Actors' Director*, p. 62.
105 Broadcasting, Entertainment, Cinematograph and Theatre Union (BECTU) History Project, No. 500, 'Lord (Richard) Attenborough', interviewed by Sydney Samuelson, 4 December 2001, BFI.
106 Author's interview with Attenborough and Clegg, 16 February 2007.
107 Johnstone, *The Arnhem Report*, p. 86.
108 Coldstream, *Dirk Bogarde*, p. 514.
109 Quoted in Johnstone, *The Arnhem Report*, p. 125.
110 Quoted in Coldstream, *Dirk Bogarde*, p. 506.
111 *Ibid.*, p. 509.
112 Jeffrey Richards, *A Night to Remember*, London, 2003, p. 56.
113 Goldman, *Adventures in the Screen Trade*, p. 296.
114 *Ibid.*, p. 281.
115 Author's interview with Major-General Ian Gill, 18 September 2005, Thorney, Cambridgeshire.
116 Ryan, *A Bridge Too Far*, p. 313.
117 Goldman, *Adventures in the Screen Trade*, p. 295.
118 James Chapman, '"The Yanks Are Shown to Such Advantage": Anglo-American rivalry in the production of The True Glory (1945)', *Historical Journal of Film, Radio and Television*, 16:4 (1996), p. 542.
119 Goldman, *Adventures in the Screen Trade*, p. 145.
120 Brian Horrocks, 'The Battle of Arnhem: Days of Grief and Glory', *The Times*, 13 June 1977.
121 DVD, *A Bridge Too Far*, MGM, 2004, VFC18970.
122 John Sandilands, 'Tanks, David Darling...', *Observer* (Magazine) 27 March 1977, p. 24.
123 *Ibid.*, p. 25.
124 Attenborough quoted in Sheridan Morley, 'Attenborough's War', *The Times*, 20 June 1977, p. 7.
125 *Ibid.*
126 Goldman, *Adventures in the Screen Trade*, p. 289.

127 *TV Times*, 83:26 (26 June 1977).
128 *Screen International*, 2 July 1977, p. 2.
129 *Screen International*, 24/31 December 1977, p. 1.
130 Street, *Transatlantic Crossings: British Films in the USA*, London, 2002, p. 195.
131 *New York Times*, 16 July 1977.
132 *New Yorker*, 20 June 1977.
133 *Filmfacts*, 20:9 (1977), p. 195; *Hollywood Reporter*, 8 June 1977, p. 3.
134 *Daily Express*, 22 February 1977 and 5 July 1977.
135 *Daily Telegraph*, 21 June 1977.
136 *The Times*, 24 June 1977.
137 *De Waarheid*, 28 June 1977. All English translations kindly provided by Professor Bert Hogenkamp, the Netherlands.
138 *Gooi en Eemlander*, 24 June 1977.
139 *Trouw*, 24 June 1977.
140 *Twentsche Courant*, 24 June 1977.
141 *The Times*, 2 July 1977.
142 *The Times*, 12 July 1977.
143 *The Times*, 22 July 1977.
144 *The Times*, 30 June 1977.
145 *The Times*, 25 June 1977.
146 *The Times*, 28 June 1977.
147 *The Times*, 7 July 1977.
148 *The Times*, 12 July 1977.
149 *Daily Express*, 2 March 1976.
150 Peter Dunn, 'The Second Battle of Arnhem', *Sunday Times*, 23 October 1977, p. 12.
151 *Ibid*.
152 *Ibid*.
153 *News of the World*, 22 May 1977.
154 *Daily Mail*, 14 June 1977.
155 Dunn, 'The Second Battle of Arnhem'.
156 Browning had then progressed to becoming comptroller and treasurer to Princess Elizabeth's household in 1948 and treasurer to the Duke of Edinburgh in 1952.
157 *Sunday Times*, 30 October 1977.
158 Quoted in Coldstream, *Dirk Bogarde*, p. 509.
159 Margaret Forster, *Daphne du Maurier*, London, 1993, p. 431; information obtained from Major-General Gill, 18 September 2005.
160 Attenborough quoted in Coldstream, *Dirk Bogarde*, p. 514.
161 *Ibid*.
162 Author's interview with Attenborough and Clegg, 16 June 2003.
163 *The 100 Greatest War Films* (Channel 4, 15 May 2005).
164 *Variety*, 6 October 1976, p. 15.
165 *Sunday Express*, 21 November 1976.
166 Quoted in Gordon Gow, 'Venturing', *Films and Filming*, 25:5 (February 1979), p. 23.
167 *Variety*, 1 November 1978.
168 Quoted in Gow, 'Venturing', p. 24.
169 *Ibid*.
170 *Scotsman*, 27 January 1979.
171 *Evening News*, 25 January 1979.
172 *Observer*, 28 January 1979.
173 *Sunday Telegraph*, 28 January 1979; *Films and Filming* (February 1979), p. 28.

174 *Monthly Film Bulletin*, 46:540 (January 1979), p. 9.
175 *New Yorker*, 11 December 1978.
176 *Variety*, 1 November 1978.
177 *Films in Review*, 29:10 (December 1978), p. 633.
178 Dougan, *The Actors' Director*, p. 70; quoted in Derek Malcolm, 'Fine and Gandhi', *Guardian*, 5 February 1979.
179 Production Notes, *Magic*, microfiche, BFI, London.
180 Sydney Edward, 'Living It up with Fats', *Evening Standard*, 26 January 1979.
181 Castell, *Richard Attenborough*, p. 26
182 Robinson, *Richard Attenborough*, p. 55.
183 Dougan, *The Actors' Director*, p. 67.

1 Richard Attenborough (Tom Curtis) in *The Angry Silence* (1960)

2 Bryan Forbes (Porthill), Richard Attenborough (Lexy) and Kieron Moore (Stevens) in *The League of Gentlemen* (1960)

3 Michael Redgrave (General Sir Henry Wilson) and Laurence Olivier (Field-Marshal Sir John French) in *Oh! What a Lovely War* (1969)

4 Simon Ward (Winston Churchill) in *Young Winston* (1972)

5 Dirk Bogarde (Lieutenant-General Frederick Browning) and Sean Connery (Major-General 'Roy' Urquhart) in *A Bridge Too Far* (1977)

6 'Fats' and Anthony Hopkins (Corky Withers) in *Magic* (1978)

7 Ben Kingsley (Mahatma Gandhi) in *Gandhi* (1982)

8 Denzel Washington (Steve Biko) in *Cry Freedom* (1987)

9 Robert Downey Jr (Charles Chaplin) in *Chaplin* (1992)

10 Anthony Hopkins (C.S. 'Jack' Lewis) and Debra Winger (Joy Gresham) in *Shadowlands* (1993)

104

11 Pierce Brosnan (Archie) and Annie Galipeau (Pony) in *Grey Owl* (1999)

12 Pete Postlethwaite (Quinlan) and Martin McCann (Jimmy) in *Closing the Ring* (2007)

Race, nation and conflict: *Gandhi* (1982), *A Chorus Line* (1985) and *Cry Freedom* (1987)

5

The 1980s marked the apotheosis of Richard Attenborough's directorial career in which he fulfilled his twenty-year ambition of realising a film on the life of Mahatma Gandhi. As well as being a personal achievement for Attenborough, *Gandhi* represented a key moment for the British film industry through its success at the box office and led to national pride by winning eight of the eleven Academy Awards for which it was nominated, the greatest acclaim to that date for a British film. The Oscar success raised hopes that the industry would be revitalised by attracting more government investment to enhance the now elevated British position which had been boosted by the previous year's success of the four Academy Awards won by *Chariots of Fire* (Hugh Hudson, 1981) and improved further by the achievements of *Gandhi*. Whereas *Gandhi* looks to racial concerns of the past, *Cry Freedom* explores the contemporary issues surrounding apartheid through the film's focus on the friendship of Steve Biko, a black activist, and Donald Woods, a white journalist, while living under the regime in South Africa. The film made a significant contribution to raising global public awareness of the realities of the apartheid regime of the time. Sandwiched between the two political portrayals, Attenborough directed his second American production, *A Chorus Line*, a musical adaptation of the stage play, which focused on contemporary racial and social concerns in America.

Attenborough's career was affected by significant changes occurring within the British cinema at the end of the 1970s. The dominance of Hollywood films saw a decline in the number of British-produced films, with a dramatic drop from sixty-one in 1979 to thirty-one in 1980. Although there were fluctuations from year to year, the decade ended with the lowest figure of thirty films being made in 1989.[1] Cinema tickets also doubled in price between 1977 and 1983 leading to changes in the class structure of the audience, from the predominantly young working class to one composed predominantly of middle classes.[2] A redistribution of ownership in the cinema chains saw Thorn EMI and the ABC circuit being absorbed into the Cannon Group, leaving the bulk of British production in the hands of independent companies. The largest of these was Goldcrest (which would later support *Gandhi*), while others included Handmade Films, Palace Pictures and Virgin Films. A further source of production, television, also became available through the emergence of Channel 4, an independent channel which began broadcasting in 1982.

The changes in the cinema also reflected the wider political environment, particularly the policies of Margaret Thatcher. The election of a Conservative government in 1979 caused significant changes to the running of the cinema by removing much of the cinema legislation Labour had introduced to support the industry. The Conservatives' attitude to cinema was in line with their economic policies for the other arts which included reduced support and encouragement for economic independence. In film this appeared to supersede all creative aspects. As John Hill observes, 'the new Conservative government was reluctant to conceive of it in artistic and cultural terms at all with the result that its policies were almost entirely concerned with the commercial aspects of the industry.'[3]

Through the 1980 Films Act and the Film Levy Finance Act of 1981, the Eady Levy continued but was eventually abolished by the 1985 Films Act. The introduction of a capital tax allowance for films in 1979, which had encouraged City investment, notably for such films as *Chariots of Fire*, *Educating Rita* (Lewis Gilbert, 1983) and *Local Hero* (Bill Forsyth, 1983), was also abolished in 1986, thus curtailing a valuable source of finance. The Conservatives also replaced the National Film Finance Corporation (NFFC) with the British Screen Finance Corporation Consortium, allocating it a grant of £7.5 million over five years.[4] The new corporation became a significant supplier of production finance, and thus occupied a key position in the industry.

Under Thatcher the cinema became affected by the leader's politics, 'Thatcherism', which advocated privatisation of state-owned industries and utilities, reform of the trade unions, the lowering of taxes and reduced social expenditure designed to halt inflation and to stimulate industrial growth. The policy combined a belief in the effectiveness of market forces, the need for strong central government and a conviction that self-help is preferable to reliance on the state, with a firm sense of nationalism. During Thatcher's tenure inflation was reduced but unemployment reached two million in August 1980 for the first time since 1935 and rose to three million eighteen months later. This was also followed by a decline in the British manufacturing industries and the curbing of trade union power.

Thatcher's premiership was also dominated by the Falklands War of 1982, when one of the last remnants of the British Empire was invaded by Argentina. The resultant conflict also had a close link to cinema in its relation to Colin Welland's remark, made at the Academy Awards on 23 March 1982, that 'the British are coming!' Two weeks later, on 2 April, the Falkland Islands were invaded and on 5 April a British task force was sent there to recapture the colony. The re-release of *Chariots of Fire* as part of a double bill with *Gregory's Girl* (Bill Forsyth, 1981) was seen as a boost to support the British war effort in its display of patriotism. Empire films has a long history in British cinema particularly during its height in the 1930s and most notably by two 'trilogies' of films, Alexander Korda's *Sanders of the River* (1935), *The Drum* (1938) and *The Four Feathers* (1939), all directed by Zoltan Korda, and those of Michael Balcon, *Rhodes of Africa* (Berthold Viertel, 1936), *The Great Barrier* (Milton Rosmer, 1936) and *King Solomon's Mines* (Robert Stevenson, 1937). These films had followed the traditional pattern of presenting the Empire as a positive concept and promoting imperialist attitudes. More recent imperial films such as *Zulu* (Cy Endfield, 1964) and the lesser acclaimed *Zulu Dawn* (Douglas Hickox, 1979) had shown a more sympathetic understanding of the colonised people. *Gandhi* moves the concept of empire further from the British colonisers by focusing, instead, on the colonised people.

Both *Gandhi* and *Cry Freedom* are largely linked to the themes of race and nation which dominated both British society and cinema in the 1980s. During the 1970s Britain had seen a number of racial attacks and demonstrations associated with the rise of the National Front, while in the 1980s disturbances occurred in several inner-city areas including Brixton, south London, Toxteth, Liverpool and Manchester. The theme of race had been much explored in cinema during the 1980s. *Chariots of Fire* portrays ethnic differences in Britain in the 1920s by its depiction of Harold Abrahams, of Jewish Lithuanian extraction, and Eric Liddell, a Scottish Presbyterian, born in China. Both men employ their athletic talents to become fully integrated as 'British'. Films such as *Local Hero* (Bill Forsyth, 1983), which explores the reactions of local Scottish inhabitants to the possible development of an American oil refinery, and *My Beautiful Laundrette* (Stephen Frears, 1985), which explores racial difference within concerns of gender and sexuality, demonstrate a thematic link with *Cry Freedom*. Both *Gandhi* and *Cry Freedom* contain overt violence and bloodshed, the inclusion of which Attenborough felt necessary to highlight the message of racial tension and point up the need for peace.

The story of the Indian Hindu leader, Mohandas K. Gandhi, who played a major role in the country's independence, freeing India of British colonial rule, was a complex topic for a cinema biography. Gandhi studied law in London before practising as a barrister in Bombay, moving to South Africa in 1907 where he began his policy of passive resistance against the government's racist policies towards Indians. In 1915 he returned to India and became leader of the Congress movement. Gandhi was imprisoned on several occasions for his political stance and also resorted to hunger strikes to help restore civil calm. In 1931 he was invited to take part in the Round Table Conference in London on the future of India. Gandhi had long concluded that independence was the only possible solution to India's problems. He later cooperated with the last viceroys, Archibald, Earl Wavell and Earl Mountbatten, for independence and partition which occurred on 15 August 1947. While many of his Hindu followers regarded Gandhi as a saint, referring to him as 'the Mahatma' or 'great soul', others deplored his acceptance of partition and rejected his pacifist philosophy. He was assassinated by a fanatical Hindu in January 1948.

The difficulties Attenborough had in coordinating all the requirements for *Gandhi* – securing finance, obtaining a suitable script and finding an appropriate actor for the principal role – were immense. The difficulties were also exacerbated by the contentious nature of the subject, both in India, due to differences of opinion on Gandhi's policies and his role in partition, and in Britain, where Gandhi had been famously denounced by Winston Churchill, who was 'revolted' by

> [T]he nauseating and humiliating spectacle of this one-time Inner Temple lawyer, now seditious fakir, striding half-naked up the steps of the Viceroy's palace, there to negotiate and to parley on equal terms with the representative of the King-Emperor.[5]

Despite Churchill's denigration, the brutal death of the peace-loving Gandhi shocked the world with many paying tribute. Mountbatten declared that 'Mahatma Gandhi will go down in history on a par with Buddha and Jesus Christ' while for Einstein: 'Generations to come, it may be, will scarce believe that such a one as this ever in flesh and blood walked upon this earth.'[6]

Attenborough's involvement with *Gandhi* began in January 1962 after he was approached by an Indian expatriate, Motilal Kothari, with a film proposal. Kothari, a devout follower of Gandhi, had been forced to leave India for his 'Gandhian' activities and came to England to work for the Indian High Commission. Kothari saw his adopted country as best placed to make the film and began 'his mission to find a professional who would spread knowledge of the Mahatma throughout the world by means of a motion picture'.[7] Although Kothari had previously discussed the project with Robert Bolt, it was Attenborough, a relatively new producer, who supported the anti-racist and anti-apartheid policies to which Kothari aspired.

The idea to make a film about Gandhi was not new. In 1923 D.W. Griffith was approached by the British government who wanted to counter Gandhi's influence and recognised the extent to which cinema could promote their cause through propaganda. While the Griffith film failed to materialise, the quest to make a film on Gandhi was resurrected after Louis Fischer's acclaimed biography, *The Life of Mahatma Gandhi*, was published in 1951. Gabriel Pascal proposed a film entitled 'The Life of Gandhi' in 1953, which was aborted after Alec Guinness turned down the role.[8] Other abandoned projects included those initiated by Otto Preminger, Michael Powell and Filippo Del Giudice. A more substantive attempt was by David Lean who had gained official support from the Indian government after meeting the Prime Minister, Jawaharlal Nehru, and his daughter, Indira, in 1958. Sam Spiegel was engaged as producer with Guinness set to play the leading role. Emeric Pressburger's resultant treatment, however, entitled 'Written in the Stars', was rejected by Lean and he and Spiegel made *Lawrence of Arabia* (1962) instead. A fictional depiction, *Nine Hours to Rama* (Mark Robson, 1962), based on a novel by Stanley Wolpert, was condemned by Nehru for its historical distortion and was consequently banned from cinemas (the ban was still in force in 1980, just prior to the production for *Gandhi*). In India, a documentary entitled *Mahatma* (Vithalbhai K. Jhaveri, 1968), made for the Gandhi Centenary Year in 1969, was not a popular success due to its sober representation which made 'no attempt to create melodrama'.[9]

Attenborough became convinced of the potential of the subject after reading Fischer's biography. He was highly influenced by one specific incident related in Fischer's book which he later recalled:

> Gandhi was walking along the pavement in South Africa with a fellow Indian and two white South Africans were walking towards them. As was expected of in those days, the early 1890s, the two Indians stepped into the gutter and the whites continued on the sidewalk.[10]

Attenborough remarked on Gandhi's reaction to the incident: '[I]t has always been a mystery to me how men can feel themselves honoured by the humiliation of their fellow beings.'[11] While the incident described in Fischer's book is not quite as Attenborough recalls (Gandhi was not referring to himself in this instance), his words nevertheless reflect his disapproval of human beings asserting superiority over others, a reaction which Fischer attributes to the word 'appeal', the key to Gandhi's politics.[12] The book inspired Attenborough to want to direct the film even though he had never directed before. Fischer supported the idea of a film and 'allowed' Kothari to purchase the film rights to the biography and another work, for the token sum of £1. Although Fischer's biography is not acknowledged in the film credits, it nevertheless provides the chronological framework for the script by beginning and ending with Gandhi's assassination.

Kothari and Attenborough became joint producers with their new company, Indo-British Films. This was where Attenborough's links with the British film industry proved helpful. In 1963, he gained support from John Davis, Chairman of Rank. Although Davis's international films were mostly adventure stories, Rank had a specific interest in colonial films having made four during the 1950s, *The Planter's Wife* (1952), *Simba* (1955), *Windom's Way* (1957) and *North West Frontier* (1959), the latter set in India in 1905.[13] While Davis questioned the feasibility of a film about 'an old man dressed in a sheet carrying a bean pole', he nevertheless gave encouragement by offering Attenborough £5,000 as initial development money to research the project.[14] This was a personal loan, given in acknowledgement of Attenborough's several acting and producing roles for Rank, and made on the condition that it would be returned if the film was made by another company. If the project failed to materialise, Attenborough was not liable to repay the loan. Attenborough later acknowledged the full implication of Davis's action: 'Without it, *Gandhi* would never have got off the ground.'[15]

The success of *Lawrence of Arabia* encouraged Attenborough and Kothari to ask Robert Bolt to write the screenplay but he declined. Instead the Irish writer, Gerald Hanley, was engaged. Hanley had lived in India and had written a novel about life under colonial control, *The Consul at Sunset*.[16] To help obtain the official permission required from the Indian government (a condition of filming in India), Attenborough received advice from Earl Mountbatten, appointed the last Viceroy to India in February 1947 and the first Governor-General between 15 August 1947 and 21 June 1948. Attenborough and Mountbatten first met on the set of *In Which We Serve* (Noël Coward and Lean, 1942) and had maintained contact since through organisations such as the Society of British Film and Television Arts (BAFTA) and the Royal Naval Film Corporation. Significantly, Mountbatten was able to provide Attenborough with the important introduction to Nehru, the then prime minister, and his daughter Indira Gandhi, a future prime minister, in 1963. Nehru, although giving his approval to the script, also wanted his views to be taken into account, the most significant being the manner of Gandhi's portrayal: 'Whatever you do, don't deify him. Show him, warts and all. He's too great a man to be deified.'[17]

Without any prospect of British funding, Attenborough looked to America and in July 1964 he engaged the support of Joseph E. Levine. In addition to being chairman of Embassy Pictures, Levine also held a production contract with Paramount who 'warmly supported the concept of the film'. Levine's support in conjunction with Paramount's enthusiasm resulted in the proposed film being given extensive publicity in the trade press. On 16 December 1964 the *Daily Cinema* reported that 'Mahatma Gandhi' will begin filming the next year on 2 October, the 96th anniversary of Gandhi's birth. There was also a full-page 'message' from Levine which publicly declared his faith in the project: 'It is my profound belief that MAHATMA GANDHI will be one of the greatest motion pictures of all time and I am proud to be associated with it.' On 21 December, a double-page spread announced the production as: 'Mahatma Gandhi – the greatest picture to be released in 1966.'[18]

The announcement was premature. Hanley's screenplay was deemed too long and too unrefined, with Levine demanding a new script. Attempts to gain the help of a support writer proved unsuccessful with Bryan Forbes, Frederick Raphael, Peter Schaffer and Bolt (again) all refusing. Difficulties also extended to the casting of Gandhi. Guinness, who was both Attenborough and Nehru's preference, rejected the role as he felt it would be better suited to an Indian actor, the same reason that he had earlier given to Lean.[19] Other actors, including Dirk Bogarde, Peter Finch, Albert Finney and Tom Courtenay, also declined. With no suitable actor and an unfinished script, the production was indefinitely postponed.

Attenborough returned to acting, starring in two Hollywood films, *The Flight of the Phoenix* (Robert Aldrich, 1965) and *The Sand Pebbles* (Robert Wise, 1966). While in America he attempted, but failed, to gain financial support for *Gandhi* from United Artists. In his absence, Kothari engaged the writer, Donald Ogden Stewart, an Academy Award winner for *The Philadelphia Story* (George Cukor, 1940). Stewart's treatment, entitled 'The Day Gandhi Died', was rejected by Attenborough for 'deserting the framework' he and Hanley had agreed upon, a decision reluctantly supported by Kothari.[20] In 1965, Kothari resigned his post at the Indian High Commission in order to devote himself full-time to the project. The strain in his and Attenborough's relationship began to show when Kothari gave Attenborough an ultimatum, informing him that unless he was prepared to 'devote himself one hundred per cent to *Gandhi*, forgoing any other engagements whatsoever', each of them having the right to continue the project on their own terms, coming together only to finalise a deal.[21] Kothari also took firmer control by engaging Bolt to write a screenplay with the right for him to approve a director, thus excluding Attenborough. After Bolt's first choice Fred Zinnemann, withdrew, Lean was appointed. In 1967, however, Bolt and Lean delayed their interest in Gandhi by making *Ryan's Daughter* (1970) first.

The date of 15 January 1970 altered the situation significantly when both Fischer and Kothari died, depriving the film of both its principal source author and its instigator. Moreover, their demise left Attenborough as the central and sole motivator of the film. In 1972 Lean's continued reticence prompted Bolt to tell Attenborough that if he could raise the finance he would now be prepared for him to direct the film based on Bolt's treatment entitled 'Gandhiji'. Contracts were drawn up with Levine and Attenborough as co-producers and Attenborough as director. In March 1973 Levine wrote to Attenborough, declaring: 'I do want to tell you that the more I think of our project, the more I love it, and I know it can do us both (especially you) much credit.'[22] It was this gesture of support that influenced Attenborough to make a momentous decision that he was later bitterly to regret. In April he signed away the rights for *Gandhi* from his control at Indo-British Films to Levine's new company Avco-Embassy, who pledged a budget of $6 million. As an incentive, Levine also gave £100,000 of his own money with the intention to start production in January 1974, but Attenborough's project was now firmly under Levine's financial control.[23] Further difficulties arose when the first draft of 'Gandhiji' was completed in April 1973 with Levine's adverse reaction to the script, which resulted in 'acrimonious correspondence' between him and Bolt. As a result, Levine halted the project. He explained his reasons in a letter to Attenborough.

> The political factors and the financial complications in connection with *Gandhi* compel me to advise you that unfortunately it is not possible to make any plans at this time to proceed with the production of this picture. I am not happy that circumstances have forced me to make this decision, as I remain confident that *Gandhi* would be one of the greatest pictures ever made.[24]

Levine's reservations were also entangled with personal politics. He claimed that he was having difficulties in raising finance due to India's alignment with the Arabs in the Middle East war. Levine, as a Jew, found this unacceptable. In November 1973, four months after obtaining the rights, Avco-Embassy formally resigned from the project.

In April 1978, Attenborough approached the American writer John Briley. Initially Briley was hesitant in accepting Attenborough's offer, commenting: 'Dickie's obsession with *Gandhi* had long been a standing joke within the film world and I couldn't be associated with another failure.'[25] He insisted that he wanted to write his own original screenplay, agreeing to keep within Bolt's basic framework but returned to Fischer's structure of beginning with the assassination (which ended 'Gandhiji') by employing a flashback technique to encompass Gandhi's life. Briley's second draft was declared by Levine to be the 'first "commercial script" he had read on the subject'.[26]

Filming appeared to be imminent with the *Hollywood Reporter* announcing in December 1978, soon after *Magic*'s release, that Anthony Hopkins had been selected to play Gandhi. However, Levine and Attenborough quarrelled, with Levine taking exception to the role of Attenborough's local banker in India, the Maharajah of Baroda, who had offered to finance the Indian 'rupee' money (the money allocated to be spent in local currency in India). Even more detrimental to the film was Levine's anger towards the Indian government's official policy which recognised the Palestine Liberation Organization. This led to Levine offering Attenborough terms for the release of the script in May 1980 for Attenborough to purchase the rights again. Attenborough was told with a sixty-day option he would have to pay $250,000 (Levine still owed him $150,000 from *A Bridge Too Far* and *Magic*) during which time if he wanted the rights he would have to pay a further $750,000 on the first day of shooting and a $1 million dollars 'plus 7.5 of the net profits, or 2.5 per cent of the gross profits, whichever was the greater'.[27] The option time was later extended to nine months after Attenborough protested at the unfairness of the terms. The once friendly relationship between Levine and Attenborough was now irretrievably damaged.

It was Briley who came to the rescue by introducing Attenborough to the transatlantic partnership, International Film Investors (IFI), run in New York by Josiah Child and, in London, Goldcrest Film International (GFI) run by Jake Eberts. Attenborough had already ingratiated himself with Goldcrest when, despite not being a member, he had addressed the first Goldcrest board meeting where he made 'an impassioned, wholly un-banker-like – indeed tear-laden – speech about his long-cherished project', which according to James Lee, chief executive of Pearson Longman, and principal backer of Goldcrest, made a 'profound impression'.[28]

IFI and GFI contributed all the non-Indian funding which amassed to two-thirds of the $22 million (£9.5 million) cost. On 21 August 1980 Indira Gandhi, now Prime Minister, officially approved a £700,000 investment in the film. This was vital to obtaining the rupee finance for providing costumes, crew and set construction. The government guaranteed the finance by using institutional finance and floated a company in partnership with the Indian National Film Development Corporation (NFDC) which supported quality film-making. To pacify any objections to the Indian government's investment in the film Attenborough insisted on a proviso that ensured that all rightful money should be passed to the NFDC and go towards future indigenous productions.

Many Gandhi followers objected to Attenborough as a British director of an Indian film as he represented the former colonial ruler. Although some opposition to Attenborough diminished after his acting role as General Outram in the Indian film *The Chess Players* (Satyajit Ray, 1977), his position was still disputed. To those who advocated a superhuman presence for Gandhi's portrayal, Attenborough's exasperation became evident when he commented: 'They'd prefer a blinding white light or a disembodied voice or something. Well, I don't give a tuppenny bugger for what this lot are on about. I'm not making a film about bloody Tinkerbell.'[29] Another protest was raised by Gopal Godse, the brother of Nathurum Godse, Gandhi's assassin. Both Godse and Madanlal Pahwa, who was also implicated in the killing, were offended for not being approached by the filmmakers as only they could give 'a true account of the events which led to the holy man's slaying'.[30] Attenborough was forced to use all his negotiating skills to overcome these problems.

The various postponements that had occurred meant that all previous actors considered for the title role were now unsuitable. It was on the advice of Attenborough's theatre director son, Michael, that Ben Kingsley (real name Krishnar Bhanji), was appointed.[31] Kingsley was an Anglo-Indian stage actor and member of the Royal Shakespeare Company whose grandfather also originated from Jamnagar (Gujarat), the birthplace of Gandhi, and thus was particularly acceptable to India. Kingsley, an inexperienced film actor, like Simon Ward in *Young Winston*, was also unhindered by previous roles. Many actors from Attenborough's previous productions were cast which helped to provide a stellar cast in supporting roles including John Mills (the viceroy), John Clements (advocate general), John Gielgud (Lord Irwin) and Edward Fox (General Dyer). Michael Hordern was also cast as Sir George Hodge. Notable Indian actors included Rohini Hattangady as Gandhi's wife, Kasturba, and Roshan Seth as Nehru.[32] The prerequisite Hollywood names were Candice Bergen as the photographer Margaret Bourke-White and Martin Sheen as the reporter, Walker.

Filming began on 26 November 1980. The production was beset with problems from the start. In December, Barclays Bank suddenly withdrew from their $8 million leasing deal which offered the bank investment by buying *Gandhi* and then leasing it back to Goldcrest/IFI.

Lee agreed to increase GFI's investment to $7.2 million to maintain the cash flow for filming to continue. In February 1981 the unnamed Indian family (later revealed to be the Hinduja brothers) who had assured $4 million, decided to renegotiate their 'rupee' deal.[33] Pearson agreed to underwrite the outstanding amount of $4 million to compensate the shortfall. To add to his difficulties, Attenborough faced accusations of racial discrimination, with members of the Indian parliament calling for his expulsion from the country.[34]

Using flashback, *Gandhi* uses a circular narrative recounting the Mahatma's life from his youth as a barrister in South Africa, his return to India and his life as a national leader until his assassination. It repeats the assassination from the beginning, cutting to Gandhi's pyre burning and his ashes scattered in the Ganges. *Gandhi* fulfils the criteria of a biopic by promoting the individual above historical events which provide pivotal points to his life. These include the 'March to the Sea', his objecting to the salt tax, participating in talks with other Congress leaders and addressing meetings. The second of Attenborough's objectives in *Gandhi* is the reassessing of the British as colonial rulers, the distance since the end of empire allowing a more critical approach. One of the most poignant scenes is the Amritsar Massacre which contrasts the British brutality with Gandhi's silent condemnation. The effect is heightened by no words being uttered: Gandhi's despair and anger at General Dyer and his men for shooting at an unarmed crowd which included women and children is expressed powerfully through expression and movement, an opportunity for Attenborough to employ his technique of 'silent dialogue' to great effect.

Gandhi can be seen to depict the British predominantly in negative terms. The anti-colonial portrayal of the Raj is further enforced by Gandhi's personal disassociation from anything British. He eschews western dress for the Indian dhoti and rejects the companionship of the English chaplain Charlie Andrews (Ian Charleson) for Indian support. Andrews, Judge Broomfield (Trevor Howard) and Mountbatten (Peter Harlowe) are exceptions in being favourably portrayed. Mountbatten is seen as the acceptable face of Britain, arbitrating meetings between Congress leaders and conversing with Gandhi. The film positions Mountbatten prominently, featuring his arrival in India and his presence in Gandhi's funeral possession. This elite positioning was partly in line with Mountbatten's importance as the last viceroy but also acknowledged his contribution in helping to gain the agreement of the Indian government, which was brought to an abrupt end with his murder by the IRA on 27 August 1978. Attenborough described Mountbatten as 'one of the most brilliant and well loved men of his time but also probably the most liberal member of the royal family that we have been fortunate enough to know'.[35] The film is dedicated to Mountbatten, Nehru and Kothari.

Mountbatten's views of Gandhi and those of Kothari influenced Attenborough beyond Fischer's book. While Attenborough upholds Nehru's plea not to 'deify' Gandhi by including moments of Gandhi's temper, such as when he upbraids Kasturba for not doing the work of untouchables, this portrayal of a Christ-like figure followed by disciples focusing on Gandhi's good qualities seems overtly hagiographic. Gandhi's negative qualities such as his vow of celibacy (Brahmacharya), or his testing it by a daily ritual of lying naked among young girls, are not referred to; nor does the film probe the difficult relationship with his sons.[36] Attenborough also elevates Gandhi's status by the epic scale achieved in the funeral sequence, the most spectacular one of the film. It was filmed on 31 January 1981, the thirty-third anniversary of Gandhi's death, the date chosen in order to encourage thousands of extras required to attend as mourners. The scene of serenity and solemnity, narrated by Walker, and filmed on the Rajpath in New Delhi, depicts epic qualities of scale, colour and spectacle with vibrant colour from the flowers contrasting with the khaki uniforms of Indian soldiers. Over 25,000 people were directed and costumed after prior rehearsal on an aerodrome.[37] On the day police estimated the numbers who turned out were between 250,000 and 350,000, while *Screen International* reported that Indian newspaper headlines claimed there was a poor turnout, the re-enactment was 'a near flop' as only '20,000 people had complied'.[38] The scene was also included in the *Guinness Book of Records* as the largest crowd scene in a film.[39]

Gandhi can be seen as a film of two halves; the first is swift in tempo, as Gandhi develops his political ideology and asserts his influence. The second half (separated by an intermission in the American version coming after the Amritsar Massacre), is considerably slower, reflecting both Gandhi's maturity in stature and in age. The film manages to combine epic scenes with intimate and poignant portrayals, supported by spectacular cinematography and inspiring music by Ravi Shankar. Above all, it is Kingsley's outstanding performance that takes precedence, providing a rich and moving character portrayal which makes him so convincing as Gandhi.

Shooting was completed on 10 May 1981 after 126 days' filming, within the allotted budget of £22 million but three days over schedule due to rain in India. By July no distributor had been found for the film, so a specially prepared two-hour sequence was shown instead, to all the major companies with Columbia outbidding the others.

Gandhi had its world première in New Delhi on 30 November 1982. The European première held in London, at the Odeon, Leicester Square on 2 December 1982, was attended by the Prince and Princess of Wales. Four North American premières were also held. Popular response was generally favourable. In London *Gandhi* rose to the top of the box-office charts, amassing £74,126 in the week of 8 January when its nearest rival *The Draughtsman's Contract*, totalled £15,149. The Academy Award nominations announced in the week of 19 February did not show any significant increase in box-office numbers, although the figures rose briefly from £42,538 to £48,017 after the awards were announced on 23 April. The total gross in Britain amounted to £7,700,000.[40]

In America *Gandhi* reached thirteenth position in its first week but could not compete with such films as *E.T. the Extra-Terrestrial* and *An Officer and Gentleman* which were showing on more screens. The box office gross for *Gandhi* in America totalled $52,767,889 with the total rental earnings reaching $25 million. It fared less well than the previous Oscar winner, *Chariots of Fire*, which grossed $30.6 million but surpassed the next Raj film *A Passage to India*, which made $13.9 million.[41]

The critical response was varied, although more markedly favourable in Britain than America. Those who praised the film included David Castell in the *Sunday Telegraph*, who observed that Attenborough had produced 'a monumental piece of filmmaking'.[42] David Robinson in *The Times* declared: 'Whatever your expectations of Richard Attenborough's *Gandhi* they are likely to be exceeded'.[43] The *Sunday Times* called *Gandhi* 'a masterpiece', and the *Sunday Express*, 'an epic in the majestic manner'.[44] Patrick Gibbs in the *Daily Telegraph* was less enthusiastic. While Gibbs praised the film for living 'magnificently up to its subject', he declared, that 'Gandhi is, I think, for all his fine qualities, seen rather too much through a rose-tinted lens.'[45] Gibbs's views were echoed by Philip French in the *Observer* who described *Gandhi* as 'a very beautiful looking movie that is maybe a little too seductive for its own good'.[46] The most disparaging opinion was given by Nigel Andrews in the *Financial Times* who declared *Gandhi* 'an eccentric wrap-around-yarn' complaining it 'does scant justice to Gandhi or to history or to Attenborough's own passion'.[47]

In America, *Variety* called *Gandhi* a 'triumph' for Attenborough 'which catapults him to the top rank of directors'.[48] The *Hollywood Reporter* declared the film 'is more than a superb movie; it's a cinematic event'.[49] For *New York's* David Denby the film had 'overwhelming power' and was the most 'emotionally wrenching political movie ever made'.[50] Dissenting voices included Andrew Sarris in *Village Voice*, who claimed he was 'more often bored than moved', describing *Gandhi* as 'a lumbering mastodon of a movie', while *Cinema* considered it a 'sterile film, squeezed of its social and political import'.[51] *The Times of India* praised the film, asserting: 'Mastery of the craft has been accompanied by a dedication that is truly rare in our age of fast foods, fads and kitsch.'[52]

The film journals provided contrasting views. For the *Monthly Film Bulletin*, *Gandhi* was '[c]aught between a bio-pic, a chronicle and an adventure story, the film elides the personal, the political and the mythical, and is consequently divested of any real focus or contemporary relevance'.[53] Conversely, *Sight and Sound* considered that the film 'measures up to its subject and breathes new life into film biography'.[54] Non-film journals were more critical. *Time Out* considered that Attenborough 'presents a highly misleading picture of both the Mahatma's life and the struggle for Indian independence', while the *Spectator* complained that the film was 'pap history, personalised history, history recreated by the stars' and 'not a success'.[55] In Britain, *Gandhi* also attracted considerable attention concerning the accuracy of its historical representation. As with *A Bridge Too Far*, *Gandhi* also served to reopen debates over blame and error during a sensitive period in British history when colonial rule ended. Articles included ones by H.V. Hodson, a former adviser to the Viceroy of India, who argued that *Gandhi's* portrayal of the British Raj was done in 'a very one-sided and hostile way'.[56] *The Times* former Delhi correspondent, Louis Heren, complained that the film was 'a gross misrepresentation of Gandhi as well as history'.[57] Paul Johnson in the *Daily Telegraph* criticised the 'hagiographic treatment of Gandhi himself' and claimed 'there is certain pretentiousness about *Gandhi*, an orchestrated campaign to present it as the truth about British rule in India'.[58] For John Grigg, in the *Sunday Telegraph*, Gandhi was by 'no means the single-minded leader' the film portrayed, instead, 'he was a mass of contradictions'.[59]

A more critical stance was voiced by Salman Rushdie, the Booker Prize-winning author of *Midnight's Children*, who described *Gandhi* as 'inadequate as biography, appalling as history, and often laughably crude as a film'. Rushdie was particularly incensed at the portrayal of the Amritsar Massacre, claiming that 'artistic selection has altered the meaning of the event. It is an unforgivable distortion.'[60] The Indian perspective was expressed by Dilip Hero, author of *Inside India Today*, who maintained that the film 'does injustice to both history and to ... Gandhi'. He quoted from an unnamed Indian critic that 'Gandhi has been assassinated again ... He has been sacrificed at the altar of crass Anglo-American commercialism.'[61] In Pakistan, *Gandhi* was considered too controversial to be shown having been condemned by the law minister as a 'denigration of the father of the nation' and 'a false presentation of his personal and political life'.[62]

Conservative MPs also entered the debate. Ivor Stanbrook claimed *Gandhi* 'gave a misleading impression of the quality of the Indian service during the period of British rule in India'.[63] Sir Penderel Moon, a former Indian civil servant, declared the film was 'far removed from reality' and complained that 'the British were made to seem rather harsh and foolish'.[64] A leader in the *Sunday Telegraph*, under the headline 'Oscars won by knocking Britain' voiced its attack at Attenborough:

> Where he has gone grievously wrong is in turning the film into a piece of straight political propaganda for India, at the expense of his own country's imperial past which is grossly traduced. If pandering shamelessly to America's anti-colonial prejudices is the only way to save the dying British film industry then perhaps its resurrection is not such as good thing after all.[65]

The Oscar success gave a temporary reprieve. *The Times* proudly announced that *Gandhi* had 'monopolised the 55th Academy Awards ceremony in Hollywood by winning eight Oscars – more than any other British film in Academy history', while the *Guardian* acknowledged the success as one of 'unstinting celebration, both for those directly involved in the making of *Gandhi* and for the resurgent British film industry as a whole'.[66] The *Morning Star* quoted Indira Gandhi who was 'delighted' with the film's success, declaring 'May the spirit of Mahatma Gandhi, which the film evokes, guide the world away from the violence and toward peace and goodwill.'[67] However, the film's proposed première showings in South Africa resulted in a fierce political debate focusing on the country's apartheid policies, particularly over Attenborough agreeing to attend a whites-only charity performance. The Labour MP, Alfred Dubs, demanded that Attenborough should not to go to South Africa. In reply, Margaret Thatcher declared that Attenborough should be free to make up his own mind, and offered her congratulations for his 'splendid achievement'.[68] Further pressure came from the anti-apartheid movement who delivered a letter of protest. A reply from the United Nations declared that 'A premiere limited to whites will be blasphemy. It will be entirely against the spirit of Gandhi and the principles of the UN.'[69] An Indian community spokesman commented: 'It is ironic that a film depicting a man's fight against racial discrimination in South Africa has become embroiled in the very political discrimination he set out to destroy in early British South Africa.'[70] Eventually, Attenborough decided not to attend the all-whites première; instead he said that he would only consider attending one in an Indian township near Johannesburg which was to benefit an Indian charity. This seemed to have been induced by a change of policy from Pen Kotze, the South African Community Development Minister, who said he would 'be prepared to grant permission for racially integrated audiences for charity performances of the film'.[71]

Gandhi's Oscar success had more positive implications for the British film industry. A meeting between the Trade Minister, Ian Sproat, and the Directors Guild of Great Britain (whose members included Attenborough) occurred a day after the Academy Award ceremony. The industry took the opportunity to attack the government and the City for refusing to back *Gandhi*, while Attenborough 'hoped international acclaim and box office success would open the City's cautious coffers to the industry'.[72] Goldcrest, which had provided £11 million of the £14 million required for *Gandhi*, was in profit for the first time, benefiting both from box-office receipts and the sale of television rights.[73]

Much of *Gandhi*'s success can be attributed to its appeal as a historical epic in the grand tradition supported by a high-profile marketing campaign. For Sarah Street, however, *Gandhi* is an example of a film 'released at times when their impact would be most effective' and 'being perceived as different from standard Hollywood productions, appealing to a specialized audience in the first instance and then "crossing over" to general release'.[74] The delay in *Gandhi*'s production was also significant as the 1980s witnessed an increased interest in empire concerns. It also allowed the best screenwriter, the right actor, and the necessary finance all to reach fruition at the same time. If *Gandhi* had been made in the 1960s, as was first intended, it is unlikely that the film would have generated the success it later enjoyed. Moreover, *Gandhi*'s success in the 1980s also initiated a Raj revival, a cycle of films that capitalised on this interest which included *Heat and Dust* (James Ivory, 1983) and *A Passage to India* as well as two prominent television series in 1984, *The Far Pavilions* and *The Jewel in the Crown*.

The confidence generated by the success of *Gandhi* persuaded Attenborough to take on a very different challenge with his next film. *A Chorus Line* is a contemporary and fictional musical which demonstrates Attenborough's particular interest in the exploration of human interactions. It also returned him to the musical, with which he had enjoyed success in *Oh! What a Lovely War*. The concept of the film is based on an audition for a new musical and explores the behind-the-scenes stories of a large group of 'gypsies' (tri-talented actor-singer-dancers) who are competing for prized places in the chorus for a new musical. The short-listed ones are then subjected to a gruelling, psychological ordeal by Zach (Michael Douglas), the choreographer/director, who forces them to talk candidly about their childhood experiences and their social inadequacies in front of their fellow contenders in order to select the final eight required. A romantic sub-plot occurs with the unexpected return to the theatre of Zach's former girlfriend Cassie (Alyson Reed), a leading dancer, who left him to advance her career in Hollywood but is now in desperate need of work and wishes to audition for the chorus.

While the narrative of *A Chorus Line* became more topical during the 1980s with the rise in unemployment in the United States, for Attenborough, the prime attraction to direct the film was his affection for the musical. Martin Baum, his agent, was keen to demonstrate that a British director could succeed in Hollywood with an American concept, especially after several American directors, including Mike Nichols, Sidney Lumet and Joel Schumacher, all declined to make the film. Although British musicals had come to prominence with the 'Oscar' success of *Oliver!* (Carol Reed, 1968), British directors regarded musicals as being somewhat inferior making it unusual for them to take on American stage adaptations. In 1982, the Broadway producers Cy Feuer and Ernest Martin offered to produce *A Chorus Line* with Jake Eberts overseeing the project in his capacity as president of Embassy Communications International, the position he held after leaving Goldcrest. The choice of Attenborough was explained by Martin: 'Anyone who can turn a difficult musical like *Oh What a Lovely War* [sic] into a movie and spend 20 years surmounting all obstacles to put *Gandhi* on the screen has to have guts as well as talent.'[75] Attenborough saw the stage version eight times before committing himself as director.

A Chorus Line was the longest-running Broadway musical at the time, opening in 1975 and closing in 1990, and grossing nearly $150 million.[76] The show won the Pulitzer Prize and a Tony Award for Best Musical. Not a conventional musical, its popularity came partly from its uniqueness and its 'cinematic staging' devised by its choreographer Michael Bennett which changed the focus of the audience's attention by the skilful use of devices including close-ups and stage dissolves and the effective use of mirrors.

The film had a budget of $16 million and featured an all-American cast. Audrey Landers, an actress known for her role as Afton Cooper in the American soap-opera *Dallas*, was cast as Val, while other roles were played by lesser known names. The only British presence for the film was the cinematographer Ronnie Taylor and the editor, John Bloom, both of whom had won Oscars for *Gandhi*. Filmed primarily at the Mark Hellinger Theatre, *A Chorus Line* is distinct from Attenborough's other films for eschewing exterior landscapes and being filmed almost entirely within a theatre. It is also devoid of his normal traditional music. There are, however, some instances of his 'silent dialogue' sequences where acting and movement are the only means that are used to convey a message to the audience. This is particularly noticeable in the selection process for the final seventeen dancers where relief and happiness are displayed through their facial expressions and their upright stance. In order to choose the final eight, Zach changes the normal arbitrary approach by making the dancers reveal their inner selves asking them personal questions of where they were born, their age, and why they started dancing. Under interrogation, the gypsies are forced to reveal their private selves. The sequence echoes the interview scenes from *Young Winston*, where an interrogator asks intimate questions. As in *Young Winston* the humiliating experience extracts from the gypsies a wide range of personal issues including childhood anxieties and racial, sexual and ageist concerns. When Zach calls out the names of eight gypsies the 'selected' ones demonstrate happiness and relief that they have been chosen until Zach informs them in a bitter twist of irony that it is the back line – those that he has not called out – are the chosen ones. It is a moment of unnecessary cruelty for those on the front line and they show their disgust at their treatment as they quickly leave the theatre.

The film demonstrates some unusual stylistic devices. Attenborough devised a technique whereby the camera is employed in a dramatic 'pigeon' shot by employing a Louma crane and a zoom lens with a camera flying backwards and forwards in the theatre. This concept was to reflect Attenborough's distinctive stylistic approach for the film – the camera producing the movement to compensate for the static stage. A variety of angles, close-ups and zoom shots were also employed to add motion and tempo in the film. Staying within the theatre was an intentional choice as Bennett had created a 'pressure cooker atmosphere of tension' in his concept. Attenborough explained: '[i]f we went outside that atmosphere the pressure would be gone, so our first decision had to be to stay within the theatre.'[77]

The real twist to the film comes in the finale when all the dancers (including those who have been eliminated) are included in the finale in what Attenborough intended as a homage to all the American gypsies. Performing to the song 'One', the sequence which cost an additional $250,000 saw the principal dancers being joined by seventeen 'look-alike doubles' all dressed in gold and sequins. The visual trickery mimics the style of Busby Berkeley using a kaleidoscope background of geometric patterns that contrasts the austerity of the backstage location, resulting in a stunning climax to the film.

A Chorus Line began filming on 1 October 1984 for sixteen weeks after eight weeks of dance rehearsals. Over 3,000 dancers were auditioned,

129 selected for the opening sequence and 17 for the chorus line all under the control of choreographer Jeffrey Hornaday, renowned for his work in *Flashdance* (Adrian Lyne, 1983). While editing of the film took place in England, American union rules stipulated that the music score had to be done in the same location as the pre-recording, and therefore was completed in Gotham.

Despite high expectations for the film, the première at the Radio City Hall in New York on 9 December 1985 was followed by some scathing reviews, many being critical of Attenborough's decision not to 'open out' the film and take it outside the theatre. Several critics also objected to a British director taking over an American show. Attenborough considered that this 'vicious cruelty' was the response to a British director delving into the 'indigenous' American musical, declaring that: '[t]he thought of a short-ass, balding, bespectacled Limey sticking his toes into the Cathedral of Broadway was more than they could manage.'[78] The *New York Times* complained that *A Chorus Line* 'is a film version that is fatally half-hearted', while *Variety* called the film 'static and confined, rarely venturing beyond the immediate'.[79] For *New York* the film was a 'strained, uncomfortable piece of work, a case of delusional vanity and of misplaced devotion to "cinema" in defiance of aesthetic logic and common sense'.[80] Not all the American reviews were disparaging. *Films in Review* praised Attenborough for his 'deft' direction and for keeping 'the proceedings extraordinarily mobile', while *Village Voice* called *A Chorus Line* 'an ensemble triumph'.[81] For Clive Barnes, the renowned dance critic, it was 'the best dance film, and for that matter, the best movie musical for years'.[82] Attenborough was convinced that much of the hostile reaction against *A Chorus Line* was due to anti-American feeling which had built up against him, particularly due to the Oscar success of *Gandhi* over *E.T.*[83] He also was aware that several American critics, who did not like *Gandhi*, had felt pressed into agreeing to award Attenborough the New York Critics Award for the film.[84] Their dislike of Attenborough may also have been made more acute after he collected an award on behalf of David Lean for *A Passage to India* as he was in New York at the time. Afterwards Attenborough performed a risqué rendition of Colonel Bogey to the New York critics which, he deduced, might not have gone down well.[85]

In Britain the film was released by Rank and opened in London on 9 January 1986 after a Royal Charity Première at the Odeon, Leicester Square. Some reviews were equally as critical as in America. The *Monthly Film Bulletin* complained that the film has 'absolutely no sense of rhythm, forever stopping, starting and trying to make up for its inadequacies'.[86] The *Scotsman* claimed that *A Chorus Line* 'proves to be Richard Attenborough's banana-skin', having 'no story, only an idea' which is 'too slight and too static for film'.[87] For the *Sunday Express* it was a 'heartbreaking miscalculation'.[88] The more favourable reviews included Philip French in the *Observer* who saw it as 'slick shallow stuff, but amusing, moderately tuneful, and well danced', and Tom Hutchinson in the *Mail on Sunday* called it 'one of the most heart-touching musicals that I have ever seen'.[89] Nigel Andrews in the *Financial Times*, praised the film for its 'visual inspiration' but disliked the end sequence, which he observes as derived from the idea of the 'multiplying crosses' in *Oh! What a Lovely War*, but which he considers 'both trivialises and misapplies it'.[90] Iain Johnstone in the *Sunday Times* claimed that the American critics were 'wrong' about *A Chorus Line* describing it 'a fine film, superior in music, choreography and dance to any of the four stage versions I have seen (including the original Broadway one)'.[91]

Although *A Chorus Line* did well on a worldwide scale, in the crucial American market the film grossed only $14,202,899, just over 25 per cent of the total that *Gandhi* amassed. For Attenborough the disappointment was more acutely felt as, according to Diana Hawkins, he considered *A Chorus Line* 'his greatest achievement as a director in terms of the use of the camera'.[92] Baum also considered that Attenborough warranted more merit than he received when he declared: 'For *Gandhi* they couldn't praise him enough and they lifted him up to the skies. And with *A Chorus Line* I believe they took pleasure in dashing him to the ground.'[93]

Although *A Chorus Line* was a personal triumph for Attenborough, like *Magic* it is a film that sits uneasily within his œuvre with a sense of awkwardness pervading the film. The intimate portrayal becomes almost too intense within the confines in a theatre, just as it was in the lakeside house in *Magic*. Both films proved critical disappointments and Attenborough did not return to fictional representations again.

The predominantly adverse reaction to *A Chorus Line* encouraged Attenborough to return to a serious subject for his next project. Like *Gandhi*, *Cry Freedom* was also politically controversial, this time concerning the interracial friendship between Steve Biko and Donald Woods. In the way that Kothari had viewed cinema as the most effective medium to bring worldwide attention to Gandhi, Donald Woods was keen to use the global impact of cinema to bring similar recognition for Biko. The principal purpose of the film was remarkably ambitious: to exert political change in South Africa, which Attenborough claimed would 'hopefully increase awareness throughout the world of the exact nature of apartheid. And following on from that, as a result, public pressure with regard to both sanctions and disinvestment will increase.'[94]

Attenborough's ambitions for the film were realised. The impact of the film made a significant contribution to raising global public awareness into the realities of the apartheid regime of the time, and indeed, hastened the speed of change.

Cry Freedom is notable as one of the first of a cycle of anti-apartheid films that explored life in South Africa. Others included *A World Apart* (Chris Menges, 1987) and *A Dry White Season* (Euzhan Palcy, 1989). *Sarafina!* (Darrell James, 1992), a South African production scripted by William Nicholson and starring Whoopi Goldberg, was different by using music and dance to highlight the troubles from the perspective of a young girl. *Cry Freedom* is also notable for its unusual narrative form which led to accusations that it had 'structural inconsistency'.[95] The film, like *Young Winston* (1972), also draws from several genres including the biopic, the adventure film, the political and the historical, but unlike the earlier film, the eclectic mix, in conjunction with the structural changes, resulted in both critics and audiences finding it difficult to comprehend. While the conflict of apartheid remains the central focus, the roles of the two characters are changed midway through the film with the sudden and traumatic death of Biko bringing Woods to the fore and switching the effect of apartheid from the black to the white population. *Cry Freedom* is also a historical account as the film identifies crucial events that surround apartheid. The film begins and ends with two major attacks by the authorities, the first at the Crossroads squatter camp on 24 November 1975 in which shanty homes were destroyed and those found without work permits ejected. It ends with the bloodshed of the Soweto uprising on 16 June 1976 which lasted for ten days and resulted in at least 176 people being killed. The two events act as a framing device to maximise the impact of what the black population endured and the extent to which the authorities were prepared to go. *Cry Freedom*'s contribution to raising awareness about apartheid is even more apparent with the South African authorities considering the film so sensitive that it was withdrawn within hours of its release. The film reels were confiscated until 1990 when political changes permitted its re-release.

Both the Thatcher and Reagan governments had economic interests in South Africa, due to key trade links. Both leaders resisted the United Nations' call for sanctions against the country. Both leaders also saw South Africa as a stronghold against Marxist forces in Southern Africa. Moreover, despite Thatcher's political standpoint, her preference for laissez-faire policies did not seek to curtail Attenborough's efforts in making the film. In contrast, South Africa employed various means in an attempt to prevent the film being made including threats and intimidation.

South Africa's political development was shaped by its British colonial past and the implementation of apartheid policies by the white minority government. The term, apartheid, was used as a slogan by the Afrikaner National Party in the South African general election in May 1948 to suggest a requirement for the enforced separation of 'whites' and 'non whites' in the country. The policy generated much hostility from other countries. In 1960, the British Prime Minister, Harold Macmillan, in his celebrated 'Wind of change' speech in Cape Town, openly criticised South Africa's policies leading to the severing of British ties. Weeks later, tensions came to a head in the Sharpeville Massacre, when South African police opened fire on demonstrators against pass laws killing 67 black Africans with nearly 200 wounded. International condemnation saw Apartheid being denounced at the Conference of Commonwealth Prime Ministers in 1961 with South Africa removing itself from the Commonwealth, becoming the Republic of South Africa.

Prior to the 1960s, the National Party government had been effective in crushing anti-apartheid opposition within South Africa by outlawing movements like the African National Congress (ANC) and Pan Africanist Congress (PAC). From the mid-1970s, a more radical generation gathered support and the South African Black Consciousness Movement (BCM) was formed. The BCM became an umbrella organisation for several groups including the Azanian People's Organisation (AZAPO), launched in 1978, and the Black People's Convention (BPC), founded in 1972 with Biko elected as honorary president.

Biko's death on 12 September 1977, the twentieth person to die in police custody in eighteen months, and the first important black leader to do so, was widely publicised in the British press with both *The Times* and the *Guardian* relaying it on their front pages.[96] His high standing and political importance was emphasised by his funeral which was conducted by the Reverend Desmond Tutu and attended by more than 15,000 mourners with thousands more banned from attending by the security forces. The official reason for his death given by the Justice Minister, James Kruger, was the result of Biko's hunger strike. Woods later stated that Biko had vowed to him never to go on hunger strike and accused Kruger of the 'ultimate responsibility' of his death.[97] His demand for a proper inquest, at which the magistrate ruled that no one was to blame, resulted in Woods being declared a 'banned person' which prohibited him from writing, moving from his own area and from being in the presence of more than one person at a time. Woods and his family were also subjected to harassment and intimidation by the security police before fleeing to England in January 1978 with the manuscript, detailing the events of Biko's life and death, smuggled out with them.

Attenborough had ambitions to make a film on the subject of apartheid long before his association with *Gandhi*. In the late 1950s he had considered a film entitled 'God is a Bad Policeman', but had declined it as the shifting perspectives of apartheid meant that the subject had 'failed to keep pace with the rapidly changing South African situation'.[98] Attenborough also believed that a positive message was essential, declaring: 'I wanted any anti-apartheid film I made to be unequivocal in its condemnation. But I still had to demonstrate that a solution was possible.'[99] The instigation of *Cry Freedom* was also rooted in Woods's desire to further publicise the truth of Biko's death and his struggle against apartheid in his works *Biko* and *Asking for Trouble*. *Biko* had originally been published in twelve languages during 1978 and 1979 but was a still a banned publication in South Africa.

The subject of Biko had been attempted by Carl Foreman during the late 1970s with both MGM and Columbia coming close to completing deals. Universal Pictures also showed interest but declined after the poor popular response to *The Wiz* (Sidney Lumet, 1978), a black musical. Woods also came close to a deal in 1979 with Columbia, but it faltered when he was denied script approval. As Woods recalled, 'Wendy [his wife] and I felt that if we lost control, commercial interests would intervene, jeopardising the story's authenticity.'[100] Other studios declared interest but none would guarantee authenticity to Woods's book with some claiming that as Biko was a public figure they could advance without Woods's approval. The close commercial links between Britain and America with South Africa, also contributed to the reluctance for studios to support a film.

Attenborough's personal interests in Africa included holding the position as chairman of the British trustees of Waterford-Kamhlaba, the first multiracial school in Swaziland. Its founder, Michael Stern, aware that Attenborough had read *Biko*, suggested that Woods send him *Asking for Trouble* as well.[101] Attenborough showed immediate interest. This interest was also timely. *Gandhi*'s success had persuaded Frank Price, the film's distributor at Columbia, who now headed Universal, that the time was right for a political film on apartheid. Moreover, Foreman's option for *Biko* also expired in 1983 leaving Attenborough free to take up the challenge.[102] To witness the apartheid situation for himself, in 1984 during an official visit to Waterford-Kamhlaba, Attenborough and his wife secretly entered South Africa to meet Biko's wife, Ntsiki, and friends, Dr Mamphela Ramphele and Peter Jones. His most memorable encounter, however, was with Winnie Mandela, wife of the imprisoned ANC leader, who was under a government banning order. Attenborough was filmed greeting Mandela and was overheard by the authorities to use the words 'when shooting begins', in reference to the film, but which was wrongly interpreted as a link to violence. The South African Broadcasting Corporation (SABC), who witnessed the encounter, then persuaded a somewhat naïve Attenborough to answer questions in a television interview.[103] The resultant programme used the interview to castigate Attenborough for touching Mandela's hand (an interracial offence). It also accused Attenborough of wanting to make 'a film in support of the ANC [and to] raise funds for the ANC abroad'. It ended by declaring: 'The sooner this man leaves our country the better.'[104] As a result of the broadcast Attenborough was pressured to leave South Africa. On his way to the airport he was physically confronted by a group of Afrikaners and subjected to verbal assaults, later recalling that he felt 'genuinely frightened. I'll never forget that, never.'[105] It was this experience that finally convinced Attenborough to make the film.

The film was three years in preparation. Funding was easier to obtain than in many of Attenborough's previous films, helped by *Gandhi*'s success. Frank Price showed immediate interest and agreed to fund a script provided an adventure theme was included as a recent poll conducted by Universal showed only 12 per cent of white Americans had heard of apartheid.[106] Woods's friend, the independent producer Norman Spencer, became co-producer and Universal the principal financial backers. Eberts was also keen that Goldcrest should also support the venture (*Gandhi* was still helping to keep the company in profit at the time) and contributed to the $22 million budget. In August 1985 Attenborough was appointed chairman of Goldcrest following the resignation of James Lee, due to the financial failure of *Revolution* (Hugh Hudson, 1985) which had cost twice its estimate of £10 million. It was the second time Attenborough had been offered the post having declined it earlier due to his commitments with *A Chorus Line*.

John Briley produced ten draft screenplays before a final shooting script was completed in 1986.[107] The screenplay was based on general incidents which Briley formed into 'background' events upon which the particular incidents involving Woods and Biko became the 'foreground', fleshed out by dialogue to produce a powerful account of South Africa. Briley promoted Biko's policy of 'non-violence' distinguishing him from other black activists while the role of the Woods family was expanded from the brief input in the book, resulting in several invented scenes. Biko's role was also made more prominent to bring it to the same level as that of Woods. For the cast, Kevin Kline was chosen for the role of Woods and Penelope Wilton for Wendy. The role of Biko was more problematic. Susie Figgis, the casting director, favoured a black South African but despite a concentrated effort to find a suitable actor, none proved suitable and Denzel Washington was cast, adding a second Hollywood figure to co-star with Kline.

The controversial nature of the film resulted in several objections raised from both black and white South Africans. Biko's former militant BCM members also objected in principle to a film being made by whites about their leader while the whites objected to an anti-apartheid film that would upset the South African government. The South African media claimed that Woods and Attenborough were 'exploiting Biko's name purely for financial gain'.[108] Peter Jones and other AZAPO members met Attenborough, at his request, in London in November 1986 to read the script after they 'threatened to "wipe the film off the screen of the world" if the movie was not to their liking'.[109] As well as gaining approval by the PAC and from Biko's mother and widow, Attenborough also received the support of Helen Suzman, who with Van Zyl Slabbert, led the Progressive Federal Party in opposition to the Nationalist Party, undefeated since it established apartheid in 1948.

Production began on 14 July with filming taking place in neighbouring Zimbabwe which had gained independence from Britain on 18 April 1980. The government under its Prime Minister, Robert Mugabe, was keen to support the film and to further establish location services for foreign filmmakers. However, the dangers of filming in Zimbabwe were soon made apparent. Since May 1981 South Africa had threatened to invade Zimbabwe if the country persisted in supporting the banned ANC in exile. In May 1986, two months before the start of production, six South African commandos crossed into Zimbabwe disguised as tourists and bombed the ANC offices in Harare, killing three people.[110] A shanty town built for the purpose of the film had to be enclosed by barbed wire and guarded by troops to prevent attacks while beach scenes planned to be filmed in Mozambique had to be abandoned for safety reasons.[111] The Biko family were also informed that the film would include 'material damaging to the honour of the family' including an extra-marital affair to make the film more commercially viable.[112] Although the South African police had made four attempts to sabotage the production, filming finished on time at $1.25 million below the original budget. As a precaution, several copies of the film were made and hidden in secret.

Cry Freedom demonstrates several similarities with *Gandhi* in displaying epic qualities of spectacular scenery and large crowd scenes. Like Gandhi, Biko is also portrayed as a quasi-Messiah silhouetted with the sunlight acting as a halo and preaching to friends who surround him like disciples. Like *Gandhi*, *Cry Freedom* contains a notable funeral sequence which included an estimated 20,000 extras. Although the scene had similar logistical concerns to the funeral in *Gandhi* it is on a much smaller scale, but equally emotional.

While the first part of the film chronicles Biko's life and work and his friendship with Woods, the film changes abruptly after Biko's violent death. Woods's quest for an inquest results in his becoming distrusted by the authorities and a banning order imposed. The restrictions under which Woods has to live, the attacks against his family (including being sent toxic T-shirts) leads to him planning a daring escape for himself and his family from South Africa with Woods disguised as a priest. The difficulties of the journey add both excitement and pace to the film as Woods struggles over a swollen river and accepts car lifts by a variety of people (including the South African police) before he meets up with his family in Lesotho, where they fly to England. As the aeroplane carrying the Woods family flies towards London, to their relative safety, the scene evokes powerful reminiscences in its simplicity and impact, of the last scene in *Oh! What a Lovely War*. The numerous white crosses of *Oh! What a Lovely War* are replaced by the names of the eighty black detainees who have died in detention, shown in a rolling list with the date and the 'official' reason of their deaths. The explanations range from 'no official explanation', to 'fell down stairs', becoming more implausible with 'fell against shower' to the physical impossibility of 'self strangulation'. Biko's name is in the middle of the list which informs the audience that deaths in detention still continued. In the script there is a reason given for the abrupt ending of the list: 'Since the re-imposition of Emergency Regulations on 11 July 1987 no further information regarding political detainees has been forthcoming.'[113] This statement is not included in the film or video but is included in the DVD version released in 2001 which also changed the end sequence. Instead of a rolling screen the names are positioned individually at the base of the screen. While this maintained the quantity of information given to the audience, the impact of the rolling format is lessened.[114]

The post-production of *Cry Freedom* is most notable for the revised format of the film which made a radical departure from the shooting script. In the script Biko's life had been portrayed retrospectively with his life seen through frequent flashback sequences, which Briley explained was 'to keep Biko alive throughout the whole course of the film'.[115] Briley returned to England after the nine-month editing period to see the film in its rough cut, still structured as the shooting script and still containing several flashback sequences. However, in the final film, the only flashback sequence to remain was the final one that Briley had written. The reason given was that following Biko's death it was decided that the audience would long 'to "mourn" for him' and his absence from the film made that possible.[116] A different problem that arose concerned the title. Initially 'Asking for Trouble' was chosen as the working title but was abandoned as it had been used in a previous British film.[117] The film then became known as 'the Biko film' which led to wrongful expectations of its content (a biography on Biko). To correct the wrong assumption several other titles were suggested including, 'For Biko' and 'Chess Game', before Universal decided on *Cry Freedom*.

In England the film was denied a royal première. An invitation to the Prince and Princess of Wales was refused officially with the excuse that they were 'too busy', although government advisers, in reality, regarded the film as 'too political'.[118] Instead, politicians, from all parties were invited. David Owen, from the Liberal Democrats, and Neil Kinnock, leader of the Labour Party, both attended but no Conservative Party member did so. Commenting on the absence of government ministers Kinnock declared: 'they were not very much against apartheid, and not very much in favour of art'.[119] The première also included the reading of a telegram from Bishop Desmond Tutu who commended the film for 'focusing the attention of the world on an evil and vicious system'.[120] The House of Commons was granted a private showing of *Cry Freedom* on 24 February 1988 organised by the Labour Foreign Affairs Committee. Its chairman, Ernest Ross, commented that the film 'shows graphically the violence and brutality of apartheid, and at a time when the true picture of South African repression is being kept from our television-screens'. He continued: 'I can think of no better place in Britain to show this film than the Houses of Parliament, where MPs, and particularly members of the Government, have the opportunity to make effective their opposition to the South African regime.'[121]

The film opened in London on 27 November 1987 at the Empire, Leicester Square and immediately headed the London charts grossing £64,494 in its first week. The reviews in Britain were mainly complimentary with many praising the political message of the film. The *Sunday Telegraph* called it 'an engulfing film' asserting, 'I defy anyone to sit through it without being gripped, excited, enlightened and moved to angry tears.'[122] For the *Mail on Sunday* it was 'the most devastating exposure of the black man's burden ever to be screened commercially.'[123] The *Observer* declared *Cry Freedom* 'a courageous milestone, a film capable of changing hearts and minds', while the *Guardian* called it 'an honourable liberal film' and an 'infinitely painstaking and fair-minded epic'.[124] For *The Times* Attenborough's conviction was an 'unequivocal indictment of racial oppression in South Africa'.[125]

The trade press and film journals were more varied. The *Monthly Film Bulletin* claimed the film 'gels remarkably successfully, for the most part, across its vast canvas'.[126] *Sight and Sound* accused the film of being 'an inevitable political compromise' with its 'appeal to mass western audiences' by including a white hero.[127] In contrast, the black British journal, the *Voice*, praised the film as 'Hollywood at its best – high drama, high tension and the kind of emotional impact that hits you like a sledgehammer.'[128]

Cry Freedom was less well received in America. The film opened at the Ziegfeld Theatre in New York on 6 November 1987 but did not attract significant interest, not helped by its limited release. By the end of December the film had grossed only $2,030,878 and Universal withdrew the film from seven theatres. It then opened the film to more screens in time for the Oscar nominations, announced in February which saw a short rise in attendances. The total gross for *Cry Freedom* in America was $5,889,797 far below that of the highest placed British film in 1987, *The Living Daylights* (John Glen), which grossed $51,185,987.

Critically the film also suffered. Those who praised the film included *Films in Review* which claimed: 'Attenborough's direction and award-caliber performances, especially by Kline and Washington, make *Cry Freedom* one of 1987's best pictures.'[129] *Black Film Review* called the film 'vintage Attenborough' with 'spectacular scenes with hundreds of extras' and 'pointedly exemplary and stagey bits of revelatory dialogue'.[130] Many less favourable reviews commented on the structure of the film. The *Hollywood Review* declared *Cry Freedom* as 'two movies, divided into almost equal parts', and a 'monumental underachievement, marred by disastrous narrative flaws which ultimately reduce its climax and impact to that of a routine escape/chase movie'.[131] *Time* described the film as 'Attenborough's stately, schizophrenic epic of South Africa'.[132] A similar metaphor was used in *Cineaste* which claimed that the film suffered 'from acute structural schizophrenia'.[133] The *New York Times* was less disparaging, calling the film 'bewildering at some points and ineffectual at others, but it isn't dull'.[134] A wider global perspective was given by the Australian journal, *Cinema Papers*, which saw *Cry Freedom* as 'an unapologetic indictment of the world's only institutionalised system of racial discrimination'.[135]

Although *Cry Freedom* grossed just under £8 million in the international market, its lack of success in America (just over £3 million) resulted in the film failing to make a profit.[136] The critical indifference to the film also showed in the awards. *Cry Freedom* was nominated for four Golden Globe Awards, two BAFTAs and three Oscars but failed to achieve any success. The disappointing response to the film in America prompted Attenborough to declare that '*Cry Freedom* was ahead of its time.'[137] This view was echoed by the editor Lesley Walker, who argued:

Part of the problem I think is that black Americans are not Africans. At that time they had not quite cottoned on to what was happening in South Africa. I think if you had waited three more years, by which time black actors, black directors, and black issues were more of a force in Hollywood, then politically they would have been interested.[138]

Despite the unfortunate critical response, Attenborough was more concerned with the global impact of the film, declaring: 'As I understand it, in one of the Scandinavian countries, West Germany and Japan, government policy was actually changed by *Cry Freedom*.'[139] The impact of the film also generated comments beyond the cinema pages of the British press. Most were disparaging in their views. Geoffrey Wheatcroft declared that Biko 'certainly deserves a better memorial than Sir Richard Attenborough's' and claimed that *Cry Freedom* was 'bitterly denounced by black critics as patronising, tendentious, "white liberal schmaltz" which it is'.[140] Richard West in the *Daily Mail*, who had covered the Biko inquest, challenged the accuracy of *Cry Freedom* arguing that the film contained 'various cardinal errors'. West claimed that the film had generated considerable 'bitter protest' from black South Africans which the film shows as a united group but which in reality are 'mutually loathing and internecine factions'.[141] Similarly, the *Sunday Telegraph* argued that the film failed to show sufficient detail of 'the "complicated, deeply divided and sometimes brutally antagonistic" black politics of South Africa.'[142]

The most surprising reaction to the film was the decision of the South African authorities to show *Cry Freedom* uncut with approval given for general release. The Publications Appeal Board approved the film for exhibition on 29 July 1988 for people 19 years or older, only coming to this decision fifteen minutes before the first performance began. White South Africans in Cape Town 'appeared stunned by police shooting black demonstrators' and were 'shocked and deeply moved' by the film.[143] Hours later the police entered thirty-five cinemas and seized all copies of the film. The Justice Minister, Kobie Coetsee, declared the banning was due to the film being 'based on the recollections of a banned white journalist, who could not be quoted in South Africa', while General Hendrik de Witt, the Commissioner of Police, claimed it would 'intensify the revolutionary climate in the country and threaten public safety'.[144] Attenborough condemned the ban as 'an outrage and justifies our original cynicism about the present South African regime ... They will say *Cry Freedom* was not the truth. But I can assure you it was – down to the last rifle butt'.[145]

Universal attempted to bring legal action against the South African government and in February 1990 the security police in South Africa returned the confiscated films to the company's overseas distributor,

United International Pictures. In May the film was released for a second time in South Africa at forty cinemas almost eighteen months after its original release. The impact of the film, however, had diminished as it had become less controversial. The timing also coincided with F.W. de Klerk becoming State President after winning a general election in September 1989, based on his proposed reform of apartheid. In 1990 de Klerk ended the ban imposed on the ANC, ordered the release of Mandela and initiated talks with black leaders to end apartheid which were repealed in the summer. In December 1993 de Klerk gained parliamentary agreement for a provisional multiracial constitution. In April 1994 a multiracial election was won by the ANC and de Klerk then withdrew from the presidency, accepting the position as second deputy to President Mandela. Both de Klerk and Mandela were recognised for their achievements by being jointly awarded the Nobel Peace Prize in 1993, six years after the release of *Cry Freedom*. To what extent *Cry Freedom* was able to aid this process cannot be accurately determined. However, the film projected the conditions of apartheid to an unsuspecting world, aided by Attenborough's skill and diplomacy in dealing with the political factions surrounding *Cry Freedom*. Attenborough's ability and success was fully acknowledged by Woods:

> Nobody else I know could have done it. The many months of diplomacy required in dealing with the various factions in the South African liberation struggle; the reserves of energy required to deal with obstacle after obstacle; the cruel accusations, destructive attacks, and campaign of damaging lies he had to put up with from certain quarters in South Africa; the physical strength and mental stamina needed to initiate, supervise, and complete *Cry Freedom* – these manifold demands were of a scale and intensity few human beings could have coped with and withstood.[46]

Cry Freedom marked the last of Attenborough's political films. The difficulties that Woods acknowledged with *Cry Freedom*, and those with which Attenborough had to contend in *Gandhi*, saw a move away from less politically active subjects to ones which saw expression in the arts.

Notes

1 John Hill, *British Cinema in the 1980s: Issues and Themes*, Oxford, 1999, p. 245.
2 James Chapman, *Past and Present: National Identity and the British Costume Film*, London, 2005, p. 271.
3 Hill, *British Cinema in the 1980s*, p. 33.
4 *Ibid.*, p. 35.
5 Quoted in Louis Fischer, *The Life of Mahatma Gandhi*, London, 1997, p. 348.

6 Quoted in William L. Shirer, *Gandhi: A Memoir*, London, 1982, n. p.
7 Production Notes, *Gandhi*, microfiche, BFI, London.
8 Kevin Brownlow, *David Lean*, London, 1996, p. 393.
9 *Film World* (India), 4:3 (Oct.–Dec. 1968), p. 51.
10 Richard Attenborough, *In Search of Gandhi*, London, 1982, p. 44.
11 *Ibid.*
12 Fischer, *The Life of Mahatma Gandhi*, p. 66.
13 Sue Harper and Vincent Porter, *British Cinema of the 1950s: Decline and Deference*, Oxford, 2003, p. 44.
14 Attenborough, *In Search of Gandhi*, p. 77 and 80.
15 *Ibid.*, p. 81.
16 *Ibid.*, p. 58.
17 Quoted in Ian Jack, 'Gandhi Gets the Hollywood Treatment', *Sunday Times*, 23 November 1980.
18 *Daily Cinema*, 16 December 1964, pp. 1 and 4; 23 December, pp. 6–7.
19 Attenborough, *In Search of Gandhi*, p. 104.
20 *Ibid.*, p. 134.
21 *Ibid.*, p. 136.
22 *Ibid.*, p. 150.
23 *Sunday Times*, 27 November 1977.
24 Attenborough, *In Search of Gandhi*, p. 152.
25 Quoted in John Higgins, 'The Man for the Gandhi Job', *The Times*, 29 November 1982.
26 Attenborough, *In Search of Gandhi*, p. 167.
27 *Ibid.*, p. 183.
28 Jake Eberts and Terry Ilott, *My Indecision Is Final: The Rise and Fall of Goldcrest Films*, London, 1990, p. 58.
29 Jack, 'Gandhi Gets the Hollywood Treatment'.
30 *Variety*, 31 December 1980.
31 Author's interview with Attenborough, 26 May 2001, Richmond, Surrey.
32 Fischer refers to Gandhi's wife as Kasturbai. The film uses the spelling Kasturba.
33 The Broadcasting Entertainment and Cinematograph Theatre Union (BECTU) History Project, Lord (Richard) Attenborough, interviewed by Sydney Samuelson, 4 December 2001, BFI.
34 *Sunday Times*, 3 May 1981.
35 Attenborough, *In Search of Gandhi*, p. 167.
36 See Fischer, *The Life of Mahatma Gandhi*, pp. 261–84.
37 *Gandhi*, BFI Special Collections, 31 January 1981 (3030001) 'Call Sheet' no. 55.
38 *Screen International*, 14 March 1981, p. 8.
39 *Guinness Book of Records of 1998*, London, 1977, p. 148.
40 AC Nielsen, Entertainment Data International (UK).
41 Sarah Street, *Transatlantic Crossings: British Feature Films in the USA*, London, 2002, p. 195.
42 *Sunday Telegraph*, 5 December 1982.
43 *The Times*, 1 December 1982.
44 *Sunday Times*, 5 December 1982; *Sunday Express*, 5 December 1982.
45 *Daily Telegraph*, 3 December 1982.
46 *Observer*, 5 December 1982.
47 *Financial Times*, 3 December 1982.
48 *Variety*, 24 November 1982.
49 *Hollywood Reporter*, 24 November, 1982.
50 *New York*, 6 December 1982, p. 166.
51 *Village Voice*, 14 December 1982, p. 74; *Cinema* (US) 12:4 (1983), pp. 45–6.

52 Quoted in *World Press Review*, May 1983, p. 8.
53 *Monthly Film Bulletin*, 49:587 (December 1982), p. 285.
54 *Sight and Sound*, 52:1 (winter 1982/83), p. 64.
55 *Time Out*, 640 (26 November 1982), p. 14; *Spectator*, 4 December 1982, p. 28.
56 H.V. Hodson, 'Errors that Count', *Sunday Times*, 17 April 1983.
57 Louis Heren, 'Gandhi: The Horror the Film Omits', *The Times*, 4 December 1982.
58 Paul Johnson, 'Gandhi Isn't Good for You', *Daily Telegraph*, 16 April 1983.
59 John Grigg, 'The Gandhi that the Film Forgot', *Sunday Telegraph*, 17 April 1983.
60 Salman Rushdie, 'Truth Retreats When the Saint Goes Marching in', *The Times*, 2 May 1983.
61 Dilip Hiro, 'Attenborough Rope Trick', *Guardian*, 13 January 1983.
62 Trevor Fishlock, 'Pakistan's Crisis of Identity', *The Times*, 5 April 1983.
63 *The Times*, 16 April 1983.
64 *Sunday Telegraph*, 17 April 1983.
65 *Ibid.*
66 *The Times*, 13 April 1983; *Guardian*, 13 April 1983.
67 *Morning Star*, 13 April 1983.
68 *Daily Telegraph*, 13 April 1983.
69 *The Times*, 15 April 1983.
70 *Daily Express*, 15 April 1983.
71 *The Times*, 16 April 1983.
72 *Guardian*, 13 April 1983.
73 *Observer*, 19 April 1983.
74 Street, *Transatlantic Crossings*, p. 215.
75 Quoted in Victor Davis, 'And Now Joining the Chorus Line – It's Audrey Landers from TV's Dallas', *Daily Express*, 21 November 1984.
76 Mervyn Rothstein, 'After 15 Years (15!), "A Chorus Line" Ends', *New York Times*, 30 April 1990.
77 Quoted in Marjorie Bilbow, 'The American Folklore of A Chorus Line Is an Englishman's triumph', *Screen International*, 25 January 1986, p. 22.
78 Quoted in Paul Jackson, 'Chorus Line Cattle Call', *Western Mail*, 18 January 1986, p. 7.
79 *New York Times*, 8 December 1985; *Variety*, 4 December 1985.
80 David Denby, *New York*, 16, December 1985, p. 76.
81 *Films in Review*, 37:1 (January 1986); *Village Voice*, 17 December 1985.
82 Quoted in *Daily Express*, 17 December 1985.
83 Quoted *ibid.*, p. 105.
84 Andy Dougan, *The Actors' Director: Richard Attenborough behind the Camera*, Edinburgh, 1994, p. 107.
85 *Ibid.*
86 *Monthly Film Bulletin*, 53:624 (January 1986), p. 7.
87 *Scotsman*, 11 January 1986.
88 *Sunday Express*, 12 January 1986.
89 *Observer*, 12 January 1986; *Mail on Sunday*, 12 January 1986.
90 *Financial Times*, 10 January 1986.
91 *Sunday Times*, 12 January 1986.
92 Quoted in Dougan, *The Actors' Director*, p. 115.
93 *Ibid.*, p. 114.
94 *Stills*, 30 (March 1987), p. 10.
95 Robinson, *Richard Attenborough*, p. 80.
96 *The Times*, 14 September 1977; *Guardian*, 14 September 1977.
97 *The Times*, 16 September 1977.
98 Richard Attenborough, Introduction, *Richard Attenborough's Cry Freedom: A*

Pictorial Record, New York, 1987, n. p.
99 Ibid.
100 Donald Woods, *Filming with Attenborough: The Making of Cry Freedom*, London, 1987, p. 7.
101 *Film Comment*, 23:6 (November/December 1987), p. 13. Stern is spelled incorrectly as Stone.
102 Robinson, *Richard Attenborough*, p. 75.
103 Michael Buckley, 'Sir Richard Attenborough: In Praise of Cry Freedom', *Films in Review*, 28:12 (December 1987), p. 593.
104 Ibid.
105 Dougan, *The Actors' Director*, p. 122.
106 *Sunday Times*, 29 November 1987.
107 Production Notes, *Cry Freedom*, microfiche, BFI. London
108 Ibid.
109 *New York Times*, 29 October 1987.
110 Production Notes, *Cry Freedom*.
111 Ibid.; *Mail on Sunday*, 27 July 1986.
112 Woods, *Filming with Attenborough*, p. 42.
113 Script S13419 *Cry Freedom*, Combined Continuity Script, BFI, London.
114 DVD, *Cry Freedom*, Universal, 2001, VFC31395.
115 *Creative Screenwriting*, 3:4 (1996), p. 6.
116 Ibid., p. 7.
117 The title was first used in 1941.
118 *Mail on Sunday*, 27 September 1987.
119 *Evening Standard*, 27 November 1987.
120 Quoted ibid.
121 Quoted in *The Times*, 24 February 1988.
122 *Sunday Telegraph*, 29 November 1987.
123 *Mail on Sunday*, 29 November 1987.
124 *Observer*, 29 November 1987; *Guardian*, 26 November 1987.
125 *The Times*, 26 November 1987.
126 *Monthly Film Bulletin*, 54:646 (November 1987), p. 332.
127 *Sight and Sound*, 57:1 (winter 1987/88), p. 49.
128 *Voice*, 24 November 1987, p. 26.
129 *Films in Review*, 39:2 (February 1988), p. 98.
130 *Black Film Review*, 3:4 (autumn 1987), p. 8.
131 *Hollywood Reporter*, 6 November 1987, p. 3.
132 *Time*, 9 November 1987.
133 *Cineaste*, 16:3 (1988), p. 38.
134 *New York Times*, 6 November 1987.
135 *Cinema Papers*, 68 (March 1988), p. 37.
136 *Evening Standard*, 21 August 1988.
137 Dougan, *The Actors' Director*, p. 120.
138 Ibid., p. 133.
139 Robinson, *Richard Attenborough*, p. 80.
140 *Sunday Telegraph*, 31 January 1988.
141 Richard West, 'Biko and bunkum', *Daily Mail*, 24 November 1987.
142 Bruce Anderson, 'How Attenborough fails to do justice to Biko', *Sunday Telegraph*, 22 November 1987.
143 *The Times*, 30 July 1988.
144 *Daily Mail*, 30 July 1988.
145 *The Times*, 30 July 1988.
146 Woods, *Filming with Attenborough*, p. 162.

Public and private identities: *Chaplin* (1992) and *Grey Owl* (1999) 6

The 1990s was Richard Attenborough's most prolific decade, directing four films with varying success. Despite all his efforts, however, Attenborough was unable to recapture the same degree of success he had enjoyed with *Gandhi*. One significant reason could be the change from the serious socio-political themes that had dominated Attenborough's productions in the 1980s, to one focusing on the people whose artistic talents held a particular personal interest for him, and, perhaps, less so for others. Of the four films two explore lives related to acting: *Chaplin*, which focuses on the comic silent screen star, actor and director, Charles Chaplin, and *Grey Owl*, which recounts the 'pseudo' life 'acted' by Archibald Belaney, an Englishman who masqueraded as a half-bred Native American Indian in Canada, in which guise he became a world renowned conservationist. Chaplin and Belaney shared several similarities. Both men were born within months of each other, Chaplin on 16 April 1889, Belaney on 18 September 1888. Both had difficult childhoods with mothers who proved incapable of looking after them and fathers who departed soon after their births. Chaplin was sent to the workhouse, Belaney to the care of two maiden aunts. Both were renowned for their unstable relationships, each marrying four times and fathering several children. Both chose to leave their native England for a better life abroad, Chaplin settling in California and Belaney in Canada. Both attracted global fame through their acting roles, Chaplin in his guise as the 'Little Tramp' and Belaney in his false persona of 'Grey Owl'.

Despite their common characteristics, Attenborough portrayed the two actors very differently. *Chaplin* represents a long period of the comedian's life from the age of 8 to 88 showing his career and his succession of wives and lovers. *Grey Owl*, instead, focuses on the two-year period of his romance with Gertrude Bernard (Pony) which changed Belaney from being a slaying hunter to a caring conservationist and protector of the beaver, Canada's national animal. Neither film attained the critical or popular success Attenborough had envisaged. *Chaplin* failed to make any significant impact at the box office, while *Grey Owl* was tarnished by being denied a theatrical release in America and going straight to video. The critical opinion of *Chaplin* was generally poor, while *Grey Owl* was almost universally slated, culminating in some of the worst reviews of Attenborough's directorial career.

The 1990s also marked a significant period in Attenborough's position within the British cinema. During the early stages of *Chaplin*'s development Attenborough's interests became directed towards the cinema industry where his position, as one of its leading representatives, competed for time and attention with his own career. At the start of the 1990s the British cinema was in decline. The late 1980s saw a reduction in the number of films produced, and a decrease in the amount of investment. Margaret Thatcher's premiership, by not supporting the arts, contributed much to its decline. The government's collective policies, including the abolition of the Eady Levy (1985), abolition of capital allowances for British films (1986) and changes to the ITV Exchequer Levy (1989) had, according to John Woodward (later director of the British Film Institute (BFI)) 'effectively brought the UK film and TV production industry to its knees'.[1]

Attenborough had recently reached several positions of authority in the industry. He was elected chair of the British Screen Advisory Council in 1987, Chairman of the European Script Fund and President of the Actors' Charitable Trust, both in 1988. From 1981 he had taken on the role of chairman of the BFI where he had been responsible for the opening of the Museum of the Moving Image in 1988, the completion of the Paul Getty Conservation Centre at Berkhamstead and the move of the BFI to Stephen Street. As chairman of the BFI and the British Screen Advisory Council, Attenborough was in a pivotal position to influence government policy. On 18 July 1989 he, together with David Puttnam, led a select group of filmmakers to discuss the difficulties with the Trade and Industry Secretary, Lord Young. The discussions included the proliferation of American films exhibited in Britain and the reduced contributions of two key sources of finance, American investment and television, all responsible for fewer British productions. In 1989 only thirty films were made, the smallest number since 1981.[2] The meeting gained only partial success. While Lord Young agreed to 'continue the government's £2 million a year support until the end of 1993', allowing British Screen, which had generated £12 million of private funds for every £1 million the government has invested, to become self-sufficient, the offer fell short of the £5 million requested by the group.[3]

Attenborough's attempts to revitalise the industry were also influenced by his own concerns as co-producer with *Chaplin*. He explained the difficulties in obtaining finance for the film to Peter Palumbo, the chairman of the Arts Council, voicing the need for American support and claiming that with *Chaplin*, 'We simply couldn't set up a film like that here. We've hardly any film industry left.'[4] In March 1990, Attenborough publicly attacked the lack of British investment for films claiming it was a 'national embarrassment' and gave the example of his own film, explaining: 'Chaplin was one of the greatest figures in the history of cinema and probably one of the greatest Englishmen in the cinema, yet I am having to go to Universal in Hollywood in order to get the money.'[5] As a result of his attack Palumbo reported Attenborough's concerns to Thatcher, who took heed of Attenborough's warning, and convened a seminar at 10 Downing Street for 15 June 1990.

The seminar was chaired by Thatcher and attended by twenty leading representatives of the film industry, including Attenborough, David Puttnam and Simon Relph, the chief executive of British Screen. The meeting ended with a regeneration plan including a £5 million pledge of government funding to help with European film co-productions and the setting up of a Department of Trade and Industry working party to ascertain how to attract more funding for British films. On 28 November 1990, however, Thatcher was succeeded as Prime Minister by John Major. Without Thatcher's recently obtained support, the impetus of the proposed changes was lost including the promised £5 million. Other difficulties followed. British Screen, which had been allotted £6 million in January 1991 did not receive its first instalment by the summer of that year and halted any co-funding of new films. In May 1991, the British Film Commission was set up with the intention of encouraging foreign filmmakers to make films in Britain. Subsequent delays, however, meant it did not come into existence until April 1992. The continuing economic difficulties of the industry continued to plague the production of *Chaplin*. During 1991 the film's progress was halted twice by the breaking of financial deals which almost resulted in the project collapsing. Although the second financial problem was resolved by a multimillion package rescue, British money was conspicuously absent with all the money coming from abroad.

Attenborough was in need of a successful film to re-establish his name in America after the poor response there to *Cry Freedom*. Despite the disappointing American box office, Universal was keen to continue its association with Attenborough and signed a three-film contract with him in a $75 million deal in November 1987. The first project involved the life story of the Victorian explorer Richard Burton, while the second concerned the life of Thomas Paine, the eighteenth century English pamphleteer and political radical, famous for his work *The Rights of Man* (1792). The third, *Chaplin*, was the only one to reach fruition, enduring a long and protracted production history that echoed the difficulties of finance, script and casting that Attenborough had experienced with *Gandhi*.

Attenborough had first encountered Charles Chaplin when he was taken to a special screening of *The Gold Rush* (1925) as a child, his father telling him that he would witness a genius who had 'an ability to make his audience both laugh and cry almost at the same instant'.[6] This film was an inspiration to Attenborough who acknowledged it as 'the film which made me want to act professionally'.[7] The story of Chaplin also appeared to be ideally suitable as a cinematic biography. A 'rags to riches' story of a child born in poverty who became famous was immortalised in his guise of the 'Little Tramp', a semi-tragic figure that was the central focus for his films. Chaplin was one of the dominant figures in the silent-film era, writing, acting, producing and directing his own films. Attenborough also shared a similar career trajectory to Chaplin. Both were English-born actors whose careers had expanded into production and direction while still maintaining their acting vocation. The two also shared similar liberal-humanist principles which emanated from their upbringing: Attenborough's largely drawn from his parents' beliefs, with Chaplin's due to his own childhood experiences.

Chaplin was the third of Attenborough's biopics forming a trilogy of lives of 'the great' which began with *Young Winston*, gained greater success with *Gandhi* and which was hoped would be a fitting celebration of Attenborough's fiftieth anniversary in cinema in 1992. As a biopic, *Chaplin* can also be linked to a more specific contemporary cycle concerning the lives of artists. These included portrayals of musicians, including Mozart in *Amadeus* (Milos Forman, 1984) and painters such as *Caravaggio* (Derek Jarman, 1986) and, in France, *Van Gogh* (Maurice Pialat, 1991). *The Buster Keaton Story* (Sydney Sheldon, 1957) had portrayed the story of another silent comic actor while Keaton had also been the subject of a recent television documentary, *Buster Keaton: A Hard Act to Follow* (1987), written by Kevin Brownlow and David Gill. Attenborough's aim was to restore Chaplin's reputation which had been tainted by allegations about his political beliefs and sexual conduct by exploring the history behind his past cinematic triumphs and to introduce the actor's legendary skills to a new generation of cinema audiences. In his position as vice-president of BAFTA, Attenborough was able to contribute to Chaplin's standing by making him a fellow. Attenborough was also 'instrumental' in Chaplin being nominated for a knighthood.[8]

Attenborough had developed a friendship with Chaplin and his wife Oona, after their daughter, Annette, worked as a production assistant on *A Bridge Too Far* in 1976. His relationship with Oona was to prove significant. After Chaplin's death, Oona held the rights to Chaplin's early short films while the rights to the renowned features, including *The Gold Rush*, *City Lights* (1931) and *The Great Dictator* (1940), were to revert to her in 1990. She also 'effectively exercised a veto over a biopic, because under American law she had to grant permission for her own screen portrayal'.[9] Attenborough, with support from Geraldine, Chaplin's eldest daughter, successfully obtained Oona's permission for a film. Oona had admired *Gandhi* and told Attenborough that she felt confident that 'there wouldn't be any exaggeration, and the story would be safe with him'.[10] She granted Attenborough exclusive rights to film Chaplin's life and also permitted him access to his letters and diaries, despite the objections of two of her children, Christopher and Victoria, the latter arguing that 'one should keep the mystery of what my father did'.[11] Between the years 1981 to 1987 the computer company IBM had gained exclusive rights to the Chaplin image. The Chaplin estate granted Attenborough the same permission to employ the image of the 'Little Tramp' for his film. The rights to two important works on Chaplin, *My Autobiography*, originally published in 1964, and David Robinson's study, *Chaplin: His Life and Art*, published in 1985, were also obtained, with Robinson also given the role of technical adviser to the film.

The idea for making a film on Chaplin originated from Diana Hawkins, Attenborough's business partner, when Attenborough was 'devastated' after his proposed film on Tom Paine was turned down by Universal in 1988. Hawkins worked secretly on a draft treatment on Chaplin before presenting to Attenborough who was 'instantly taken with the idea'.[12] Bryan Forbes was engaged as scriptwriter, beginning with the disappearance of Chaplin's body after burial and the ransom demand for its return.[13] The script, described as strong on Chaplin's early days, and 'a terrific piece of construction' by Attenborough, although 'somewhat on the lengthy side', was sent to Universal whose script-reader raised objections.[14] It transpired that the studio management preferred an American writer, with Attenborough conceding to their demands. This rejection of Forbes's work resulted in a rift between him and Attenborough, with Forbes declaring that he felt 'betrayed and resentful' and that working on *Chaplin* had 'blighted one of my oldest and most valued friendships'.[15] The rift was also exacerbated by the later engagement of William Goldman, who had had an unhappy relationship with Forbes on *The Stepford Wives* (Forbes, 1974). Forbes claims that Goldman wrote some 'nasty things' about him that he claimed were 'grossly rude and offensive'.[16] This contrasted Attenborough's good working relationship with Goldman on both *A Bridge Too Far* and *Magic*. In 1984 Goldman had claimed that Attenborough 'is by far the finest, most decent human being I've met in the picture business'.[17] In July 1990 Universal approached William Boyd, instructing him to write 'an entirely new script, both shorter and of a wholly different temper'.[18] Boyd produced several draft scripts before a shooting script was finalised. Five weeks before filming was due to start, Universal decided they wanted Tom Stoppard to apply a 'pre-production polish' to Boyd's script. The degree of change that Stoppard bought is unclear although it is acknowledged that he 'contributed to some dialogue'.[19] Some of the changes are evident from Boyd's draft script dated January 1991 which although structurally similar to the finished film, show some marked changes to the dialogue.[20]

As with *Young Winston*, *Chaplin* required three actors of different ages. Several actors had shown interest in the adult role including Dustin Hoffman, Billy Crystal and Robin Williams before Robert Downey Jr was selected by Attenborough. Despite being American, Downey possessed the necessary qualities which Attenborough demanded:

> [H]e had to have a brilliant ear, he had to be able to dance like Nijinsky, and he had to be able to be made up to look like the Little Tramp. I would have liked an English actor, but Robert leapt off the screen.[21]

Although Downey had only one previous starring film role, with Mel Gibson in *Air America* (Roger Spottiswoode, 1990), his inexperience was a critical factor in Attenborough's choice.

Universal, however, refused to sanction Downey's casting, preferring an acclaimed name instead. Attenborough decided to give Universal a twenty-four-hour ultimatum – 'either finally to sign Robert or I would not go ahead with the film'.[22] Universal refused to change their mind, and the film entered a state of 'turn-around' (collapse), halting the project. Although Universal had spent an estimated £4 million ($8.5 million) in pre-production costs, their unwillingness to sanction Downey was an excuse to withdraw from the project coming soon after the studio had suffered a significant loss with *Havana* (Sydney Pollack, 1990). Tom Pollock, head of Universal, also insisted that the reason for Universal's withdrawal was 'never about the project. It was only about the cost', asserting that 'We had approved it with Downey *at a specific budget.*'[23]

In 1991, Pollock suggested to Attenborough that he should contact the chairman of the independent company Carolco Pictures, Mario Kassar. Carolco, which had taken over Cannon in 1990, required a prestigious film with Oscar potential after producing such films as *Terminator 2:*

Judgement Day (James Cameron, 1991) and *Basic Instinct* (Paul Verhoeven, 1991). Kassar welcomed the opportunity to work with Attenborough, claiming: 'The chance to have one of the greatest directors of our time create an epic about one of the most brilliant and fascinating legends in Hollywood was simply too good to pass up.'[24] After Carolco stipulated that Boyd's script had to be shortened, Attenborough engaged Goldman, who expanded upon the director's idea of introducing a fictional character, George Hayden, as a narrator, providing continuity throughout the film. According to Goldman:

> I decided that since Chaplin wrote an autobiography, and since he was a famous man living in Switzerland, it would not be ridiculous if his book editor came from London to discuss final revisions. The editor could ask whatever questions we wanted to get us to the next dramatic sequence. And could also, if possible, shoulder some of the dreaded exposition that infiltrated the story.[25]

Goldman was the fourth writer to embark upon the project. The complicated sequence of the writers' different contributions for the film was later explained by Boyd:

> The basic structure and narrative of the film and most of its major scenes and key emphases were evolved and written during my seven-month collaboration with Attenborough and Hawkins; some interpolations and scenes were subsequently written by Hawkins and Goldman, and various traces of Stoppard's polish are to be found. Goldman is solely responsible for the Switzerland scenes.[26]

Continuing financial difficulties delayed the start of filming. Attenborough offered to defer 60 per cent of his salary to help while Downey announced they all (the cast) were paid less than they were originally contracted. Terence Clegg, in charge of production, cut costs further by reducing the shooting schedule by two weeks. Some cost-cutting decisions appeared ill-judged. Carolco refused to finance a day's shooting for the London street scene at an estimated cost of $200,000, despite the fact that $250,000 had been spent on the original set and there was a projected cost of $60,000 to dismantle it. To rebuild it, according to Clegg, they spent 'about a third as much' resulting in a set totalling nearly half a million dollars used for one day's filming.[27] Universal also made legal demands for payment concerning the film's rights and assets which resulted in a settlement for an immediate $4 million with a further $4.5 million to be repaid after the film's release. Further negotiations reduced the latter fee to $2.5 million.[28]

After many delays, Carolco officially sanctioned *Chaplin*'s go-ahead in the autumn of 1991, funding the film for $37 million. Under the deal,

Kassar and Attenborough were joint producers, Hawkins associate producer and Clegg co-producer. The delays had resulted in problems with casting. The actor playing the young Chaplin had outgrown the role, while Winona Ryder, who was contracted to star in *Dracula*, became unavailable and was replaced by Moira Kelly. While the casting was largely Attenborough's choice, Carolco insisted that 'certain names' were required including Anthony Hopkins (the editor), Kevin Kline (Douglas Fairbanks) and Dan Aykroyd (Mack Sennett).[29] The most significant casting, however, was that of Geraldine Chaplin, in the role of Hannah, her real grandmother, who declined into insanity and was committed to a mental asylum. The choice of Geraldine was also a diplomatic move on Attenborough's behalf, to help ensure permission to film in the Chaplin house in Switzerland.

The casting of Moira Kelly in the dual role of Hetty Kelly, Chaplin's first girlfriend, and Oona, his greatest love, last of his four wives and mother of eight of his children, was unusual but not unique. Michael Powell had employed Deborah Kerr to play three characters in *The Life and Death of Colonel Blimp* (1943) playing Blimp's first love Edith, his wife Barbara, and, after her death, his driver Angela. Another significant appointment was that of Sven Nykvist as director of photography. Nykvist was regarded as one of the world's greatest cinematographers after making his name working for Ingmar Bergman, winning two Oscars under the director for *Cries and Whispers* (1972) and *Fanny and Alexander* (1982). His preference for 'small-scale, low-tech filmmaking', was well suited to Attenborough's own approach. Attenborough also needed the support of reliable 'old hands', including Stuart Craig, in charge of production design for his third Attenborough film, while for David Tomblin, Attenborough's trusted first assistant director, *Chaplin* was his fourth production for the director.

Production began on 14 October in California at Fillmore, near Hollywood. While the production was overshadowed by the recent death of Oona, on 27 September, more worrying was the state of Carolco's financial position. In December, with news of the company's difficulties about to appear in the trade press, Attenborough decided to draw on his acting skills in order to disguise the off-set problems to the crew. In his words, he produced 'a tremendous performance', by announcing that *Chaplin* was 'not bankrolled by Carolco per se but through a separate "venture" created by Carolco, Le Studio Canal+ of France, and RSC Video of Italy, with additional funding from Japan Satellite Broadcasting'.[30] The performance paid off with both cast and crew remaining unaware of the depth of the problems until such time that Carolco had raised the necessary finance to ensure the film was safe. For Attenborough, the performance was purely employing the training and skills he had learned for his profession, commenting: 'I am first and foremost an actor. An actor must be able to come on stage in a farce with his trousers down, even though he has just been told his aunt has died.'[31]

The film's focus on Chaplin's private life demonstrates certain weaknesses which undermined his public persona. Chaplin's relationships with teenage girls, his left-wing political leanings, and his refusal to seek American citizenship led to his being despised by many of the cinema fraternity. His relationship with Joan Barry, an affair which ended in mutual loathing and Chaplin being sued for paternity, resulted in a case that was proved scientifically incorrect but was nevertheless carried by a Californian court, while his public support for socialist principles also showed him to be out of touch with the then changing political climate by voicing his opinions in inappropriate directions. The film shows Chaplin as a victim of the political climate which made him a prime subject of an internal security investigation. According to Robinson, the basis of FBI chief J. Edgar Hoover's interest was that Chaplin's films focused on 'the homeless, the unemployed and the slum-dwellers – the underbelly of society'.[32] Concern was also shown with Chaplin's progressive films, such as *Modern Times* (1936), which depicted the growing industrialisation of society, and *The Great Dictator* (1940), a satirical denouncement of fascism which won Chaplin praise from the *Daily Worker*, the voice of the British Communist Party, but which aroused considerable hostility in America. Although *Chaplin* does not refer to this specifically, it does reflect the paranoia of Hoover, whose proclamations are voiced in the film, that *The Great Dictator* is not about Germany but about America.

Chaplin explores several themes relating to identity. Chaplin's guise of the 'Little Tramp' provides his public face, while his image as a filmmaker and actor is depicted as one who has set his own moral standards, sexual desires and political beliefs. The question of national identity provides a secure link with Chaplin's home country by being influenced by the dominant values to which the British aspired. As Jeffrey Richards observes: 'Every nation has a set of national values, desirable qualities that derive from the national identity and the national character'.[33] Chaplin is shown in the film to have many 'values' – political, moral, and social – providing a personal creed. He also retains his identity to define his individuality against the American people among whom he resides. Moreover, despite his vast fame and fortune being achieved in the country, Chaplin refuses to adopt American citizenship, a factor that is disliked (and distrusted) by the authorities. It is this reason that is employed legally to prevent his re-entry to America in September

1952 after he departed to London for the première of his film, *Limelight* (1952). The action was based on the 'US Code of Laws on Aliens and Citizenship', which 'permitted the barring of aliens on grounds of "morals, health or insanity, or for advocating Communism or associating with Communist or pro-Communist organizations"'.[34] Chaplin's decision to live in exile in Switzerland also indicates that he had become distanced from England. On an earlier return to the country, he was castigated in a public bar for not supporting his country in the First World War, after which, in the film he declares, 'I had no home so I put down roots in America.'

Chaplin uses flashback to recount the comedian's life from childhood to old age. The story of Charles Chaplin is interspersed with recollections from the older Chaplin who recounts his past through conversations with the editor of the autobiography he is completing. Chaplin's 'two' lives merge into one when the past and present come together in the award of his honorary Oscar at the Academy Awards in 1972 bringing the film to a rousing conclusion. As a background to Chaplin's life, the film also provides a history of the development of cinema in America as it progressed from the silent era to the advent of sound. This is further emphasised with editorial devices and the attention paid to historical authenticity including sequences of actuality footage, excerpts of Chaplin's own films, the use of historic buildings and captions providing specific information relating to time and place. The film also includes several examples of the qualities which have come to characterise Attenborough's films: picturesque landscapes, the English countryside, and the grounds of grand houses, including, in a gesture of authenticity, scenes filmed at Chaplin's palatial house in exile, the Manoir de Ban, in Corsier-sur-Vevey, Switzerland. These images are contrasted against scenes of social deprivation, the austere living conditions of London depicting Chaplin's own childhood.

Attenborough's own socio-political principles are also reflected in the political attitudes of the film. Chaplin is seen to dismiss the proclamations of Hoover, and publicly attack a German for his pro-Nazi proclamations, commenting after being accused of being a Jew that he does not 'have the honour' of being one. Chaplin is also unaware of his own position as only 'a guest' in America by dismissing his brother Sydney's warning concerning his proposed film, *The Immigrant* (1917). Sydney berates Chaplin for 'kicking an immigration officer up the backside', asking – 'do you think that's funny' and reiterating: 'there's a war on remember. Now you make a million a year while British boys are dying in France. Do you want the same thing to happen here?'

Although *Chaplin* portrays the life of a comic genius it is not a comic film. A publicity statement that preceded the film warned: 'He made the whole world laugh and cry. He will again'. Humour and pathos merge together in a reflective depiction of Chaplin's life. This is most evident in the sequence involving the editing of *The Kid* (1921) which includes a section speeded up to resemble a Keystone Cops routine with Chaplin embracing the disguise of a wheelchair-bound woman both as a deception and as a comical turn. The insertion of the film clip of *The Kid* also demonstrates the pathos of Chaplin's own life, a semi-autobiographical film which captures the distress of a child taken from his family to the workhouse, made more overt by the silent but readable words of the child crying out for his mother.

On 15 November 1992, a month before *Chaplin*'s British release, ITV broadcast a *South Bank Show* special entitled 'Action Darling' to commemorate Attenborough's fiftieth anniversary in cinema. The programme provided publicity for the film and included scenes being rehearsed and filmed. Also included were some interesting opinions on Attenborough from colleagues. The critic Philip French claimed that Attenborough 'has Napoleonic ambitions. His thinking is about movies influenced by the war – something he hasn't been able to shake off.' For David Puttnam, Attenborough 'is seen in Hollywood as a unique proposition, he is what he is: hugely respected, massively tenacious. He doesn't let go.' Puttnam continued:

> Dickie, as indeed with Stanley Kubrick, is probably a better producer than a director. But he directs more than competently. Dickie is a storyteller. He sets out to tell stories. He tells them in an accessible way, not in a particularly stylish way or certainly not in a particularly modish way. And of course, if you do that you are always going to be accused of, to a greater or lesser extent, of being a little old fashioned. But I happen to think this is a quality not a defect.[35]

Using his preferred venue of Twickenham Studios, *Chaplin* marked the first occasion on which Attenborough employed computer-generated imaging (CGI). The device was employed most notably in the scene featuring Chaplin with Fairbanks who is seen climbing over the large 'Hollywood' sign. The production only had use of the lower half of the sign built for the set with the higher part added later. The post-production period was also beset by problems. The film required drastic editing to reduce its length to below the maximum as stipulated by Carolco. Since the success of *Gandhi*, Attenborough had been granted the privilege of 'final cut' of all films he directed by which the distributor has to accept his editing with the final length not exceeding 2 hours and 15 minutes. Kasser added his own stipulation that the Swiss scenes had to be included in the final film. Although Attenborough had employed a renowned editor, Anne V. Coates, a niece of J. Arthur Rank and best known for editing *Lawrence of Arabia* (David Lean, 1962), a significant mistake occurred with the film's length, completed at 147 minutes instead of the required length of 135 minutes. The problem was exacerbated as Chaplin's life was so integrated that it was difficult to omit any part without the whole structure collapsing. Attenborough took full responsibility for the error, commenting 'I got the timing wrong and it was entirely my mistake.'[36] The subsequent removal of several small parts of the film, as no single section could be extracted, had inevitable consequences with the film losing continuity as well as significant footage, which 'damaged the picture significantly' and resulted in an inferior film.[37]

A further and unforeseen problem occurred with the script credits. Attenborough had expected that Hawkins would be credited for writing the story, and Boyd and Goldman for the screenplay. The Writers Guild of America agreed to acknowledge Hawkins's input but had to arbitrate for the screenplay credit and consulted all previous scripts of the film. In October 1992 the Guild dictated that the credits should read as written by 'William Boyd and Bryan Forbes and William Goldman'.[38] The preciseness was important with the crucial 'ands' (as opposed to the ampersands) which established that they were not a writing team. While Boyd acknowledged that the reason for Forbes's inclusion was a normal procedure as the Writers Guild 'always recognises the work done by the first writer on the project, whether it was used or not', he declared that the inclusion of Forbes's name (who wrote no part of the final script) 'saddles *Chaplin* with a ridiculous absurdity'.[39] Forbes commented that although 'surprised' he was pleased at the credit as 'there's poetic justice involved. I spent a year producing five drafts.'[40] The last comment was questioned by Attenborough who ascertained that while Forbes 'may have revised his original script a bit, but he certainly didn't write five drafts'.[41] Similarly, while Attenborough acknowledged that Stoppard contributed to the dialogue, 'there was never any question of a credit.'

Yet another difficulty concerned the film's title. During production the film was entitled 'Charlie' but after the editing processes were almost completed, Attenborough was threatened with legal action if the title was not changed. This action was instigated by the actor, Cliff Robertson, who had received awards for his portrayal of a mentally retarded man in the Oscar-winning film, *Charly* (Ralph Nelson, 1968), and who objected to the same title (albeit a different spelling) being used again.[42] Two months before the film was released, it was renamed *Chaplin*.

Chaplin was chosen for the 46th Royal Film Performance on 16 December 1992 in the presence of the Queen and the Duke of Edinburgh.

The film opened in Britain on 18 December 1992 at the Odeon, Leicester Square, and was released nationally from 15 January 1993. The total amount taken from the British box office was £1,813,792. It fared badly with other British films competing at the time including *The Crying Game* (Neil Jordan) which grossed £2.020 million and *Howards End* (James Ivory) £3.7 million. In America *Chaplin* opened on 25 December 1992, on the fifteenth anniversary of Chaplin's death. Although the film had a disappointing opening weekend, taking $43,839 in New York and $40,830 in Los Angeles, after January the film was given a wider release resulting in *Chaplin* becoming the fifth most successful British film at the American box office in 1992 grossing a total of $8,272,368.[43]

The British reviewers were predominantly critical of the film although there was almost universal praise for Downey's performance. The *Observer* called him 'as remarkable as Ben Kingsley was [in *Gandhi*]' while the *Guardian* considered that Downey offered 'a brilliant impersonation of Chaplin rather than a valid interpretation of him'.[44] The *Independent on Sunday* claimed that Downey has 'a perfect ear for the Chaplin accent' and a 'perfect boot and fist for the slapstick'.[45] For the *Daily Telegraph*, Downey's performance was 'nothing short of remarkable'.[46]

Many of the reviews appeared more concerned with the subject of Chaplin rather than providing an opinion of the film itself. This could be attributed to the number of articles that appeared in the quality press at the time of the film's release. The film's technical adviser David Robinson, in *The Times*, focused on the personal war vented on Chaplin by J. Edgar Hoover, making Chaplin a marked man in America and resulting in the actor's enforced exile.[47] This sympathetic view of Chaplin's life was contrasted by John Diamond, also in *The Times*, who challenged the film's 'celebration of the great man', disputing Chaplin's comic abilities by claiming that Chaplin 'wasn't funny' as a comedian.[48] Diamond's views were echoed by George Perry in the *Sunday Times* who argued that while '[t]he comedy of Keaton and Laurel and Hardy still works, Chaplin's has wilted'. For Perry, Chaplin 'means little to today's generation of film-goers, or indeed, filmmakers.'[49] The questioning of Chaplin's humorous skills also concerned some reviews. The *Sun* declared Chaplin 'the world's unfunniest comic', while *Today* did not find Chaplin 'remotely funny'.[50] *The Times* appeared to assume the opinion of the readership when it declared: 'We may admire Chaplin's pantomime skills, his blending of slapstick with sentiment. But we actually laugh at Buster Keaton.'[51] Writing in the communist publication, the *Morning Star*, Jeff Sawtell added a political element to Chaplin's reputation by quoting from the Russian film director, Sergei Eisenstein:

'Chaplin stands equally and firmly in the ranks of the greatest masters of the age-long struggle of Satire with Darkness.' For Sawtell, *Chaplin* had a deeper message: 'As the danger of fascism once again stalks Europe, *Chaplin* might prove an inspiration to those who never knew of the Little Tramp who could smite the "Goliaths of Villainy and Obscurantism".'[52] A different perspective was taken by Alexander Walker in the *Evening Standard* who used his review to launch a personal attack on Attenborough's reputation.

> Throughout his career, and indeed his life, he has manifested a reluctance to speak ill of anyone, especially the heroes of his boyhood, his country or his liberal sentiments. A commendable virtue in a human being. But a crippling one for an artist.[53]

Anthony Lane from the *Independent on Sunday* claimed that *Chaplin* showed 'an uncanny ability to leapfrog over real interest and hit the dull spots'. Lane pointed to the end of the film with Chaplin's return to Hollywood where the actor is seen to 'pretend to cry with pride' as having 'little to do with Chaplin, and an awful lot to do with Sir Richard Attenborough; it's his idea of the perfect end to a lovely life'.[54]

The press book described *Chaplin* as '[e]ntertaining, dramatic and revealing'. Many critics challenged this perspective. The *Sunday Telegraph* declared that '[s]eldom can such an action-packed life have been turned into such a tepid biopic'.[55] *The Times* described *Chaplin* as 'a valiant but deeply flawed film', while for the *Mail on Sunday* it was 'homage without humour'.[56] Philip French in the *Observer* was rare in his almost universal praise for the film, declaring that 'Attenborough's admirable film acknowledges the stature of a life, art and presence to which no one can be indifferent.'[57] The *Daily Telegraph* called the film 'a labour of love; a big, glossy, old-fashioned bio-pic, well acted and skilfully mounted', but criticised it for falling 'somewhere between homage to the genius of silent cinema and an attempt to penetrate the mystique'.[58] Of the journals *Sight and Sound* was the most constructive, declaring that *Chaplin* is a film 'that is always watchable, and always manages to stay the right side of hagiography'.[59] In contrast *Empire* claimed that *Chaplin* 'ultimately fails either to illuminate the genius of its subject or to excite it as a story'.[60] For Attenborough the British reviews reflected a national obsession, asserting: 'I think, in a strange way, particularly in the Metropolis, there is a requirement to denigrate our heroes and people who have some kind of reputation.'[61]

Many of the American reviews took a similarly hostile opinion. *Village Voice* complained that Attenborough had made 'another big, bland biopic'.[62] The *New Yorker* called it 'diffuse, gimmicky, and damnably respectable', while Roger Ebert in the *Chicago Sun-Times* called *Chaplin* 'a disappointing, misguided movie that has all of the parts in place to be a much better one'.[63] Vincent Canby in the *New York Times* was overtly critical, asserting: '*Chaplin* is to serious biography, even to Mr Attenborough's *Gandhi*, what unfortified cornflakes are to real food. It's slick packaging around what is mostly warm air.'[64]

Despite the adverse critical opinion *Chaplin* was nominated for three Academy Awards, Best Actor (Downey), Best Art/Set Design (Stuart Craig and Chris A. Butler) and Best Original Score (John Barry) but failed to win in any category. Downey and Geraldine Chaplin had also been nominated for Golden Globe Awards held in January, losing out to Al Pacino in *Scent of a Woman* (Martin Brest) and Joan Plowright in *Enchanting April* (Mike Newell). Downey, however, had success in Britain by winning a BAFTA award.

The divisive perception of *Chaplin* had significant implications on how the film was received. Chaplin's name was celebrated by the unveiling of two plaques, one outside his former London home in Kennington High Street and the other in Leicester Square by Sir Ralph Richardson. A compilation of unseen Chaplin films entitled *Unknown Chaplin* was released in Britain in 1983 and in America in 1986. In 1989 there were worldwide celebrations of the centenary of Chaplin's birth. *My Autobiography* was also republished by Penguin to coincide with the opening of the film. However, there was also evidence of hostility towards Chaplin. In 1988 a letter to the *Daily Telegraph*, entitled 'Cry Chaplin!', responded to the proposed film and gave an indication that it would not be universally welcomed. The letter, employing a sarcastic tone, declared Attenborough as the 'hope of the oppressed, whose works (*Gandhi, Cry Freedom, Cry Attenborough!* etc) ... has acquired the right to make a film about Charlie Chaplin'. It continued:

> With his smug Left-wing politics, his prodigious vanity, his absurd belief that he was a world-class thinker, his sheer unfunniness in any role but that of clown (and his second-rate ability in that), Chaplin is an ideal subject for Attenborough's talents.[65]

Chaplin's sexual and political activities were also of concern in America. In 1991, the *Hollywood Reporter* related concerns of Chaplin's past, predicting that the role of Chaplin in the film would be a 'bittersweet' one. It reminded its readers that '[t]here was considerable moral outcry and press attention focusing on Chaplin's extramarital pursuits – many of them with beautiful teenagers' and 'the subject of a paternity suit in 1944'. The article continued to record other 'concerns', including Chaplin's refusal to acquire American citizenship, and his later subpoena by the House Un-American Activities Committee to testify about his alleged communist activities.[66] The anti-Chaplin feeling was also evident during filming in California when Robinson was asked: 'Why are you making a film about that damned commie?'[67] Robinson, however, claimed that Chaplin 'was never disliked and despised as much as he was in Britain'. This view was earlier endorsed by Chaplin's widow who maintained that: '[i]f Charlie had died drunk, broken and miserable, (the British) would have adored him, but they will never forgive him for dying wealthy and happy.'[68] While Attenborough later declared that making *Chaplin* was 'one hell of a film' and 'the toughest of my life', the film was nevertheless a disappointment.[69] While *Chaplin* suffers from an uneven narrative, the film's several remarkable performances all serve to enhance it. In addition to Downey's convincing interpretation of Chaplin, Geraldine Chaplin as Hannah, Kevin Kline as Douglas Fairbanks and Paul Rhys as Sydney Chaplin all provide notable supporting roles. The result is a sensitive, although arguably, too hagiographic representation, of Chaplin's life.

Although Attenborough had filmed two further biopics *Shadowlands* (1993) and *In Love and War* (1996), with differing critical and popular success, he continued with the genre by embarking on *Grey Owl*. Like Chaplin, Archie Belaney also had a problematic reputation in Britain. While *Chaplin* explored the life of the professional stage and screen actor, *Grey Owl* looked at a performer whose clever impersonation as a Native American Indian convinced a worldwide audience of his tribal authenticity. The 'acting' was deemed so credible that his true English origins were only discovered by a journalist from the *North Bay Nuggett* in 1936 when Grey Owl was at the height of his popularity. Out of respect for Grey Owl's conservation work, his fraudulent existence remained a secret until the day after his death in April 1938, when the news broke and resulted in astonishing disbelief. His deception even tricked the British Establishment. At the request of Princess Elizabeth, Grey Owl was invited to give a private performance to the Royal Family in 1937. The Court Circular declared that it was in the presence of 'Their Majesties, and Queen Mary, the Princess Elizabeth and the Princess Margaret'.[70]

Attenborough witnessed Grey Owl's 'act' when he and his brother, David, saw a performance at De Montfort Hall in Leicester during his second world tour. Attenborough recalls being totally besotted by him: 'the fascination for me lay in his showmanship, in his stage presence, which was phenomenal'.[71] He also recalled Grey Owl's striking appearance as 'an impossibly exotic figure in those pre-war days of 1935', for a population who, before the war, had only seen white people in

Britain.[72] Part of the attraction was that interest in Grey Owl's conservation methods had grown since articles were published in magazines and periodicals such as *Country Life*. The press, too, were keen to publicise his work. In 1931 an article in *The Times* related Grey Owl's almost Damascene conversion from a trapper, described as 'one of the most prolific and profitable fur-bearers of the Canadian wilds' to becoming a conservationist, when the saving of the beaver from extinction became his life's work.[73] The conservation message later expanded into an environmental cause which was relayed to the world through Grey Owl's numerous publications and by two world tours in 1936 and 1937.

The man who became known as the 'modern Hiawatha' and 'first eco-warrior' was born Archibald (Archie) Stansfeld Belaney in Hastings, England in 1888.[74] Archie was brought up in a strict disciplinarian regime by his maiden aunts, Ada and Carrie, after his father's early departure and his mother's difficulties in bringing him up. At the age of 17, Archie moved to Canada where he was adopted by the Ojibwas tribe who bestowed on him the name 'Grey Owl'- 'he who flies by night'. Archie absorbed himself into their community by observing their customs and traditions and married a native Indian, Angele. The couple had a daughter before Archie formed another relationship with Marie Gerrard with whom he fathered a son. At the start of the First World War, Archie joined the Canadian Army, enlisting in the 13th Montreal Battalion, but, after suffering a gunshot wound to his foot, he returned to the Canadian hospital in Hastings to recover. There he married Ivy Holmes (who later divorced him for bigamy) before returning to Canada where he met Pony, a half-Canadian, half-Iroquois waitress and bestowed on her the Indian name Anahareo before 'marrying' her in a native Indian ceremony in June 1926. Pony was credited for changing Archie from a traditional hunter and trapper to a conservationist after she was appalled at the cruelty inflicted on the beavers, whose fur was used in the fashionable top hats in Europe. As Donald B. Smith later commented, '[h]er concern slowly had its effect on Archie, gradually weakening his resolve to trap'.[75] Although the film focuses on Archie's two-year relationship with Pony, there is no mention of the couple's daughter, Dawn, born in 1932, nor to the events leading to their separation the same year. A further inexactness occurs when the film shows Archie confessing his true identity to Pony. In reality, Pony claims that she did not learn the true identity of Archie until after his death.

Grey Owl's false identity was later claimed to be one of the major hoaxes of the twentieth century. The hoax was much debated in *The Times* after the newspaper, itself taken in by the deception, published an appreciative obituary of Grey Owl's conservation work on 14 April

1938, the day after his death. On 18 April, an article entitled, 'Was Grey Owl an Englishman?' responded to the allegations made in Canada that he was not a genuine Indian. While evidence to support this claim had come from several people, the article claimed that its most 'disturbing evidence' was Grey Owl's 'correct English accent'.[76] On 20 April, a letter from Lovat Dickson, Grey Owl's publisher, denied any suggestions of him being English. Dickson, who also claimed Grey Owl as a friend, categorically denied the story, backing it up with a 'biography' of his life, maintaining he had been born in Arizona. Dickson also maintained that '[t]ruth was a passion with Grey Owl. That grave and kindly face could not have hidden a deceit like this.'[77] On 21 April, *The Times* revealed that while Dickson's claim had been backed by Major J.A. Wood, Superintendant of the National Park in Prince Albert, it pointed out that this claim was questioned by the Misses Ada and Carrie Belaney of Hastings, asserting that Grey Owl was their nephew. Another letter, from Bill Gribble, an acquaintance of Grey Owl's, asserted that if a fake, Grey Owl 'must indeed have been one of the greatest actors of all time' to have lived a deception.[78] Attenborough was able to recall his mother's stoical reaction to Grey Owl's deception, to which she had declared: 'His identity doesn't mean a damn. The only important thing is what he came to tell us.'[79] The significance of her remark encouraged him to make the film, intending, as he had hoped with *Chaplin*, to restore Grey Owl's reputation for a modern-day generation.

Grey Owl's success in maintaining his lengthy disguise and convincing so many people of his fake ancestry was an astounding feat of acting. By focusing on the contrasting identities of the private Archie and the public Grey Owl, the name given to his pseudo-image, the picture emerges of a man who is unhappy living the conventional life he was born into in England. Using his adopted life *Grey Owl* explores the issue of Archie's national identity, which contrasts with that of Chaplin. Whereas Chaplin maintained his original links (by refusing to give up his British citizenship), Archie actively rejects any association. By denying his true ancestry, Archie effectively becomes a free person eschewing any claims to the dominant values to which British people may aspire. Although there is no mention in the film, Archie 'served with distinction as a sniper and crack shot' in the First World War, while Chaplin is perceived to have been happy not to participate.

Grey Owl is a partial biopic as it restricts its focus to a specific era of Archie's life. It is also a part-romance film with its exploration of Archie's relationship with Pony and may also be considered a historical film, through its exploration of environmental issues that existed in the 1930s. *Grey Owl* is characteristic of Attenborough's films through its high production values which feature the picturesque landscapes of the Canadian wilderness, the detailed exploration of the traditional American Indian lives through meticulous (some would argue slow and methodical) attention being paid to detail of native costumes, traditional dances and ethnic ceremonies which offers a specific image of the past. Andrew Higson argues that this form of 'visual perfection' of films and their 'fetishization of period details create a fascinating but self-enclosed world'.[80] In *Grey Owl* the audience become voyeurs on the private life of the American Indians as a contrast to the more conventional societies that many of the audiences live within.

Grey Owl employs a flashback technique with a circular narrative, in a similar manner to *Gandhi*. The film begins and ends with a journalist informing Grey Owl that he knows his true identity, thus ending the public life of the performer, and allowing the audience to know of the deception. The narrative of the film explains the circumstances, viewing Grey Owl's lifestyle and his developing romance with Pony. Picturesque images are held together by George Fenton's music, both rousing and tranquil, the score interposing First Nation Indian music with a classical style merging the two traditions together, a technique that had been successfully employed previously in *Gandhi* and *Cry Freedom*. Attenborough also makes use of actuality footage which changes into modern reproductions, thus confusing the true identities further. The technique, used in *Gandhi* and in *Chaplin*, is employed, most notably, with Grey Owl's visit to Buckingham Palace, the authenticity of the original aided by the authoritative tones of the narrator in the voice-over.

As with *Chaplin*, the original idea for *Grey Owl* came from Diana Hawkins who, after reading an article in *Country Life*, saw the potential for a film that had 'the most wonderful story with a phenomenal twist to it'.[81] The 'twist', the revelation of Grey Owl's true identity, added the cinematic entertainment factor to the more serious theme and message of conversation that the film was to deliver. The theme of conservation was particularly topical for the 1990s. Conservation and environmentalism had gained momentum over the last three decades with national and international organisations formed to deal with the issues. These included the World Wildlife Fund, founded in 1961; Friends of the Earth, launched in America in 1969, and Greenpeace, originally known as the Greenpeace Foundation, which was founded in Vancouver in 1971. The collective work of these non-political organisations influenced the Thatcher government in the late 1980s when it became receptive to environmental concerns that tallied with the free-market economic policies they supported. In 1990 the Environmental Protection Act was passed covering a wide range of issues concerning global warming and climate control. The same year the Prince of Wales featured in a documentary programme for the BBC, *The Earth in Balance: A Personal View of the Environment*, broadcast in May. The Prince made a 'personal, impassioned call for a reassessment of man's relationship with the natural world'.[82] This message echoed similar concerns that Grey Owl had raised in the 1930s. Another significant individual concerned with animal conservation at the time was David Attenborough, Richard's younger brother. David had a long history in broadcasting wildlife programmes, joining the BBC in 1952 and making a series of programmes called *Zoo Quest* which brought images of wildlife into public viewing. In 1965 he became Controller of BBC2 and after a spell as Director of Programmes for BBC Television he returned to making nature programmes becoming the leading presenter of wildlife programmes including *Life on Earth* (1979), *The Living Planet* (1983) and *The Private Life of Plants* (1995).

As a conservation film *Grey Owl* can be said to be part of a small cycle which began with *Born Free* (James Hill, 1966) and continued with its sequel, *Living Free* (Jack Couffer, 1972). In the 1980s, *Gorillas in the Mist* (Michael Apted, 1988) revived the theme, while in the 1990s *Free Willy* (Simon Wincer, 1993), which relates to the concerns of a captured Orca, continued it. The 1990s had also witnessed attempts to restore Grey Owl's name and reputation. In 1994, *The Times* declared Grey Owl 'a remarkable English eccentric who fooled 1930s Britain, King George VI and *The Times* into thinking he was a Red Indian brave', but, despite the scandal, the 'message of his conservation work survived'.[83] On 4 January 1995 the story of Grey Owl was told on the BBC1 children's programme, *The Really Wild Show*, a collaboration made between the BBC's Natural History Unit and Children's Television. The documentary was repeated, for the benefit of adults, the following day on BBC2. A film, released at the end of the decade, thus appeared well timed to take advantage of the newly established interest in Grey Owl.

In the 1990s, the hostile reception which *Chaplin* had received had been tempered by the greater success of *Shadowlands*, which had re-established Attenborough's credibility as an adept director of biographical films. *In Love and War*, however, despite its comparable theme and subject to *Shadowlands* and similar traditional style, the film failed to gain success at the box office or critical approval. Despite this disappointment, Attenborough continued a similar formulaic pattern for *Grey Owl*, again focusing on a romance which had life-changing consequences for the male protagonist. One notable and critical difference was Attenborough's reliance on only one star actor, Pierce Brosnan, in the title role, using an unknown actress, Annie Galipeau, as the female lead. Although Attenborough had successfully selected non-cinematic names for the leading roles for *Young Winston* and *Gandhi*, both Simon Ward and Ben Kingsley were experienced stage actors. Both films had also employed experienced film actors in several minor roles thus giving the star a supporting framework throughout the film on which to aid their performance. In *Grey Owl* Stephanie Cole and Renée Asherson, both acclaimed British actresses, had only cameo roles as Archie's two aunts. The additional minor roles were all assigned to Canadian actors, who were predominantly unknown outside their own country. The employment of only one 'name', in conjunction with Attenborough's quest to produce a film that was devoid of any sex or violence, nor enhanced by special effects, had a significant impact on the marketing of the film and its failure to gain theatrical release in America.

The gestation of *Grey Owl* lasted eight years before production commenced, the second longest of any Attenborough film after *Gandhi*. On 21 August 1995, *Variety* announced that *Grey Owl* was to begin filming in the spring of 1996, but financial difficulties halted the project. The chance to reunite the working partnership of Attenborough and Jake Eberts, who had supported *Gandhi*, was a welcome reprieve. Eberts was now the owner of Allied Productions as well as being an independent producer based in Canada and, thus, ideally placed for filming *Grey Owl*. Eberts's keenness to work with Attenborough again was apparent:

> This is a man I adored being in business with, and someone who has a remarkable talent for directing actors. Very few directors today have the patience, experience and skill to get an actor to perform at his peak. Richard is someone who attracts actors. Secondly, I knew he genuinely *felt* this story.[84]

Eberts also revealed *Grey Owl* as 'the perfect project', explaining that '[w]ithout being overtly political, it has a very strong message of hope, about how important this fragile earth is and how important animals are to our existence.'[85] Attenborough also reinstated the name 'Beaver', employed with his first production company, Beaver Films, formed with Bryan Forbes in 1958, by forming Beaver Productions for *Grey Owl*. The filmmaker's first major task was to obtain the rights to the two principal biographies of Grey Owl, *The Land of Shadows* by Donald B. Smith and *The Wilderness Man: The Amazing Story of Grey Owl*, by Lovat Dickson, published in 1973. While Smith's study was easy to obtain, Dickson's work, which had been under the control of several film and television companies, was more problematic requiring difficult and lengthy negotiations and 'tons of money in legal expenses'.[86]

William Nicholson was appointed as scriptwriter, due to his success with *Shadowlands* and his long-standing interest in American Native life. Brosnan was chosen for the title role, having the 'correct profile' and the physical abilities that the role demanded. Other actors who were also considered included Daniel Day-Lewis, who had previously played a major Indian role in *The Last of the Mohicans* (Michael Mann, 1992), Alan Rickman, Kevin Kline and Aidan Quinn. Attenborough's decision over Brosnan had been made before the actor had appeared in the James Bond film *GoldenEye* (Martin Campbell, 1995), so was not influenced by his success or characterisation in the part. Brosnan was also keen for a different role:

> It is an actor's dream to do such a role as this ... He was an amazing man, and a fine writer. And I do believe he was a great man in many respects, in what he stood for. What he wanted for this planet was profound. It's a rather complex part and, for an actor, it plays on many different levels.[87]

Brosnan was equally impressed by Grey Owl's environmental concerns being a conservationist himself. He had worked on several environmental campaigns, including one in Mexico to preserve breeding areas of the grey whale and had also supported the work of his long-term partner (and now wife), Keeley Shay-Smith, a committed environmental speaker.

In 1994, however, financial negotiations with *Grey Owl* broke down and in June 1995 the production was announced to be 'indefinitely delayed'. For the next two years there was little progress. Nicholson became involved with writing other scripts and Brosnan made his second Bond film *Tomorrow Never Dies* (Roger Spottiswoode, 1997). Attenborough also returned to acting in *The Lost World: Jurassic Park* (Steven Spielberg, 1997) and *Elizabeth* (Shekhar Kapur, 1998). In the autumn of 1997, the situation altered when Eberts, an investment banker by profession, observed a change in financial regulations whereby new tax advantages in Canada for Anglo-Canadian co-productions became available, which resulted in a saving of nearly 10 per cent of the budget. Eberts assumed total financial control of the project himself and succeeded in securing a deal with Largo Entertainment, an American subsidiary of JVC, the Japanese electronics company who dealt in film distribution in 'foreign' markets, outside North America. This enabled Largo to negotiate deals in Germany, Italy and Spain and in Canada with a Montreal company, Prima Film. The deals, once secured, enabled pre-production to begin.

During the hiatus, Brosnan's fame had risen to star status and, as a result, had become less available for filming. He had also set up a film company, Irish Dream Time, with his production partner, Beau St Clair. Brosnan produced and acted in *The Nephew* (Eugene Brady, 1998) and his company produced the remake of *The Thomas Crown*

Affair (John McTiernan, 1999) with him taking the starring role. These extra commitments resulted in the role of Grey Owl being offered to Brosnan three times before he finally accepted it. Brosnan's delay in accepting the role also helped to cast Galipeau to play the role of Pony/ Anhareo who, after initially being dismissed as 'too young', was now sufficiently mature. Attenborough had been determined to cast a First Nation Canadian actress, claiming that because he was making a film about a 'phony Native Canadian, the one who was real (in the story) had better be real.'[88] Although Galipeau as half-Indian fulfilled this requirement, she had little film experience, her one small role being in *Map of the Human Heart* (Vincent Ward, 1992).

Production began on 17 March 1998 and lasted for twelve weeks. Filming took place predominantly in Quebec, taking advantage of Canada's spectacular natural landscapes, and ended with three days in Hastings. The weather caused several difficulties. Late-falling snow that was slow to clear required rescheduling of the planned order of filming, while an ice storm, resulting from the El Niño sea current, damaged trees and new locations had to be found. The worst problem, however, concerned the principal action scene which involved a canoe battle between Grey Owl and a group of men opposed to his environmental stance. The battle had been prepared and rehearsed by professional stuntmen but on the day of filming, on the last Saturday at the end of a two-week location stay, they failed to arrive. It was later discovered that their previous film had overrun its time and the stuntmen were offered financial incentives to stay and complete the assignment. Attenborough attempted to film the sequence with local actors, but it failed to reach his required standard and the scene was deleted from the final editing.[89]

Another major problem was the difficult relationship between Brosnan and Galipeau. During filming, Attenborough declared that the chemistry between them was 'wonderful', but he later conceded that 'the scenes between them don't work as they should'.[90] Much of this was due to Galipeau's language difficulties due to her native French, although her lack of acting experience was also a factor. Although Attenborough had been initially convinced that the language problems could be overcome, he later conceded that 'because she was always translating into English, she could never get the colloquial flow of dialogue'.[91] Brosnan also thought Galipeau's voice inadequate and requested that it should be 're-voiced' during editing, a request that was refused.

Brosnan developed a good relationship with Attenborough. He praised Attenborough's direction claiming that '[h]e is everything that has been spoken about him or written about him', and commented that he 'gives care and consideration to the details of the performance'.[92] The meticulous preparation, careful construction of scenes and continual reviews of the script was the basis of Attenborough's policy:

> I tend to do more setups than some directors because I love painting and composition. Composition in film must be attractive and also serve the telling of the story and the facility of the actors. When I talk to the actors before a scene, it's really only about how the characters will react to that moment, how that scene relates to other scenes. A great deal of work is done before we come anywhere near the floor, the exploration of the character, the motivation. An actor must know his character backwards before arriving on set, and of course, the lines must be very sure.[93]

The film was produced at a cost estimated to be $30 million.[94] Distribution rights had not been obtained before production but this was not unusual for films produced by Eberts who claimed, 'I still think there's a market for good, intelligent stories and in *Grey Owl*, we had a top director, a great story and an international star.'[95] Although films featuring American Indians were known to have a 'limited market', *Dances with Wolves* (Kevin Costner, 1990) challenged this assumption by grossing $184,208,848, becoming the third most successful film in America that year.[96] Like *Grey Owl*, *Dances with Wolves* featured a star name (Costner) alongside native actors. Twentieth Century-Fox, MGM and Warner Bros. all showed interest but despite the vigorous publicity campaign that Canada provided, *Grey Owl* failed to gain theatrical release in America, instead going straight to video through Twentieth Century-Fox Home Entertainment. The presence of Brosnan outside of his James Bond persona was not sufficient to persuade the executives to distribute the film. Moreover, *The Nephew*, Brosnan's former film, had also been refused distribution. Although *Grey Owl* succeeded in gaining a limited distribution on the art-house circuit, without general release it became a commercial failure and labelled as one of the costliest video premières in America.

Canada, however, was particularly proud to be associated with *Grey Owl*. The chief executive of the Canadian Distributor, Remstar, Andrew Austin, paid $900,000 for the Canadian rights.[97] *Grey Owl* opened in Canada on 1 October 1999 and was distributed by Miramax. With no general release in the United States, Canada was responsible for the bulk of North American opinion. Most reviewers were unimpressed with the film, although many commented favourably on the picturesque scenery. The *Calgary Sun* praised the 'breathtaking portraits of Canadian landscapes' but complained that the film 'doesn't have much bite'.[98] *Macleans* magazine delighted in Attenborough's framing the film 'with majestic images of the Canadian North' but remarked, 'it's a shame that such an unconventional hero receives such conventional treatment.'[99]

The *Montreal Gazette* questioned how the filmmakers could take 'such an intrinsically intriguing story and make it seem so mundane?'. It also criticised Galipeau for not being 'up to the task at hand' and for delivering her lines 'in wooden fashion'.[100] The *Toronto Sun*, in contrast, praised her performance, asserting that she 'projects an innocence that keeps everything grounded and believable'.[101] Further criticism came from The *Globe and Mail* which blamed Attenborough's casting of Brosnan as 'trading in his 007 finery for a headdress and braids, the conclusion is unmistakeable: Seems that, out to save the planet from doom, Grey Owl is just Bond in buckskin.'[102] The *Vancouver Sun* was less harsh, declaring that 'Seeing Brosnan in braids and buckskins takes some getting used to, but once you accept him, you discover that he is the strongest thing in the movie.'[103] For the *Ottawa Citizen*, Brosnan 'demonstrates an inner fire we haven't seen before'.[104]

The response from America was particularly unfavourable. *Variety* described the script as 'lacklustre', the direction, 'old-fashioned' and the casting 'seriously questionable'.[105] The *Georgia Straight* attacked the film for 'the problem of emotion', declaring: 'It is a peculiarity of Attenborough's cinema that his movies often straddle the fine line between sentimentality (unearned emotion) and awkward feeling (genuine sentiments that strike our sophisticated brains as embarrassingly mawkish).'[106] *Entertainment Weekly* praised the 'superlative production design' and the 'stunning location photography', but was critical of the pace declaring that watching the film was 'akin to swimming through an enormous vat of caramel'.[107]

Grey Owl opened in Britain on 3 November 2000, thirteen months after its opening in Canada, receiving some of the worst reviews of any of Attenborough's films. Many reviewers were influenced by a British press screening where laughter was heard at the sound of the word 'beaver', with its contemporary and colloquial sexual context overriding the reference to the animal. Peter Bradshaw in the *Guardian* referred to the 'tittering' at the screening which he explained related to the term beaver, as employed in *The Naked Gun* (David Zucker, 1988). In the film, Frank Drebin (Leslie Nielson) looks at Jane (Priscilla Presley) and declares 'nice beaver', to which Jane replies, 'thanks I've just had it stuffed' before handing him the now inanimate object. While Bradford declared he could hear the whisper of 'split beaver' in the stalls when Brosnan is seen holding the two beaver kittens, he also criticised the actor's dancing, describing it like 'the Bishop of Bath and Wells doing the funky chicken'.[108] The *Independent on Sunday* claimed that by presenting 'Pierce "007" Brosnan playing the man responsible for all this beaver-love [and] you've got an audience helpless with giggles'.[109] Other reviews were equally critical. Philip French in the *Observer* dismissed the portrayal of Grey Owl's life as 'sentimentalised and Disneyfied'.[110] *The Times* asked the question, 'why is Attenborough's film an epic slice of *Boy's Own* blandness?'[111] Alexander Walker described *Grey Owl* as 'one damn dull scene after another, relieved mainly by sentimental overkill pushed to the extreme of unintended hilarity'.[112] For the *Independent*, *Grey Owl* 'goes horribly awry'.[113] Of the journals *Sight and Sound* was the most positive, asserting that Brosnan was 'excellent in an unlikely role' and claiming that the film 'abounds with genuine pleasures'.[114] *Film Review* thought *Grey Owl* was a 'fascinating tale' but complained that 'Attenborough was not the man to bring his story to the screen, nor Brosnan the actor to play him.'[115]

The lack of an American theatrical release was a bitter disappointment to Attenborough and to Brosnan. Attenborough criticised the American distributors for their methods on BBC Radio 4, claiming 'they don't know how to sell it – and by that they mean it doesn't have the supposed pre-requisites of commercial success.' Although his disappointment was evident, Attenborough declared that he was not going to compromise his personal standards, asserting: 'I don't accept the pornography of violence under any circumstances and if that's a rerequisite to getting a distribution in America, I'll accept the non-distribution.'[116] Brosnan maintained that *Grey Owl* 'was made for the cinema', and criticised the American distributors for 'lacking in imagination' and attacked their explanation that they could not come up with a strategy to sell the film to American audiences.[117] The *Toronto Star*, however, indicated that Brosnan was not totally happy with the film's strong focus on romance at the expense of Grey Owl's other life experiences, an omission which he saw as detrimental to the film, claiming: 'You lose out Archie's experience of the war, you lose out the demons of the booze and you lose out the bigamy and all the women he had in his life.'[118]

With the limited release in America, the audience figures available offer only a partial view of the popular response. *Variety* gave the reported figures for the week 11–17 October 1999 as $235,901. The total box office in America was $632,617.[119] In Britain the film gained a box-office total of £150,934 with the opening weekend of £46,873, the lowest figures for any of Attenborough's films.[120] Other British films which fared better at the time included *The Golden Bowl* (James Ivory), *Topsy Turvy* (Mike Leigh) and *Billy Elliot* (Stephen Daldry), the top-grossing British film, which made £16,661,492.[121]

The lack of a pivotal action sequence appears to be a significant factor in the poor response to *Grey Owl*. The film's nostalgic portrayal of a simple lifestyle is so divorced from the pace of modern life in the 1990s that it is a total contrast to the action-packed thriller films that dominated the decade, with *Gladiator* (Ridley Scott) and *Crouching Tiger, Hidden Dragon* (Ang Lee) being the most popular films in 2000.[122] Another factor can be attributed to the press, both in America and in Britain, which published pre-production articles advertising the fact that James Bond, rather than Pierce Brosnan, was to play Grey Owl. Headlines such as 'British Knight Brings 007 to Quebec' and 'James Bond to star as Red Indian in Hastings' indicated that the film would be associated with 'Bondian' qualities that would have interested a different audience (young and predominantly male) rather than one middle class/middle aged at which *Grey Owl* was targeted.[123] *The Times* review, which claimed that Brosnan 'looks like James Bond with a couple of tasty pigtails hanging down his back', did nothing to detach Bond from Grey Owl in the public consciousness.[124] The contradictions between the public and perceived identities which *Grey Owl* explored were also a significant factor in the film's lack of appeal to both critics and audiences.

Grey Owl is a much better film than the critical response would suggest. The strength of the narrative, the stunning photography and the incorporation of Native American Indian ceremonies and customs, provide an enjoyable and also informative production, despite the absence of the key action scene. While criticism of Gallipeau's performance is to a degree justified, she nevertheless presents an engaging and vulnerable contrast to Brosnan's tough masculine role. Commercially, however, *Grey Owl* was a failure. It would be another nine years before Attenborough was to direct again.

Notes

1. John Woodward, 'Cinema 1989–90: Production Focus', *Film and Television Handbook*, London, 1991, p. 25.
2. Alexander Walker, *Icons in the Fire: The Rise and Fall of Practically Everyone in the British Film Industry, 1984–2000*, London, 2004, pp. 96–7.
3. *Sunday Times*, 23 July 1989.
4. Walker, *Icons in the Fire*, p. 113.
5. *Evening Standard*, 12 March 1990.
6. Richard Attenborough, *In Search of Gandhi*, London, 1982, p. 31.
7. Richard Brooks, 'Charlie Is Dickie's Darling', *Observer*, 15 November 1992.
8. *Daily Telegraph*, 4 January 1992; *Observer*, 15 October 1992.
9. Andrew Billen, 'Dickie, Charlie and a Movie Make Three', *The Times*, 28 December 1988.
10. David Gritten, 'Making a Proper Charlie', *Daily Telegraph*, 4 January 1992.
11. Gritten, 'Lady and the Little Tramp', *Daily Telegraph*, 16 December 1992.
12. Brooks, 'Charlie Is Dickie's Darling'.
13. Chaplin's coffin was stolen on 1 March 1978 and was recovered on 17 May.
14. Brooks, 'Charlie Is Dickie's Darling'.

15 Bryan Forbes, *A Divided Life*, London, 1992, pp. 296 and 298.
16 Forbes interviewed on *The Stepford Wives*, DVD, Paramount Pictures, 2004, VFC61794.
17 William Goldman, *Adventures in the Screen Trade: A Personal View of Hollywood*, London, 1984, p. 279.
18 William Boyd, 'Give Credits Where They're Due', *The Times*, 12 December 1992.
19 David Robinson, *Richard Attenborough*, p. 85.
20 Script S17786, 'Charlie' (*Chaplin*), January 1991, BFI, London.
21 Quoted in Minty Church, 'Little Tramp Rides Again', *Sunday Telegraph*, 13 December 1992.
22 Brooks, 'Charlie Is Dickie's Darling'.
23 Quoted in Cyndi Stivers, 'Trampled', *Premiere* (USA) (emphasis in original), 6:5 (January 1993), p. 69.
24 Press Book (small) *Chaplin* microfiche, BFI.
25 Goldman, *Which Lie Did I Tell: More Adventures in the Screen Trade*, London, 2001, p. 332.
26 Boyd, 'Give Credits Where They're Due'.
27 Quoted in Stivers, 'Trampled', *Premiere* (USA), 6:5 (January 1993), p. 69.
28 *Ibid.*
29 Andy Dougan, *The Actors' Director: Richard Attenborough Behind the Camera*, Edinburgh, 1994, p. 141.
30 Quoted in Stivers, 'Trampled', p. 65.
31 Brooks, 'Charlie Is Dickie's Darling'.
32 Robinson, *Chaplin: His Life and Art*, London, 2001, p. 317.
33 Jeffrey Richards, *Films and British National Identity: From Dickens to Dad's Army*, Manchester, 1992, p. 2.
34 Robinson, *Chaplin*, p. 622.
35 Quoted on *The South Bank Show* 'Special', ITV (Granada) 15 November 1992; *League of Gentlemen*, DVD, Granada Ventures, 2007, VFC55197.
36 Quoted in Dougan, *The Actor's Director*, p. 143.
37 *Ibid.*
38 Brooks, 'Charlie Is Dickie's Darling'.
39 William Boyd, 'Give Credits Where They're Due'.
40 *Evening Standard*, 5 November 1992.
41 *Ibid.*
42 *Screen International*, 25 September 1992; Brooks, 'Charlie is Dickie's Darling'.
43 AC Nielsen, EDI (UK box-office returns), 2004, New York; BFI, London.
44 *Observer*, 20 December 1992, p. 40; *Guardian*, 17 December 1992.
45 *Independent on Sunday*, 20 December 1992.
46 *Daily Telegraph*, 17 December 1992.
47 *The Times*, 5 December 1992.
48 John Diamond, 'News from the Front', *The Times*, 12 December 1992.
49 George Perry, 'A Funny Thing, Comedy', *Sunday Times*, 6 December 1992.
50 *Sun*, 18 December 1992; *Today*, 18 December 1992.
51 *The Times*, 17 December, 1992.
52 *Morning Star*, 19 December 1992.
53 *Evening Standard*, 17 December 1992.
54 *Independent on Sunday*, 20 December 1992.
55 *Sunday Telegraph*, 20 December 1992.
56 *The Times*, 17 December 1992; *Mail on Sunday*, 20 December 1992.
57 *Observer*, 20 December 1992.
58 *Daily Telegraph*, 17 December 1992.
59 *Sight and Sound*, 3:1 (January 1993), p. 43.

60 *Empire*, 43 (January 1993), p. 20.
61 *Glasgow Herald*, 19 December 1992.
62 *Village Voice*, 29 December 1992, p. 60.
63 *New Yorker*, 28 December 1992, p. 204; *Chicago Sun Times*, 8 January 1993.
64 *New York Times*, 25 December 1992.
65 *Daily Telegraph*, 17 November 1988.
66 *Hollywood Reporter*, 17 January 1991.
67 Quoted in Geoffrey Macnab, 'Charlie Chaplin Rides Again', *Guardian*, 16 May 2003.
68 *Ibid*.
69 Quoted in Brooks, 'Charlie Is Dickie's Darling'.
70 'The Court Circular', *The Times*, 11 December 1937.
71 Attenborough, 'Animal Magic', *Guardian*, 27 October 2000.
72 *Ottawa Citizen*, 30 September 1999.
73 *The Times*, 13 August 1931.
74 Stansfeld was given as a middle name after his grandmother's uncle, George Stansfeld Furnish.
75 Donald B. Smith, *From the Land of Shadows: The Making of Grey Owl*, Saskatchewan, 1990, p. 82.
76 Ottawa Correspondent, 'Was Grey Owl an Englishman?', *The Times*, 18 April 1938.
77 *The Times*, 20 April 1938.
78 *The Times*, 22 April 1938.
79 Attenborough, 'Animal Magic'.
80 Andrew Higson, 'Re-presenting the National Past', in Lester Friedman (ed.), *Fires Were Started: British Cinema and Thatcherism*, Minneapolis, 1993, p. 113.
81 Production Notes, *Grey Owl*, microfiche, BFI, London.
82 Information obtained from website: http://ftvdb.bfi.org.uks, accessed 20 April 2008.
83 Alexandra Frean, 'Indian Brave Was Hoaxer from Hastings', *The Times*, 23 December 1994.
84 Production Notes, *Grey Owl*.
85 *Ibid*.
86 Jeremy Eberts, Dane Lanken and Anthony Hobbs, *The Making of Richard Attenborough's Grey Owl*, Ottawa, 1999, p. 7.
87 Production Notes, *Grey Owl*.
88 Tyler McLeod, 'Galipeau Is the Genuine Article', *Calgary Sun*, 5 October 1999.
89 Attenborough interviewed on '*True Brit*': Richard Attenborough and the British Cinema, Part 2, BBC Radio 4, transmitted on 25 April 2002.
90 Production Notes, *Grey Owl*; Robinson, *Richard Attenborough*, p. 104.
91 Robinson, *Richard Attenborough*, p. 104.
92 Production Notes, *Grey Owl*.
93 Eberts *et al*., *The Making of Richard Attenborough's Grey Owl*, pp. 27–8.
94 *Ibid*., p. 11. Other sources vary. *Variety*, 4 October 1999 estimated the budget was 'about $40 million', while the *Sunday Times*, 21 June 1998, gave it as $30 million (£18.75m.).
95 Eberts *et al*., *The Making of Richard Attenborough's Grey Owl*, p. 6.
96 www.boxofficemojo.com, accessed 28 August 2008.
97 *Playback*, 4 October 1999.
98 *Calgary Sun*, 1 October 1999.
99 *Macleans*, 4 October 1999.
100 *Montreal Gazette*, 1 October 1999.
101 *Ibid*.; *Toronto Sun*, 1 October 1999.

102 *Globe and Mail*, 1 October 1999.
103 *Vancouver Sun*, 1 October 1999.
104 *Ottawa Citizen*, 30 September 1999.
105 *Variety*, 4 October 1999.
106 *Georgia Straight*, 7 October 1999.
107 *Entertainment Weekly*, 526 (18 February 2000).
108 *Guardian*, 3 November 2000.
109 *Independent on Sunday*, 5 November 2000.
110 *Observer*, 5 November 2000.
111 *The Times*, 2 November 2000.
112 *Evening Standard*, 2 November 2000.
113 *Independent*, 3 November 2000.
114 *Sight and Sound*, New Series, 10:12 (December 2000), p. 48.
115 *Film Review*, 600 (December 2000), p. 29.
116 bbc.co.uk/1/hi/entertainment/981169.stm,1 November 2000, accessed 20 April 2008.
117 *Ibid.*
118 *Toronto Star*, 1 October 1999.
119 IMDb, www.imdb.com/title/tt0128239, accessed 20 April 2008.
120 AC, Nielsen EDI Ltd 2004, *Entertainment Data International*, UK Box Office Returns, BFI.
121 wwwbfi.org.uk/filmtvinfo/stats/boxoffice/ukfeatures-00, accessed 23 April 2008.
122 *Screen International*, 15 December 2000 and 14 January 2001.
123 *Georgia Straight*, 7–14 October 1999; *Daily Telegraph*, 19 January 1998.
124 *The Times*, 2 November 2000.

Brief encounters: *Shadowlands* (1993), *In Love and War* (1996) and *Closing the Ring* (2007)

7

Shadowlands and *In Love and War* continued Attenborough's interest in historical individuals by exploring the lives of two famous authors. Each was very differently received. *Shadowlands*, which portrayed the late-in-life romance of C.S. Lewis and the American Joy Gresham (née Davidman), was both critically and popularly acclaimed and became acknowledged as Attenborough's second most successful film. *Shadowlands* was also the film which gave Attenborough his greatest personal fulfilment. He declared: 'When people ask me which film I am most proud of, I can truthfully say that this is the one I am least ashamed of.'[1] Despite sharing several similar characteristics with *Shadowlands*, the similarity in form *In Love and War*, which recounted the brief romance of the author, Ernest Hemingway and Agnes von Kurowsky, the nurse who played a significant part in his recovery, failed to generate any significant popular or critical acclaim. Both films were unusual in Attenborough's later career for being initiated before he was engaged as director, thus denying him a controlling hand throughout the early stages of development. Both films had derived from other media. *Shadowlands* had been successful on television and in the theatre, while the story of *In Love and War* had been portrayed in fictional form in two versions of Hemingway's novel, *A Farewell to Arms*. *In Love and War* was also thematically linked to Attenborough's final production, *Closing the Ring*, filmed ten years later, in portraying a brief romance against a background of war.

The films were produced in contrasting economic climates. *Shadowlands* was produced in the early 1990s at a time when the cinema industry was in a poor economic state. *In Love and War* was produced in the middle of the decade, towards the turbulent end of seventeen years of Conservative government. Although the film industry had benefited from the launch of the National Lottery in 1995 which became a key source for funding films, it was becoming more difficult for British producers to obtain release for their films. *Screen Finance* reported in 1998 that '[n]early 60 per cent of British films involving a UK producer that went into production in 1996 have yet to be screened at a UK cinema.'[2] By virtue of its American registration, *In Love and War* formed part of the 70 per cent of American films that contributed to 80 per cent of the British box-office takings.[3] *In Love and War* was also made at a time when the industry was enjoying the results of the success of films such as *Four Weddings and a Funeral* (Mike Newell, 1994) and just prior to the release of *The Full Monty* (Peter Cattaneo, 1997) and *Shakespeare in Love* (John Madden, 1999). *Closing the Ring* is more related to Attenborough's own life, made following a time of personal tragedy following the deaths of his daughter and granddaughter in 2004. All three films returned Attenborough to the format of the intimate biography allowing him an opportunity to engage with the heritage film, a cycle which had gained momentum during the 1980s and early 1990s.

Attenborough was in great need of a successful production to restore his standing as a director after *Chaplin*. He had good reason to believe that *Shadowlands* would be the film to do this as the story had already been 'tested', first as a television play and later on stage, with both forms achieving popular and critical acclaim. *Shadowlands* was also an opportunity to explore people's behavioural patterns when severely tested coping with serious illness and impending death, a prospect that Attenborough relished. As he explained:

> I'm fascinated by people who've changed our lives ... I feel desperately deeply about what I want to say and the revealing of human frailty, one to the other, and the introduction of concern into the public arena is something that I love doing, and that works, I believe, more satisfactorily through fact rather than fiction.[4]

Shadowlands recalls the relationship between the British writer, C.S. (Jack) Lewis, and the American writer and poet, Joy Gresham. Their relationship was instigated by Joy who wrote to Lewis, beginning a long correspondence. Both shared intellectual interests as writers and held a common fascination with the Christian religion. Joy had been particularly attracted to Lewis's religious works, particularly *The Screwtape Letters* which she likened to her own 'Damascene' conversion. Although Joy had been born into a Jewish family, she became a communist while at university, later converting to Christianity after her marriage to a fellow New York writer, William Gresham. Lewis and Joy's relationship developed into a close friendship, after her arrival in England with Lewis agreeing to marry Joy to allow her to remain in the country after her divorce. Their friendship developed into romance after Joy was diagnosed with terminal cancer and they married 'properly' in a religious service held in Joy's hospital room. The couple enjoyed a limited time together before Joy's death on 13 July 1960.

The film follows the private life of the couple by exploring the various themes of national identity, class, religion, romance and death. It follows the couple's relationship as it progresses through correspondence, friendship, romance and finally death. The climax of their relationship is their hospital marriage, followed by Joy's period of remission from her illness, which allows the couple to enjoy a delayed honeymoon near the 'Golden Valley', the place depicted in the painting in Lewis's study. After a short period of marital happiness, Joy's condition rapidly deteriorates, and her life ends following an intensely emotional death scene; Jack's grief is contained and repressed until he and Douglas, Joy's younger son, find comfort in each other and cry openly together in the privacy of the attic, releasing their pent-up emotions. Although devastated by Joy's death, Lewis is later seen to find solace in his work and in his capacity as a stepfather to Douglas.

Shadowlands can also be seen in the context in the 1990s of other emotionally challenging films such as *The Remains of the Day* (James Ivory, 1993) and *The Age of Innocence* (Martin Scorsese, 1993). The film also revived an older 'genre' of the 'male weepie' which Nick James claims is 'the unrecognised genre of cinema'.[5] James detects the 'genre' beginning with *It's a Wonderful Life* (Frank Capra, 1946) and *Rebel Without a Cause* (Nicholas Ray, 1955). Both films were American productions which provided a contrast to the 'buttoned-up' emotions evident in British films at the time. *Shadowlands* may be termed a 'male weepie' as it openly exposes male feelings to the audience. This was in direct contrast to the reserve and restraint of emotions that British cinema had embraced in the past. *Brief Encounter* (David Lean, 1945), the story of a romantic relationship between two already married people, gives no outward display of emotion as decorum dictated at the time, with both characters remaining equally restrained. A similar restraint is detected in the original version of *The Browning Version* (Anthony Asquith, 1951) where Michael Redgrave is seen to break down with his back to the camera. In the remake of 1994, directed by Michael Figgis, the male protagonist played by Albert Finney weeps towards camera thus portraying the new openness of the time. William Nicholson, the scriptwriter for *Shadowlands*, observed that the reason for the plethora of films aimed at men was a reaction against feminism. He declared: 'No longer can men use their sense of responsibility as a reason for suppressing emotion. Men think in terms of powerful relations and I think that's okay as long as they don't deny their feelings.'[6] The practice of displaying open emotion is considered particularly 'non British', but one that Attenborough openly embraces. Richard Dyer has observed that 'Attenborough is a curious case in British film culture, an intensely emotional and absolutely mainstream figure in a supposedly unemotional national tradition'. For Dyer, Attenborough's public performances at award ceremonies are 'effusive, generous and lachrymose.' Dyer further comments: 'Such performance qualities also characterise his work as a director – and direction is only another kind of performance.'[7] Anthony Hopkins, who was engaged for his fifth film and second starring role under Attenborough's direction, admires and appreciates these qualities, declaring: 'It is unfashionable in this England to be positive. Richard Attenborough is the epitome of positive thinking, he has massive enthusiasm and genuine love for people. I like Attenborough because he overwhelms people with enthusiasm and affection.'[8]

Shadowlands can be said to have been responsible for initiating a trend of films linked to the heritage cycle through its exploration of literary figures. These films included *Tom and Viv* (Brian Gilbert, 1994) which portrayed the marriage of the British poet T.S. Eliot and his wife Vivienne Haigh-Wood, and *Carrington* (Christopher Hampton, 1995) which focuses on the relationship between the artist Dora Carrington and the writer Lytton Strachey. Like *Shadowlands*, *Carrington* first appeared as a television play for Channel 4, six years before it was released as a film.

Shadowlands is also difficult to position within a specific genre. By exploring a particular part of Lewis's life the film is most easily associated with the biopic. However, Attenborough claims that *Shadowlands* is 'not *quite* a biopic', acknowledging that it also contained fictional elements.[9] The film's representation of Britishness/Englishness also positions *Shadowlands* as a heritage film. Moreover, *Shadowlands* also displays several similarities to *Young Winston*. Both films display qualities that Andrew Higson has identified as characteristic of heritage films:

> The narratives of these films are typically slow moving and episodic, avoiding the efficient and economic causal development of the classical film. The concern for character, place, atmosphere and milieu tends to be more pronounced than dramatic, goal-directed action. Camerawork generally is fluid, artful and pictorialist, editing slow and undramatic. The use of long takes and deep focus, and long and medium shots rather than close-ups, produces a restrained aesthetic of display.[10]

While many of Higson's characteristics can be applied to *Shadowlands*, the film also emphasises additional British qualities. These include the depiction of tradition and ceremony with classical and rousing music featuring prominently using the combination of the sounds of Elgar and the national anthem. The ceremonial rituals of the University of Oxford, including the May Day chorister singing from Magdalen Tower and the 'Pageant of Learning', the latter a sequence of splendour set in the Sheldonian Theatre, further emphasise the quintessential Englishness. The grand traditions of Oxford are contrasted with the private world and sombre conditions of Lewis's house, still trapped in an era of post-war austerity.

Shadowlands is also rare as a heritage film without literary origins, and can therefore be linked to *Chariots of Fire* (Hugh Hudson, 1981) which was based on the events leading up to the 1924 Olympic Games portraying primarily real rather than fictional characters. Colin Welland, the screenwriter of *Chariots of Fire*, admitted that he exercised dramatic licence swapping and adapting historical facts to produce a better storyline. With *Shadowlands*, however, fiction is restricted to supporting figures and personal dialogue. The fiction also allows an exploration of class and social relevance through the character of Peter Whistler (James Frain), a student who challenges Lewis's authority and high moral stance. Whistler's working-class origins differentiate him from his fellow students. He is depicted as a loner, eating separately in the refectory and staying awake all night to sustain his passion of reading. He also steals books, as, he explains to Lewis, they are 'meant to be read, not left unopened on shelves'. Whistler's life is bound by his father's philosophy, 'we read to know we're not alone', a perspective which Lewis takes on board himself and one which he passes on to other students.

While Lewis enjoyed success during his lifetime he achieved greater acclaim after his death. During the 1980s a plethora of his works was published as well as several biographical studies. The instigation of national centres to store Lewis memorabilia, the C.S. Lewis Foundation (a British religious body), the Bodleian Library in Oxford and the formation of an American foundation assured a continued Anglo-American interest and the development of a C.S. Lewis industry in both countries.

The origins of *Shadowlands* resulted from the growing interest in Lewis's marriage to Joy which inspired the BBC director Norman Stone to research the possibility of the story becoming a television film. Stone, a committed Christian, decided to base the film on the religious aspects of Lewis's life. The BBC, however, refused to provide the £1 million budget required and the money was eventually obtained by a religious television foundation. Brian Sibley, who had originally worked with Stone on the project, produced a script. This was rejected by the BBC who commissioned William Nicholson to rewrite it, retaining Sibley as a nominal consultant. Nicholson was initially reluctant to become involved in the project due to his personal reservations based on his mother's bad experiences with Lewis. As he recalled: 'My mother was taught by Lewis at university and hated him. She thought he was an argumentative, woman-hating pig.'[11] Nicholson, however, changed his mind when he discovered strong similarities between his own life and that of Lewis. As he explained: 'At that time I was in my mid-30s, unmarried and reluctant to make a commitment ... I found myself empathizing with Lewis, identifying with the man locked in an emotional prison of his own making.'[12] Nicholson also wrote the theatre script before being commissioned to write a screenplay. The three versions contain variations in the narrative. Nicholson explained the changes required for the film version in a memo included with the script:

> The story is based on events that occurred in the lives of two real people – C.S. Lewis and Joy Davidman – but it is not a documentary drama. I have used part of their story, not used other parts, and imagined the rest. This is not because I'm careless about facts, but because I know that any story version of a life can only present a fragment of the reality. Rather than offer what a lawyer might define as the truth – a sequence of selected actions and quotations, every one of which can be proved to have originated from the real people, but which remains lifeless – I have tried to create dramatic characters that exist in their own right.[13]

The film, as demonstrated in Nicholson's preface, does not claim to be a true account. However, his statement is contradicted by the caption at the start of the film which states: 'This true story takes place in the University of Oxford in 1952', an assertion which Simon Jenkins in *The Times* argued:

> Had Sir Richard wished to attain a state of Keatsian grace, he had only to drop the claim to truthfulness and change the name of his characters. The story could have stood as fiction and been no less moving, no less enjoyable, for that.[14]

Shadowlands was first broadcast on 21 December 1985 on BBC 1 as part of the *Everyman* series starring Joss Ackland as Lewis and Claire Bloom as Joy. The play was voted as best television Play of the Year by BAFTA with Bloom named as Best Actress. She was also awarded an international Emmy award. The success of the television play led to a stage production which opened in Plymouth on 5 October 1989 and transferred to London at the Queen's Theatre on 23 October. Lewis was played by Nigel Hawthorne and Joy by Jane Lapotaire. Although the critic Michael Billington considered that *Shadowlands* was more suited to television, the production was awarded the *Evening Standard* Award for Best Play, while Lapotaire won the Best Actress category in the Variety Club

Awards. The play had success on Broadway with Hawthorne winning both a Tony and a New York Critics Circle award. *Shadowlands* was also later staged in several other countries. The universality that the show offered and the international success it gained in the theatre prompted Eastman and Nicholson to adapt the play for the cinema. Initially, Attenborough was invited to co-produce the film with Brian Eastman, and Sydney Pollack asked to direct. When Pollack withdrew Attenborough undertook the role of director.

Although Attenborough considered that Hawthorne 'was wonderful' in the theatre production, the actor had yet to make an impact in the cinema. This pre-dated his starring role in *The Madness of King George* (Nicholas Hytner, 1994) so Attenborough chose Anthony Hopkins to play Lewis instead. Hopkins initially refused the role as he wanted a break from filming after his role as Dr Hannibal Lecter in *The Silence of the Lambs* (Jonathan Demme, 1991), but after reading the script he changed his mind: 'I read the script and it was so good I thought, yeah I would like to do that.'[15]

The attraction of engaging a major star of the calibre of Hopkins enabled a distribution deal, in the form of a verbal agreement, to be completed within two days, which prompted Attenborough to declare, 'I have never in my life had a film come together so easily.'[16] Although Attenborough had personally helped the project by guaranteeing nearly $3 million of his personal finances to keep the project moving, written contracts, however, proved difficult to obtain, resulting in lengthy negotiations. Martin Baum, Attenborough's agent, described the negotiation process as 'a tough one', with eight sets of lawyers involved in the process.[17] Eastman negotiated the financial deal initially with Columbia Pictures, under Frank Price's leadership. Price was a founding partner of Savoy Pictures and his company, together with Spelling Films International, co-financed the film. As with *Chaplin*, all the finance for *Shadowlands* was obtained from non-British sources.

Attenborough chose Debra Winger to play Joy. Winger's American nationality was considered more important for the part than her being non-Jewish, a contrast to the television casting of Bloom who is Jewish but British. Winger's feisty temperament matched Joy's legendary abrasiveness and she also had previous cinema experience of performing a 'dying' role in *Terms of Endearment* (James L. Brooks, 1983). However, Winger had a reputation for being difficult on film-sets and Attenborough had to convince the other actors (particularly Hopkins) of Winger's promised cooperation by insisting on a strict code of behaviour.[18] The role of Douglas, Joy's son, was given to Joseph Mazzello who had recently played the grandson of Attenborough's character, Dr Hammond, in *Jurassic Park* (Steven Spielberg, 1993), while the part of Lewis's brother Warnie was given to Edward Hardwicke. Hardwicke, an occasional cinema actor, was more familiar to British television viewers for his portrayal of Dr Watson to Jeremy Brett's Sherlock Holmes in the Granada television series after he took over the role from David Burke. His role as Watson readily transferred to Warnie, as elder brother and often voice of reason to Lewis.

In adapting the story for film Nicholson made use of published sources to enhance the script, including two works by Lewis, *A Grief Observed*, published in 1961, and *The Problem of Pain*, in 1940. Nicholson also received advice from Douglas Gresham, who had witnessed his mother's relationship with Lewis. Attenborough was quick to praise Nicholson's ability in transferring from theatre to screen commenting:

> I think it is very difficult to transfer theatre into movies since such a piece of work of any real calibre is usually created for one particular medium. I really did quake a little when I heard the writer of the play, Bill Nicholson, had also written the screenplay. That's even worse because very often they are so rooted in their original creation that they just can't reconceive it. One of the miraculous things about this script is that you really do believe it was written once only, for the cinema.[19]

Several draft versions were written before a shooting script was finalised. The second draft displayed many similarities to the television play. Both this draft and the shooting script provide an insight on how Nicholson viewed the film including additional details of emotions, expressions, mannerisms and movements of the characters. There are also particulars, relating to the background, buildings and properties he envisaged. Lewis's abode, 'The Kilns', which he shared with Warnie, is described as 'not very old, not very beautiful' while the interior is dictated as being 'modest and uncluttered, its interior decoration untouched for fifteen years'. Similar attention to detail is applied to the character of Whistler, described as being 'a little older than the others, mid-twenties, a skinny man with burning eyes and a wild air about him'.[20] Not all of Nicholson's ideas were adopted by Attenborough. The depiction of Christopher Riley, a fellow university colleague of Lewis, was described as being 'a deceptively sweet-natured don' but Attenborough transformed him into a pompous character who enjoys asserting his authority over others.[21] Another change Attenborough instigated was the location of the last scene which portrays Lewis and Douglas together after Joy's death enjoying a country walk. In the second draft the scene was intended to be located at the 'Golden Valley'. In a change of location, perhaps to prevent the scene being over sentimentalised, the scene was transposed to a place of less significance – 'a road outside the Kilns'.[22]

Douglas Gresham was appointed as an unofficial adviser to the film. The gesture was partly a courtesy but also a safeguard for the film as Gresham was the 'quality control' and 'copyright infringement consultant' to the C.S. Lewis Estate. Gresham was also able to observe the accuracy of the script, claiming that '[t]he emotional content of the film is absolutely right – that to me is the most valuable thing about it.' He also explained the omission from the film of his elder brother, David, claiming: 'He's not in the film due to dramatic necessity. If you add another child into that situation, you have to deal with several different reactions. And after all, the story was not about the children's reaction.'[23] The 'dramatic necessity', however, was not deemed such a problem for the television production which featured both brothers.

Principal photography began in April 1993 at the Randolph Hotel in Oxford, portraying the tearoom where Lewis and Joy first meet. Filming continued for six weeks in Oxford and its environs, in Herefordshire, and for four weeks at Shepperton Studios. Additional scenes were filmed in Loughborough on the Great Central Railway, which doubled for Oxford station after the war, the 'Golden Valley' which was filmed on the Herefordshire–Welsh borders, and in London. Attenborough decided that he did not want to be influenced by the previous two versions of the story. The decision was both calculated and circumstantial. As he explained:

> I deliberately did not see the BBC version until our screenplay was ready. At that point, it seemed sensible to take a look and see if there was any little thing that William hadn't put in that we could use from the original script.[24]

The production of *Shadowlands* ran without significant problems. Winger's reputed behavioural difficulties did not materialise with Attenborough declaring: 'Her dedication, devotion, commitment to the subject was unequalled and unequivocal.'[25] The greatest challenge for Attenborough was dealing with the disparate techniques of the two stars, Hopkins preferring minimal rehearsal to enhance the spontaneity of his performance while Winger wanted several rehearsals before she felt confident to be filmed. One further difficulty he had to overcome was finding a way of animating Joy's relative immobility, resulting from her illness. To enhance the scenes Attenborough decided to employ the technique of cross-cutting and to shoot the film on the widest possible ratio using different focuses to point attention to the characters. This technique was new to him. As he explained:

> I'd never seen focus used in quite such a way before, or indeed to that extent. It was quite an innovative style in a way but I think it was worth

it because it worked not merely as an integral part of those particular scenes but ultimately in terms of the wider emotional impact of the film.[26]

Shadowlands centres around three pivotal scenes which highlight the emotional context, each gaining more in intensity. The first is in the chapel where Joy's presence, during the 'Pagent of Learning', is the realisation of Lewis's feelings for her. The second involves Joy's highly charged death scene, while the third relates to the climactic scene in the attic where Lewis and Douglas openly emote to each other, united in their grief. The emotion is highlighted by the imposing score. Lesley Walker, the editor, asserted that music was essential to maintain a balance between 'sentiment and sentimentality'.[27] George Fenton, working on his third film for Attenborough, was supported in his music by the choristers of Magdalen College, Oxford. He also composed an original piece for the opening anthem for the film eschewing all traditional Tudor music that had been considered.

Despite its sad subject matter, *Shadowlands* can also be considered one of Attenborough's most humorous films, the humour adding to both the film's intensity and allowing greater entertainment for the audience. The humour ranges from sarcasm, as exemplified by Warnie telling Joy that Lewis is 'dying to listen to her poetry', to satire as when Joy, having been told that she will die, asks Lewis: 'I'm a Jew, I'm divorced, I'm broke, I've got cancer. Do you think I'll get a discount?' Humour plays a pivotal part in the Christmas party scene where Joy becomes the centre of attention, dressed in a scarlet gown which contrasts the drabness of the other female attire. Professor Riley's arrogance manifests itself in the manner of his dismissal of Joy's work as a poet while also revealing his misogyny, declaring: 'where men have intellect, women have soul'. Joy's reply is quick and cutting, and concludes, 'Are you trying to be rude or are you merely stupid?' The sequence ends with Lewis attempting to stifle his laughter and Riley turning towards the camera, lost for words, his expression showing that his ego has been totally thwarted.

Shadowlands was produced under budget at a cost of $22 million (£15 million) and was released to coincide with the thirtieth anniversary of Lewis's death in 1963 (Lewis had died on 22 November, the same day as President John F. Kennedy). It opened in America on 29 December 1993, gaining a final American box-office gross of $25,842,377. In London the film opened on 4 March 1994 at the Odeon Cinema in Leicester Square, the British box office totalling £4,862,314. The response in Britain was better than Attenborough usually received. He also revealed an interesting introspective opinion of his work:

> I don't get good reviews on this side of the Atlantic. I think people think I'm mundane – not banal necessarily – but mundane. And I think that the cinema aficionados don't find in my work the innovative or undisciplined form of cinema that tends to be in vogue.[28]

The majority of critical opinion applauded the film. The *Sun* claimed that *Shadowlands* was 'Dickie Attenborough's best movie ever' and 'British film-making at its best'.[29] In a similar tone, Derek Malcolm in the *Guardian* praised *Shadowlands* as 'a first-class piece of film-making' and 'the best piece of direction [Attenborough] has ever accomplished'. Malcolm, previously a harsh critic of Attenborough, further extolled the film by declaring that *Shadowlands* 'exhibits all the virtues of the often underrated British cinema of the past and very few of the overly theatrical vices'.[30] Malcolm's views were echoed by Philip French in the *Observer* which praised Attenborough for his 'unobtrusive directorial style and a sympathetic way with actors, both brought into play in a beautifully crafted movie that gleams like a newly-made antique'.[31] The *Mail on Sunday* called *Shadowlands* 'gentle, decent, sad, slow, and sweet, the sort of film you can recommend to older relatives', yet was critical of Hopkins for finding it 'hard to come to terms with himself as a sexual being'.[32]

The few adverse reviews included the *Independent on Sunday*, which complained that 'with its contempt for complexity of feeling and a mawkishness masquerading as honesty, *Shadowlands* is a tear machine.[33] The *Financial Times* declared the film 'substantive twaddle, bar the performances'.[34] The most dissenting voice, however, belonged to Alexander Walker in the *Evening Standard*, who claimed that: 'There are moments in *Shadowlands* that touch you, but very few move you.' Walker also took the opportunity to attack Attenborough's directorial style in general:

> It is Richard Attenborough's strong point. Soften the blows, tenderise the traumas, sieve the lumps, blend the feelings, dilute the facts, filter the message: his career seems to contain a built-in strainer. He can be guaranteed to produce a cheering infusion out of the unlikeliest substances. The Great War, Churchill, the Second World War, Gandhi, apartheid, Charlie Chaplin: all have been stretched to the limits (but no farther) of midbrow appreciation, educated taste, liberal-minded concern, healthy emotion, elevating enjoyment. Quality viewing for AB viewers.[35]

The film journals were generally positive about *Shadowlands*. *Sight and Sound* described it as a 'grandiose, beautifully crafted film', while *Screen International* noted that Hopkins and Winger 'give perfectly judged performances and keep the film from slipping into sentimentality'.[36] In America, *Variety* claimed that 'the film's greatest achievement was that it neither comes across as an abstraction or type', commending Attenborough for his 'modest, unobtrusive direction that serves the material – and actors'.[37] For the *New York Times*, *Shadowlands* 'offers a gratifyingly soapy love story, handsomely told'.[38] *Village Voice* was less enthusiastic, declaring *Shadowlands* 'an exercise in rampant donnishness and cozily cloistered Sceptered Isle-ism, is still less grandiose than director Sir Richard Attenborough's customary tub-thwacking'.[39]

Shadowlands attracted comment in Britain from other sources. These were mainly concerned with factual inconsistencies, including the length of Joy's illness which lasted for six years but was reduced for filmic purposes to six months, and the place of her death which was altered from hospital to home. Douglas's age was also changed from being a teenager to a 9–year-old in order to parallel that of Lewis's own age when his mother died. David Sexton in the *Sunday Telegraph* used A.N. Wilson's biography of Lewis to substantiate claims of inaccuracy. For Sexton, both the film *Tom and Viv* and *Shadowlands* were examples where 'the writing is made to seem little more than a mask for the "real" story which is the writer's life in society.'[40] The historical interpretation was also questioned in many of the reviews. Walker recounted that Lewis was in reality 'an academic sourpuss, theological bully and public demagogue', while he considered that Lewis's relationship with Joy was not as platonic as displayed in 'Attenborough's bonk-free version' which, in his opinion, drew heavily from the influence of the director's mentor, Noël Coward, in *Brief Encounter*.[41] Philip French also listed several inaccuracies, including his claim that '*Shadowlands* is false to the Britain of the 1950s, the life of universities, the relationship between Lewis and Joy, and the character of Lewis all in the interest of shaping a heart-wrenching love story for a popular audience.'[42]

The *Evening Standard* presented the views of A.N. Wilson. Wilson's principal criticisms were of omissions, particularly the absence of Lewis's old friends, who 'deserted him on his marriage because they simply could not stand Joy Gresham and, in particular, her graceless foul language'. David, the younger son also absent, after reverting to Judaism, developed a problematic relationship with both Lewis and his mother. For Wilson, however, 'Attenborough has made a visually pleasing, emotionally satisfying work of art. To have told the unvarnished truth would not have been possible because of the English libel laws.'[43]

Wilson's views were also echoed by Humphrey Carpenter, author of a study entitled *The Inklings*, the name given to the group of university friends, which included both Lewis and J.R.R. Tolkien. More significantly, Carpenter revealed himself as the son of the Bishop of Oxford who had refused to marry Lewis as Joy was a divorcée, a decision which caused much personal pain to Lewis, but one that Carpenter was able to clarify further after his father explained to him the reasons behind his decision. Although the Bishop was sympathetic to Lewis's plight, he nevertheless did not consider Lewis an exception to the Church rule. There were also concerns regarding Lewis's public position, as Carpenter explained: 'If permission were given to such a public figure (argued my father), everyone would demand the right to follow suit.' The film omits any reference to the Bishop's refusal, unlike the television version. Carpenter also criticised the exclusion of 'much of the tear-jerking part of the real story', with the return of the cancer 'a full two and a half years after the bedside marriage, not just a few months as the film implies'. As Carpenter asserted: 'The film should not be regarded as a documentary account of his marriage. The truth was far more elaborate, and far more dramatic'.[44]

Despite the questioning of historical accuracy, *Shadowlands* did much to restore Attenborough's directorial career. The film was nominated for two Academy Awards for Winger (Best Actress) and for Fenton (Best Music). Attenborough's greatest disappointment, however, was that Hopkins failed to be nominated for *Shadowlands*, for what he considered 'the best piece of work Tony has ever done in his life'.[45] The disappointment was even greater with Hopkins nominated for *The Remains of the Day* in which he played Stevens, the butler, a similar repressed character. However, Hopkins received a BAFTA for his role while Attenborough and Eastman won the Alexander Korda Award for the most outstanding film of the year.

The success of *Shadowlands* encouraged Attenborough to continue with the same intimate formula with his next film, *In Love and War*. Like *Shadowlands*, *In Love and War* also explores a brief romance which had a similar profound effect on an author's life. During the First World War Ernest Hemingway was serving as a volunteer and working on a rolling canteen which delivered sweets and commodities to the troops on the front line. While on duty he became seriously wounded helping to evacuate an Italian soldier and was hospitalised in Milan. Agnes von Kurowsky became responsible for helping Hemingway back to health, and in particular, saving his leg from amputation by her modern nursing skills which prevented the spread of gangrene. The couple's romance developed into a close relationship. Although it was only of a short duration, Agnes became acknowledged as Hemingway's great love and was later fictionally portrayed in Hemingway's novel, *A Farewell to Arms*, published in 1929. The relationship ended after Agnes became betrothed to Domenico Caracciolo, an artillery officer, but portrayed as a surgeon in the film.[46] Despite his four marriages, Hemingway later claimed that he never again attained the same intensity of feeling as he had for Agnes.

In Love and War shares many similarities with Shadowlands. Both films focus on the emotional side of the relationships. Both use the hospital as the site where romance competes with the dangers of illness and the finality of death. Agnes's sudden attraction to another man whom she later declined to marry had a similar devastating effect on Hemingway as Joy's death did on Lewis. Like Lewis, who conveyed his feelings in A Grief Observed, Hemingway wrote about his experiences in A Farewell to Arms, with Agnes and Hemingway represented by two fictional characters, Catherine Barkley and Frederic Henry. In Love and War also demonstrates structural similarities with Young Winston by exploring the early years of a man who was to achieve greatness in later life. Whereas Young Winston covered a period of twenty years, In Love and War concentrates on a few critical months of Hemingway's youth.

The incentive for directing In Love and War was partly due to the intensity of emotion that the subject demanded. In declaring that he loved people who could 'stand up and be counted' Attenborough distinguished two types: 'Some like Gandhi or Churchill change our very destinies. Others simply illuminate our lives, and the complexities and difficulties and confrontations that we inevitably have to face. Hemingway is one of those.'[47] War was also a popular theme at the time of In Love and War's production with The English Patient, which shared the similar theme of romance intertwined with injury, hospital and death. As well as being closely linked thematically to the film, In Love and War also, by virtue of being based upon the same source, is closely connected to A Farewell to Arms, which was produced first in 1932 (Frank Borzage) and was remade in 1957 (Charles Vidor), both Hollywood productions. The film also bears comparison with Reach for the Sky (Lewis Gilbert, 1956) in the close relationship that developed between Douglas Bader and one of his nurses aiding his recovery after losing both legs as a result of a flying accident. In Love and War also returned Attenborough to the First World War, the topic of his first film, Oh! What a Lovely War. The subject of the First World War was also prophetic. During the late 1990s a resurgence of interest in the conflict appeared in cinema with two notable productions, Regeneration (Gillies MacKinnon, 1997) and The Trench (William Boyd, 1999), both of which focused on the tension and psychological suffering rather than the actual fighting, thus continuing the themes explored in In Love and War.

In Love and War is also linked to Shadowlands by its inclusion of heritage characteristics, including the architecture of grand buildings, pictorial landscapes and elegant historical costumes. The film looks to the past, showing the splendours of architecture as a contrast against the austere hospital buildings where the war injured are tended. More specifically, the film can also be identified as belonging to a cycle of historical films featuring Italy by engaging with the culture and employing the pictorial landscape as a background to the narrative. This cycle began in the 1980s with *A Room with a View* (James Ivory, 1986), based on the book by E.M. Forster. It continued in the 1990s with another Forster adaptation, *Where Angels Fear to Tread* (Charles Sturridge, 1991), based in Tuscany, followed by *Enchanted April* (Mike Newell, 1991), which was located on the Italian Riviera, *Wings of the Dove* (Iain Softley, 1997) filmed in Venice, and *Tea with Mussolini* (Franco Zeffirelli, 1999) based in Florence.

Attenborough was not involved from the outset of *In Love and War*; instead, he was appointed as director after the project was instigated. This was to be a significant factor which went against the success of the production. Attenborough's independence and artistic freedom came under the control of the production company New Line, while there was also strong influence exerted by the producer, Dimitri Villard. The situation was similar to Attenborough's experience with *Young Winston*, with Villard's excessive personal involvement mirroring that of Carl Foreman. Villard's father, Henry, had witnessed the romance between Hemingway and Agnes and therefore could claim greater background knowledge of the subject as Foreman had done previously. Another factor that caused Attenborough major concern was the script. The production company's insistence on employing a team of scriptwriters went against Attenborough's preference for one writer, thereby creating a situation that mirrored the difficulties of *Chaplin*.

The origins of the film came from the discovery of a lost diary, written by Agnes von Kurowsky, which was presented to Henry Villard by her widower, William Stanfield. Agnes and Henry had maintained a regular correspondence since occupying adjoining rooms in hospital. Henry was also a rival for Agnes's affections. After her health declined, Stanfield wrote to Henry, now an American diplomat, to seek his help for her wish to be buried in the Soldiers Home National Cemetery at Arlington, Washington, DC. Permission had earlier been refused but Henry, using his diplomatic influence, succeeded in overturning the decision before Agnes died in 1984. In appreciation of Henry's help, Agnes's diary was sent to him. In 1989, in conjunction with James Nagel, a Hemingway scholar, *Hemingway in Love and War: The Lost Diary of Agnes Kurowsky*, was published. Hemingway had died in 1961.

Dimitri Villard, Henry's son, was keen to expand on Hemingway's romance for cinema audiences but the proposal was rejected by

Hollywood in 1989. This was partly due to the structured form that Henry requested. As he explained: 'I felt the film should really be told from Agnes's romantic point of view. But at the end of the 1980s the studios were only interested in big action pictures.'[48] In 1991, with audience attitudes changing, Villard approached New Line with a different film treatment and the film rights were secured. The script was initially approved by Diana Hawkins. Although Attenborough had concerns with it, 'requiring a lot of work to be really cinematic', he was impressed with the concept, claiming that 'the subject, the context and personalities were just magical'.[49] Attenborough's appointment as director to the film was announced at the Cannes Film Festival in May 1996. With a sizeable budget of $40 million, Villard was hopeful of success to improve his reputation in a critical industry. Scott Collins of the *Chicago Tribune* had referred to Villard's career as 'chequered' with *In Love and War* being the 'biggest coup' for him.[50]

The company's policy for a multi-author approach for the script caused several problems. Villard was responsible for writing the first draft of the screenplay, entitled 'Hemingway in Love', which was further developed by the Scottish writer, Allan Schiach, under his pen name, Allan Scott. Scott's non-writer cinematic commitments involved being a governor of the British Film Institute and chairman of the Scottish Screen Agency. The time involved in both roles was extensive and Scott was unable to complete any further work on the script. New Line's screenwriter, Clancy Sigal, also made further adaptations before it was taken over by Anna Hamilton Phelan. Phelan was inspired by the poems and the histories of the Red Cross during the war and based the film in a hospital. She recalled: 'I wanted to take as my thread for the character of Agnes the idea that she was drawn sexually, almost obsessively, to this young man', to which Attenborough replied, 'Go for it.'[51]

There were several disagreements over the script. New Line wanted the film to be focused around the couple's romance to attract a better box office, while Attenborough favoured war as the pivotal theme. There were also difficulties with the ending. Hemingway and Agnes's last sighting of each other was at a station on Hemingway's departure for America by train. Although there is a clear parallel to the end of the romance in *Brief Encounter*, it was decided that this would not be a suitable conclusion for cinema in the 1990s. Attenborough suggested an invented scene with Agnes visiting Hemingway's grave soon after his burial in 1961. This was rejected as being 'too mournful'. The chosen ending depicted Agnes visiting Hemingway at his home in 1919 where she voices her love for him but he is too proud and distressed to accept her advances. Although the ending is historically inaccurate, it had the necessary requirements for cinema. Attenborough later explained: 'The end is made up, but with films based on real life you do have to make compromises. Yet as long as the essence remains true, it's fine.'[52]

There were also contentious issues concerning the two leading actors. Chris O'Donnell was chosen to play Hemingway, prior to Attenborough's appointment. O'Donnell had won a Golden Globe nomination for his role in *Scent of a Woman* (Martin Brest, 1992), but he had achieved greater prominence through his role in *Batman Forever* (Joel Schumacher, 1995). O'Donnell's youthful looks allowed him, at the age of 26, to play the role of the teenaged Hemingway. He also had the advantage of a strong physical resemblance to the writer. O'Donnell was particularly keen to work with Attenborough, claiming: 'The story was wonderful, but getting to work with Richard Attenborough was the primary driving factor to become involved.'[53] New Line had also put pressure on Attenborough to cast Julia Roberts as Agnes (Villard's choice) but negotiations failed. Attenborough's preference was for Sandra Bullock, who shared a similar antecedence to Agnes, having one German and one American parent. Bullock was secured for her first European production with a reported payment of $10 million. For Bullock, too, the prime attraction of the film was working with Attenborough. As she explained: 'It was the lure of Dickie. I wanted to find some director strong enough to take me out of what I have become too comfortable with.'[54]

The only British presence in the film was the actress Ingrid Lacey who took the part of the Scottish nurse Elsie 'Mac' MacDonald. Lacey was familiar to British television audiences as Helen in the BBC comedy *Drop the Dead Donkey*. There were several Italian and American actors in minor yet pivotal roles. Finance was a critical factor with the choice of locations. New Line preferred Budapest as it was cheaper, but Attenborough asserted his directorial status and insisted on Italy to achieve the authentic background and correct atmosphere. He also maintained his usual quest for historical accuracy by engaging experts to advise him. These included a Red Cross consultant, a volunteer nurse historian from the American Red Cross headquarters in Washington and a Mobile Army Surgical Hospital (MASH). Army surgeons were engaged in operating theatre scenes, troops from the Aviano Air Force Base in Italy were drafted in to play First World War soldiers, while a local priest ensured that the last rites were performed correctly.

Filming began on 22 May in Italy at Vittorio Veneto, at the base of the Dolomites, with sequences filmed in Venice; it lasted eleven weeks. The production moved to London for studio locations at Shepperton Studios, and then to Montreal and Quebec in Canada. As with *Young*

Winston many of the scenes were filmed in two versions to comply with the wishes of the production company who would then be able to instigate changes if required. Attenborough had initially wanted to open the film with the press coverage of Hemingway's funeral, as he had with *Gandhi*. A selected audience were asked to give their preference. They favoured one depicting American Red Cross soldiers bringing in nurses to help in the hospitals in northern Italy, and Attenborough was forced to accept their decision. The result meant that the biographical details of Hemingway and the black-and-white portrait photographs of him ageing had to be transposed to the end of the film.

Attenborough brought the theme of war into prominence by the stark images displayed at the start of the film and in the fighting sequences. Although he claims that he is 'not fascinated by the pyrotechnics of cinema', this claim is challenged by the production which contains some gruesome war images. To justify the inclusion he declared:

> In my judgement, the pornography of violence is simply dreadful, but this was a true story that took place during World War 1, which was one of the bloodiest battles of this century. I felt that the violence and blood were necessary to the story.[55]

In Love and War depicts the dangers of war through the fast tempo and vivid images as is portrayed when the trench in which Hemingway is sheltering is attacked. Hemingway is seen carrying his Italian friend, Roberto, across the field amid shells and gunfire, showing his bravery until he is wounded in the leg and falls. After being rescued, Hemingway is moved to safety and the label 'Sì' is attached to him, while Roberto, lying next to him is given one depicting 'No'. The scene is reminiscent of *Oh! What a Lovely War* with the label 'No' replacing the red poppy as an indication of impending death. Further graphic scenes occur in the field hospital where several patients are being operated on simultaneously. The difficulties of providing a realistic depiction of war had to be balanced with what was considered acceptable for the middlebrow audience usually attracted to Attenborough's films. To reduce the 'pornography of violence' a particular camera technique which Attenborough and cinematographer Roger Pratt devised was employed. Attenborough explained: 'I've discovered that, if you make the cut away so quickly that the audience is almost not sure they saw it, then what you do show on-screen has to have tremendous reality but you don't have to show much.'[56]

The use of specialist extras continued Attenborough's policy of portraying 'total credibility' as it improved the actors' involvement in the specific circumstance. Thus the soldiers 'spoke and acted like real surgeons' because they were playing themselves. It was also saved time and cost. In this they were helped by a genuine war, employing surgeons recently returned from the conflict in Bosnia. Another of Attenborough's aversions, the depiction of gratuitous sex, is one that is skilfully avoided. The difficulties of conducting a relationship during wartime and the forced separation of the couple are handled with skill and aplomb. Agnes meets Hemingway on his final night in Italy at a brothel, the only available place for them to be alone. While Hemingway is embarrassed, she understands the reasons for such places, 'where men are desperate for sex and women for money'. The scene, despite the squalid background of the brothel, is tastefully portrayed to the sounds of an accordion playing in the background. The couple partially undressing in a passionate scene is enhanced by the camera closing in towards them. A cut to the couple embracing as they move together in a slow waltz to the sounds of the accordion, concludes the sequence.

The vintage impression of the film was achieved through the techniques devised by Pratt. In a similar way that Gerry Turpin had achieved a period feel by developing his Colorflex technique for *Young Winston*, Pratt concentrated on softening and muting the image by the technique he devised in using Christian Dior stockings as a diffusion tool to provide a muted effect. The age and condition of the historic buildings in Venice, however, caused concern as to whether they could support the equipment required. To prevent damage, the Italian government stipulated that they had to be supplied with detailed information regarding the weight of the cameras and the related equipment from the crew.

Attenborough's employment of computer-generated imagery (CGI) prevented the need of the numerous extras that he had required for the epic crowd scenes in *Gandhi* and *Cry Freedom*. The technology was employed twice, first in the battle sequence, where two hundred servicemen were 'increased' to give the illusion of 13,000, and second for the night-time scene in Venice when a number of gondolas were 'filled' with candles. The purpose of the scene was to convey the elation felt at the prospect of the imminent end of the war.

During post-production New Line continued to exert further pressure on Attenborough to produce a final cut that emphasised the love theme rather than the war elements in order to attract a plentiful female audience. Despite the pressure, Attenborough maintained his stance and the prominence of the war remained. Additional tensions arose concerning the screenwriting credits which echoed similar difficulties with *Chaplin*. Negotiations between the writers and New Line failed and the matter had to be resolved legally. The result was that the screen story was credited to Scott and Villard with Hawkins's name omitted and the screenplay attributed to Scott, Sigal and Phelan. A caption added to the film informed audiences that *In Love and War* is 'based' on a true story. The word 'based' is significant as its omission in *Shadowlands* generated criticism that it was not an authentic representation.

In Love and War opened in Los Angles on 24 January 1997 after an earlier preview in the city on 18 December 1996. The film opened on a 'Super Bowl weekend', the sporting attraction competing against cinema audiences. The date was set to allow the film a one-week screening in December to qualify for possible Oscar nominations. It had a moderate opening weekend totalling $5.9 million but declined rapidly thereafter in the face of competition, including from *Jerry Maguire* (Cameron Crowe).[57]

In Britain the film had its première on 12 February 1997 at the Empire Cinema in Leicester Square, London, in the presence of Diana, Princess of Wales. Proceeds from the evening went to support the Red Cross campaign to outlaw landmines. A second première was held in Scotland, on the Isle of Bute, near the Attenboroughs' holiday home. The film opened on 14 February and received an opening weekend total of £357,024. Although it reached fourth position in the British charts, it soon dropped before exiting the charts at the end of the month. The total British box-office gross was £1,141,157, less than a quarter of *Shadowlands*.

The critical response in America was influenced by the stance taken in an early review by Kenneth Turan in the *Los Angeles Times* who described the film as a 'tepid story' and considered that 'In Love and Snore' would be more fitting title: 'Not even Richard Attenborough ... can make a moving love story out of such uncompromising material'.[58] Many criticisms were pointed at the casting and performance of O'Donnell and Bullock. The *San Francisco Chronicle* employed a food metaphor, claiming that 'the vanilla yoghurt' of O'Donnell and the 'strawberry syrup' of Bullock 'make for a sticky concoction'.[59] For the *New York Times* Attenborough makes the film 'too muted for either character to come alive'.[60] In contrast, the *Daily News of Los Angeles* described the film as 'an intimate, emotional affair' and praised Attenborough for staging the battle scenes with 'a hard-hitting brutality that more than makes up for any misleading romantic ideas about war'.[61]

In Britain there was an equally hostile reaction. The *Observer* claimed that 'largely due to the inadequacies of a contrived, overly romantic script that plays fast and loose with known facts, *In Love and War* falls short of his [Attenborough's] finest work.'[62] The *Sunday Telegraph* saw the film as 'another example of bombastic movie-making', while the *Guardian* complained that the screenplay 'falls far short of Hemingway's standards'.[63] Alexander Walker in the *Evening Standard* called the film 'a handsome looking story' but listed its shortcomings, claiming: 'It is a film that provides the sensation of war but not the pain, the presence of literature but not the sweat, the romance of the flesh but not the sex – or at least not very visibly so.'[64] The *Sunday Times* praised the film, declaring that 'Attenborough's craftsmanship skilfully stages the intimate encounter against a spectacular backdrop of war, marching armies, and travelogue Venice, a reminder of his credentials in the David Lean school of British filmmakers.'[65]

The journals were more positive. *Film Review* called the film a 'big love story in a well thought-out wartime drama', while *Empire* claimed that it was 'not without its merits'.[66] Philip Kemp in *Sight and Sound* compared *In Love and War* favourably with *Shadowlands* finding 'the two films, taken together, dovetail perfectly, each illuminating and complementing the other.' Kemp also considered a changing emphasis in Attenborough's reputation as a director:

> It may seem odd, even perverse, to treat Attenborough as some kind of *auteur*; for years the films he's directed have been condescendingly dismissed as 'stolid', 'worthy' or at best 'workmanlike', products of the old-fashioned mainstream school of British film-making: Lean without the flair. But these two latest films suggest that he may be a more interesting director than has been allowed; more interesting, perhaps than he's hitherto allowed himself to be.[67]

The film also generated debate away from the cinema press. Most of the controversy was centred on the brothel scene, which questioned the film's historical accuracy. Several Hemingway aficionados claimed that Hemingway's relationship with Agnes remained unconsummated, while others considered that despite the strict moral code of the times, the impact of war and the imminent prospect of death would have influenced the relationship. The differing opinions also divided the Villard family. Henry, who remained in contact with Agnes until her death, recalls that she considered the relationship 'a flirtation'. He also observed that 'Standards were pretty strict and moral in those days. We were all very much virgins.'[68] Dimitri Villard, however, disputed his father's views claiming they were constrained by social convention and declared:

> My father was a gentleman of the old school. But, in the discussions with me, he admitted that he could not know for sure. After all, every patient in the hospital was in a separate room with a door that shut. Given the passion in the letters, I think it is hard to imagine that love-making didn't take place.[69]

Dimitri's views were challenged by his sister, Alexandra De Borchgrave, who recalled in 1977: 'Daddy's theory was that Hemingway was very, very deeply affected by this love, but he fiercely maintained that Hemingway and Agnes never consummated it.'[70] Attenborough's views concurred with those of Dimitri believing they had a physical relationship as is depicted in the film. He also added, 'I don't think there is any doubt about it from the letters she wrote to Hemingway. Their affair absolutely destroyed Hemingway. He told all his wives that his only love was Agnes.'[71]

While *In Love and War* failed to live up to New Line's expectations, for Attenborough much of the blame was due to their interference. Attenborough particularly attacked the studio's policy of using multiple scriptwriters:

> If only they'd left us alone. If they had allowed us to make the film we originally wanted to make, our original script. But they have these ridiculous script doctors. They bring in these people who write an analysis and then are given the right to rewrite the screenplay, which they did in our case – I think three times.[72]

Attenborough also declared that his lack of control as a director was also significant in the poor response to the film, explaining: 'I was not entirely my own boss, and certainly not able to avoid the whims and critiques of those who made the law of that company.'[73] The film also suffered from sharing common thematic concerns with *The English Patient* which was released one month earlier, setting a standard against which *In Love and War* could not compete. The greatest impact was felt by New Line. At the beginning of March 1997, it was put up for sale.[74]

The decade that had brought Attenborough renewed success with *Shadowlands* ended in disappointment with the critical and popular failures of *In Love and War* and *Grey Owl*. Yet Attenborough continued to look for another project undaunted by the response and his advancing years. At the age of 83, he began production for *Closing the Ring* in 2006. The brief wartime romance was remarkably close in subject to *In Love and War* as well as forming Attenborough's third 'brief encounter' film. While *Closing the Ring* marked a significant departure from the biographical portrayals that had been the basis for Attenborough's last five films, the theme of war remained as the common narrative thread of his films. *Closing the Ring* engaged with the subject of war through its depiction of internal strife during the IRA campaign in Belfast during the 1980s and 1990s. The title, itself, was also directly related to war. Winston Churchill had chosen *Closing the Ring* as the title of the fifth volume of his major study of the Second World War.[75]

Closing the Ring is based on a true event of the Second World War. On 1 June 1944, a B-17 bomber with a crew of ten, crashed in fog into Cave Hill in Belfast with no survivors. Following the chance discovery, fifty years later, of an airman's wedding ring in the wreckage, it was returned to the man's widow in Louisville, Kentucky. Alfred Montgomery, who found the ring, was granted the freedom of Louisville and the date, 22 September 1996, became Alfred Montgomery day in the city.[76] The story that instigated the screenplay was publicised by a commemoration service in 2006 in Belfast which attracted the attention of the television writer, Peter Woodward (son of the actor Edward), who produced a screenplay. Attenborough was attracted by the quality of the writing, which he acknowledged as the best first script he had ever read. For Attenborough: 'The script is everything. You can make a reasonable picture with a good script, but with a bad script, no matter how skilful you are, you have no chance.'[77]

The script used flashback to integrate the story of the 1940s romance into events in the 1990s (when the ring was discovered) which reignites the whole affair again, in the contemporary setting of Northern Ireland. The themes of lost love, redemption and sacrifice were also particularly poignant for Attenborough. In 2004, Attenborough's eldest daughter, Jane, and his granddaughter, Lucy, were both killed in the Boxing Day Tsunami while on holiday in Thailand. The film, as well as fulfilling his work as a director, also acted as a therapy for Attenborough to cope with his loss.

Closing the Ring also provided Attenborough with an opportunity to be reunited with several former colleagues, including the American actress Shirley MacLaine, who had the starring role as Ethel Ann, with whom he had co-starred in *The Bliss of Mrs Blossom* (Joe McGrath, 1968), and Pete Postlethwaite, with whom had acted in *The Lost World: Jurassic Park*. MacLaine had won an Academy Award for her role in *Terms of Endearment*, while Postlethwaite had been nominated for an Oscar in Jim Sheridan's film *In the Name of the Father* (1993). Brenda Fricker, the Irish actress who had won an Academy Award for Best Supporting Actress in *My Left Foot* (Jim Sheridan, 1989), had the part of Grandma Riley. The film also featured the Canadian actor, Christopher Plummer, most noted for his role in *The Sound of Music* (Robert Wise, 1965), and the British-born actress Mischa Barton, most renowned for her Hollywood television role in *The OC*, who plays the young Ethel Ann. Other cast members included the Belfast actor Martin McCann in the role of Jimmy Riley, the young boy who discovers the ring, and Stephen Amell who played the young Teddy, the love of Ethel Ann. Despite its acclaimed cast and being granted a Christmas release in Britain, *Closing the Ring* attracted only moderate popular success. The film also shared the same adverse fate as *Grey Owl* in failing to gain American distribution and going straight to DVD, under licence from Universal Pictures and released in May 2008.[78]

Closing the Ring can be seen as belonging to a cycle of films that portrayed 'brief encounter' romances, which had significant and long-term impacts on the characters involved. The cycle began in the 1990s, most notably with *The English Patient*, and continued in the early years of the millennium, with *Enigma* (Michael Apted, 2001) and, later, with *Atonement* (Joe Wright, 2007) released at the same time as *Closing the Ring*. By its engagement with the political scene of Northern Ireland in the early 1990s, the film can also be identified as belonging to a cycle of films that explored the world of the IRA, which included *The Long Good Friday* (John Mackenzie, 1981), *The Crying Game* (Neil Jordan, 1992), *In the Name of the Father* and *Puckoon* (Terence Ryan, 2002) in which Attenborough himself was cast.

The film had a long gestation period before it came to fruition. Many of the cast members had been signed as early as 2003, but after several false announcements, production finally started in 2006, caused by a delay in securing finance.[79] The film was given a budget of £13 million ($23,500,000). It was jointly funded by the UK Film Council, to the amount of £2,091,886 (which included a National Lottery Award of £25,886l), by Scion Films, the Northern Ireland Film and Television Commission, and Content Film International forming an Irish/English/Canadian co-production.[80] Attenborough produced the film with Jo Gilbert, who with Judy Gilbert co-owned the Titanic Studios in Belfast. Martin Katz was named as co-producer. The crew contained many of Attenborough's usual team including Clegg, Pratt, Walker and Jonathan Bates while new additions included Jeff Danna (music composer) and Tom McCullagh (production designer). Significantly, Attenborough was without Diana Hawkins, a prominent presence in previous productions who was not involved on the set, but held the role of script consultant.

Filming began on 27 March 2006, starting in Belfast on location and at the city's new Titanic Studios, and in Canada in both Toronto and Ontario. The film was aided by receiving additional publicity through tabloid newspaper interest in Barton's proposed nude scene. The *Sun* headline read: 'Mischa to break out big guns', while for the *News of the World* it was 'Mischa bare-ton', bringing a new sexual perspective to Attenborough's work but overriding the more serious concerns of the film.[81]

Closing the Ring also contributed to a new era in the British film industry after the 'disastrous 2005' which witnessed a decline in filmmaking. The year 2006 saw an increase in American money spent on

British productions which benefited such productions as *The Bourne Ultimatum* (Paul Greengrass), an American film with a British director, and *The Golden Compass* (Chris Weitz). The film also benefited the industry in Northern Ireland. At the start of filming, Gilbert hailed the event as 'a land-mark co-production' with Canada and an 'incredible opportunity for the film industry of Northern Ireland'. She also acknowledged the benefits of having a well-known director and a stellar cast:

> To have a British film icon like Richard Attenborough, and actors and filmmakers the calibre of Shirley MacLaine and Roger Pratt filming this movie here in Belfast with local crew and actors, is a phenomenal achievement for this community. In addition to forging a new and strong link with Canada, it will show the rest of the world that Northern Ireland has a vibrant film industry and that we are indeed open for business.[82]

The *Daily Telegraph* also welcomed the event for Northern Ireland as part of its regeneration in the light of its past history of conflict.[83] The article declared that in peaceful times Ulster has become one of Europe's busiest film locations. It also claimed that *Closing the Ring* is considered 'the most glamorous film produced in Northern Ireland and is becoming one of the most high-profile productions of the year'. The filming also brought echoes of the Troubles to Belfast again. The film set was within range of the notorious Antrim Road, near the New Lodge district where the first British soldier was killed thirty-five years ago. The campaign had resumed its activities on 18 August 1969, until a ceasefire, originally negotiated in 1994, was restored on 20 July 1997. The discovery of the ring had also occurred during the IRA terror campaign in Northern Ireland. Nonetheless, the film's 'staged explosions' and 'gun-wielding extras' were welcome. The article observed that '[s]uch a scenario would have been unthinkable a few years ago when Belfast was engulfed in terrorist conflict and the closest locals came to Hollywood was on day trips to the nearby Co Down garrison town of the same name.'[84]

Closing the Ring contains several features that have come to characterise Attenborough's films. The film is enhanced by a background of pictorial landscapes, a high standard of acting and moments of 'silent dialogue' that allow the full emotional impact to be received. It also employs a slow tempo, the effect of which is heightened through the action scenes which include the dramatic sequence of the air crash in which Teddy is killed and the bomb blast in Belfast which also provides Ethel Ann with a form of redemption for her past guilt at not loving the man she married after Teddy's death. The end scene is reminiscent of Attenborough's first film, *Oh! What a Lovely War*, in its simplicity but with less impact. In the place of plain white crosses a circle is formed by two birds flying in a ring formation highlighting the message that deep love does not end through death but remains alive through memories. The film is supported by a strong musical score, the tone of which provides a dual purpose of creating a rousing atmosphere but accompanied by a slow tempo emphasises the sadness which is evident throughout the film. The classical-style music is also accompanied by traditional Irish melody, linking the two nations of Ireland and America together.

The film was first shown at the Toronto Film Festival on 14 October 2007 and then in Britain at the 51st BFI London Film Festival on 21 October 2007. It had its world première in Belfast at the Waterfront on 13 December 2007, distributed by the independent company, The Works. *Closing the Ring* also 'opened' in other countries throughout 2008 including in Australia, Spain, Brazil, the Netherlands and Japan. Attenborough himself embarked on a countrywide tour to publicise the film which also included an interview at the London Film Festival in which he described himself as 'not an *auteur*, but a simple teller of stories'.[85] In Edinburgh, he explained why he undertook the tiring job of publicity himself:

> If you don't have blockbuster money behind you then of course you have to do it on the cheap. That's why I'm out and about promoting this film myself. We just don't have the money to advertise it. If the film's a dog then it will crash and burn. But I don't believe it will. That's why even at my age I'm travelling up and down the country to tell people about it.[86]

The December date for the release of the film represented a difficult personal time for Attenborough, close to the third anniversary of his daughter's and granddaughter's deaths, but he conceded it was out of his hands, commenting: 'I was taken aback because it is such an important time for me, but they insisted it was the right film for that time of year.' However, he also recognised the connection between the film and his own circumstances when he observed:

> It definitely is a movie which makes you think about your loved ones. Pain and loss is a bewildering problem that so many of us have to face – especially when it's someone so young you lose for no reason at all. Of course pain has touched my own life, but it's how you deal with it that counts.[87]

Attenborough's personal grief was also commented on in articles in the press. The *Daily Mail* related one particular scene of the film to Attenborough's own predicament, where Ethel Ann refuses to believe that her husband, Teddy, has died. For his own part, Attenborough said: 'People ask, "Does it get any better?", but it doesn't'. You just become more capable of dealing with it.'[88] Attenborough also acknowledged that working with MacLaine was a therapeutic experience:

> Shirley was hugely sympathetic. We talked about the grieving process as a way of understanding her character. In the film she clings to the hope that her husband might not be dead because his body wasn't found. Then the ring arrives. I felt able to talk to Shirley about what she had to assimilate by virtue of what had happened to Poppy [Lady Attenborough] and me.[89]

Many reviewers found the film commendable but uninspiring. Sheila Johnston in the *Daily Telegraph*, reviewing *Closing the Ring* from the London Film Festival, called it 'gentle, unpretentious and life affirming'.[90] The *Observer* found the script 'more than a little contrived' and 'over-emphatic' but praised Attenborough for his direction which 'infused it with warmth and mature insight'.[91] Henry Fitzherbert in the *Sunday Express* hailed the film as one of the director's 'most heartfelt and moving pictures'. For Fitzherbert, *Closing the Ring* had the necessary ingredients:

> The hallmarks of an Attenborough picture . . . brilliant, intuitive casting and superb performances ... are in evidence here ... The production values, period detail and cinematography are first class, while Attenborough's direction shows many imaginative flourishes. If it lacks the simplicity and sheer heartache of one of his finest films, *Shadowlands*, it is still nevertheless a fine romantic drama.[92]

Empire commented favourably that after recent disappointments 'Attenborough is back on better, albeit old-fashioned, form.'[93] The *News of the World* praised the film calling it '[s]mall in scale but big in emotional impact, *Closing the Ring* is a gentle masterpiece.'[94] Less favourable reviews included the *Daily Telegraph*, which declared that '[n]o one could accuse Richard Attenborough of not having a heart, but this tragic Second World War love story has more of that snuffly organ than it knows what to do with'.[95] *The Times* was also unforgiving when it described the film as an 'interminable melodrama' which is 'tortuously corny, insanely contrived and deeply unconvincing'.[96] For *Screen International*, '*Closing the Ring* is a drama that aspires to achieve epic status but ultimately delivers too little.'[97] Opinions from abroad were also varied. The *Irish Times* was critical of the performances, claiming '[t]he acting by the younger Americans is woeful', the film helped by 'the senior actors, who almost manage to make the incredible credible'.[98] *Variety*, reviewing the film in Toronto, complained that the film 'is too bland to score any meaningful degree of emotional impact'.[99] For the *Toronto Star*, the film 'seems like it belongs to another era'.[100]

Despite the overt disparaging criticism, *Closing the Ring* was nominated in two categories in the Irish Film and Television Awards announced on 15 January 2008 for Best Film (Gilbert and Attenborough) and Best Production Design (McCullagh), although none were winners. A more significant disappointment was the box-office returns, not helped by the delayed and limited release in America. *Closing the Ring* made a poor start making £23,339 on its opening weekend while its total box office was given as £152,000.[101]

While there are several similarities between *Shadowlands* and *In Love in War*, *Closing the Ring* failed to reach the heights of the former and became more associated with the negative qualities of slow tempo and cloying acting styles of the latter. As well as sharing similarities with *The English Patient*, *Closing the Ring* also suffered greatly from its thematic and stylistic similarity with *Atonement* which was more critically and popularly acclaimed. *Atonement*'s director, Joe Wright, and the popular British actress, Keira Knightley, both represent the new generation in British cinema and proved more of an attraction than the veteran partnership of Attenborough and MacLaine, despite the popular interest in Barton. However, while the film is guilty of a very slow tempo at times, there are tremendous moments of excitement, especially during the air crash scene, which brings added tension and exhilaration to the film. *Closing the Ring* thus returns Attenborough to a film containing some 'great moments' that were characteristic of *Oh! What a Lovely War*, but falls short of concluding his career with 'a great film' as would have been his wish.

Notes

1 David Robinson, *Richard Attenborough*, London, 2003, p. 94.
2 *Screen Finance*, 14 May 1998, n. p.
3 James Chapman, *Past and Present: National Identity and the British Historical Film*, London, 2005, p. 301.
4 Quoted in Jeff Dawson, 'The Crying Game', *Empire*, 58 (April 1994), p. 81.
5 Nick James, 'The Tracks of Their Tears', *Observer*, 26 December 1993.
6 Quoted *ibid*.
7 Richard Dyer, 'Feeling English', *Sight and Sound*, New Series, 4:3 (March 1994), p. 19.
8 Production Notes, *Shadowlands*, microfiche, BFI, London.
9 Quoted in Dawson, 'The Crying Game', p. 80.
10 Andrew Higson, 'The Heritage Film and British Cinema', in Higson (ed.), *Dissolving Views: Key Writings on British Cinema*, London, 1996, pp. 233–4.
11 *Ibid*.
12 Production Notes, *Shadowlands*.
13 Script, *Shadowlands*, S19308, dated 5 April 1993, BFI.
14 Simon Jenkins, 'Stories that Get in the Way of Facts', *The Times*, 12 March 1994.

15 Production Notes, *Shadowlands*.
16 Andy Dougan, *The Actors' Director: Richard Attenborough Behind the Camera*, Edinburgh, 1994, p. 156.
17 *Ibid.*, p. 117.
18 Author's interview with Attenborough, 26 May 2001, Richmond, Surrey.
19 *Ibid.*
20 Script, *Shadowlands*, S18338, Second Draft, 22 October 1991.
21 Script, *Shadowlands*, S19308.
22 Script *Shadowlands*, S18338.
23 Quoted in Jo Berry, 'Dad!', *Empire*, 58 (April 1994), p. 80.
24 *Film Review*, February 1994, p. 44.
25 Robinson, *Richard Attenborough*, p. 96.
26 Quoted in Dougan, *The Actors' Director*, pp. 157–8.
27 *Ibid.*, p. 170.
28 *Daily Telegraph*, 10 March 1994.
29 *Sun*, 4 March 1994.
30 *Guardian*, 3 March 1994.
31 *Observer*, 6 March 1994.
32 *Mail on Sunday*, 6 March 1994.
33 *Independent on Sunday*, 6 March 1994.
34 *Financial Times*, 3 March 1994.
35 *Evening Standard*, 3 March 1994.
36 *Sight and Sound*, New Series, 4:3 (March 1994), pp. 48–9; *Screen International*, 28 January 1994, p. 16.
37 *Variety*, 13 December 1993.
38 *New York Times*, 29 December 1993.
39 *Village Voice*, 4 January 1994.
40 David Sexton, 'Making a Waste Land of Eliot', *Sunday Telegraph*, 10 April 1994.
41 *Evening Standard*, 3 March 1994.
42 *Observer*, 6 March 1994.
43 A.N. Wilson, 'Skeletons in the Wardrobe', *Evening Standard*, 3 March 1994.
44 Humphrey Carpenter, 'Of More than Academic Interest', *Sunday Times*, 27 February 1994.
45 Dougan, *The Actors' Director*, p. 162.
46 Henry S. Villard and James Nagel, *Hemingway in Love and War*, Boston, 1989, p. 41.
47 Quoted in Publicity Notes, *In Love and War*, microfiche, BFI, London.
48 Quoted in *Screen International*, 20 September 1996, p. 27.
49 Publicity Notes, *In Love and War*, March 1997, microfiche, BFI, London.
50 Quoted in John R. Bittner, 'The Hemingway Biography on the Silver Screen: Richard Attenborough's Film, In Love and War', *Hemingway Review*, 19 (spring 2000), University of Idaho, n. p.
51 Production Notes, *In Love and War*.
52 Quoted in Richard Brooks, 'A War, a Nurse, a Wounded Hunk – Dickie at the Kleenex Again', *Observer*, 2 February 1997.
53 Publicity Notes, *In Love and War*.
54 *Guardian*, 16 May 1996.
55 Mary Hardesty, 'Hemingway *In Love and War*', *American Cinematographer*, 78:2 (February 1997), p. 82.
56 Quoted in Hardesty, *Directors Guild of America Magazine*, 22:1 (March/April 1977), p. 62.
57 *Hollywood Reporter*, 27 January 1997. AC Nielsen gives the amount as $82,515 for the opening weekend.

58 *Los Angeles Times*, 18 December 1996.
59 *San Francisco Chronicle*, 24 January 1997.
60 *New York Times*, 24 January 1997.
61 *Daily News of Los Angles*, 24 January 1997.
62 *Observer*, 16 February 1997.
63 *Sunday Telegraph*, 16 February 1997; *Guardian*, 14 February 1997.
64 *Evening Standard*, 13 February 1997.
65 *Sunday Times*, 16 February 1997.
66 *Film Review*, Special Year Book, 22 (1997–98), p. 50; *Empire*, 93 (March 1997), p. 33.
67 *Sight and Sound*, New Series, 7:3 (March 1997) pp. 50–1.
68 Sue Reid, 'Nursing a Passion', *Sunday Times*, 31 March 1996.
69 *Ibid.*
70 Hugo Gurdon, 'The First Casualty of War', *Daily Telegraph*, 7 February 1997.
71 Quoted in Reid, 'Nursing a Passion'.
72 Robinson, *Richard Attenborough*, p. 100.
73 *Ibid.*
74 *Hollywood Reporter*, 3 March 1997.
75 Winston Churchill, *The Second World War, Volume V, Closing the Ring*, London, 1950.
76 *Mirror*, 2 June 2006 (Ulster Edition).
77 *Ottawa Citizen*, 20 June 2006.
78 *Closing the Ring* did obtain limited distribution in America in January 2009.
79 Information gained from author's conversation with Richard Attenborough, 15 June 2003, Richmond.
80 *Screen Finance*, 19:7 (5 April 2006), p. 3.
81 *Sun*, 24 March 2008; *News of the World*, 23 March 2008.
82 news.bbc.co.uk/1/hi/northern_ireland, dated 28 March 2006, accessed 29 May 2008.
83 Tom Peterkin, 'Belfast Welcomes Latest Shooting by Attenborough Troubles as Stars Shine on Belfast Streets', *Daily Telegraph*, 22 April 2006.
84 *Ibid.*
85 *Daily Telegraph*, 23 October 2007.
86 Matt Bendoris, 'He Might Be Jurassic but Dickie Will Never Retire', *Sun*, 29 December 2007.
87 *Ibid.*
88 'My Christmas Tsunami Grief, by Attenborough', *Daily Mail*, 24 December 2007.
89 Quoted in Nigel Farndale, 'The Trouper Cinema', *Sunday Telegraph*, 23 December 2007.
90 *Daily Telegraph*, 23 October 2007.
91 *Observer*, 30 December 2007.
92 *Sunday Express*, 30 December 2007.
93 *Empire*, 223 (January 2008), p. 74.
94 *News of the World*, 23 December 2007.
95 *Daily Telegraph*, 26 December 2007.
96 *The Times*, 27 December 2007.
97 *Screen International*, 18 September 2007.
98 *The Irish Times*, 28 December 2007
99 *Variety*, 1 October 2007.
100 *Toronto Star*, 14 September 2007.
101 www.ukfilmcouncil.org.uk, accessed 29 May 2007 and 28 December 2011.

Conclusion

The main objective of this study has been to explore Richard Attenborough's work as a significant producer and director in British cinema. By directing twelve films and by producing a further five, over a long period of five decades, he has shown that he has been able to adapt to both the far-reaching changes within the film industry and in the nature of popular film culture. While it would be fair to say that Attenborough has experienced mixed critical and popular success, the critical discourse around his films has been dominated by their often controversial content, particularly in respect of their representations of history and historical figures, with less attention paid to Attenborough's style.

Attenborough has employed his many skills of negotiation, persistence and patience to achieve many of his objectives. His long quest to realise *Gandhi* and the Oscar success he enjoyed has made Attenborough internationally renowned, and provided the pivotal point of his career. Yet, *Gandhi*'s Oscar success appears to have lessened his standing in scholarly terms, leading, at least partially, to his subsequent academic neglect. While Attenborough appears not sufficiently innovative or stylised for him to be considered an *auteur* director, a claim with which he himself concurs, there is sufficient evidence to show that his films do contain several auteurist characteristics, particularly in his focus and emphasis on performance from his actors (who have benefited from Attenborough's own acting experience) as well as several examples of the use of 'silent dialogue' to enhance, through skilful acting techniques, inner feelings of characters. Nevertheless, Attenborough's career might have taken a different path if he had continued with the innovation in style and technique demonstrated in his first film, *Oh! What a Lovely War*. But this was not a mode that Attenborough wished to pursue, instead his future productions tended to eschew fantasy for the realism he preferred.

The biopic has emerged as Attenborough's preferred genre and filmic form. In many of his own instigations, including *Gandhi*, *Cry Freedom*, *Chaplin* and *Grey Owl*, Attenborough has employed the biopic in the manner of Lord Reith 'to inform, educate and entertain' his audience as well as fulfilling his personal ambition of projecting his heroes on film. The films that were ready-made projects, including *Young Winston*, *Shadowlands* and *In Love and War*, instead indulged his personal wish to delve into the complexity and interaction in human relationships despite the overbearing hands of producers whose influence constrained, to different degrees, his directorial control. Attenborough's other preference has been the war film which he has portrayed in differing forms, from extreme stylisation (*Oh! What a Lovely War*), drama based on real events (*Closing the Ring*) to documentary-style realism (*A Bridge too Far*). These films are motivated by Attenborough's 'Reithian' designs to bring past events to a new audience. With *Cry Freedom*, however, it was the events of the present that he succeeded to bring to the attention of a global community.

By the very nature of their subjects Attenborough's films are more attractive to a middlebrow, middle-class and middle-aged audiences, thus bypassing the younger generation who form cinema's main following. The absence (or near absence) of sexual encounters and aspects of violence and pyrotechnics make the films unattractive to an audience more used to hyperbole. Attenborough's biopics tend towards a sanitised portrayal showing the subject in a favourable rather than unflattering light which may fulfil Attenborough's personal views of his heroes rather than providing an objective depiction for audiences. By this they satisfy an audience eager to remember the past in a nostalgic rose-tinted hue thus failing to employ the cinema as a means of reappraising the subject. Attenborough's personal crusade to rehabilitate boyhood heroes whose reputations had suffered due to human frailties, especially *Chaplin* and *Grey Owl*, succeed in revealing their lives, particularly their harsh childhoods which shaped their futures. Whereas both these films can be commended for their intentions, their lack of critical success, and indeed the popular and critical indifference to the films, questions whether the subjects were suited to the times in which they were made.

Another significant factor which has been considered is the proliferation of Attenborough's roles within the cinema. In front of the camera he is both actor and spokesman. Behind he is producer, director, negotiator and spokesman. His degree of multitasking has, to some extent, detracted from his standing as a director putting him at a disadvantage when compared to other directors whose work is channelled in one specific area.

The title of Attenborough's last film, *Closing the Ring* is a prophetic title with which to end his directorial career. Advancing years, poor health and lack of financial support have prevented further projects being realised, including his other long-held wish to make a film on Thomas Paine. Philip French's review of *Closing the Ring* concluded with a plea to the film industry for someone to 'give Attenborough the money to realise his dream of a film about Tom Paine'.[1] Although this dream will not now be fulfilled, Attenborough's lasting legacy is the significant body of work that he has already produced making him, unquestionably, a major and important director in the history of British Cinema.

Note

1 *Observer*, 30 December 2007.

Filmography

Films as actor and producer

The Angry Silence (1960), 95 min.

Beaver Films/British Lion
Producers: Richard Attenborough, Bryan Forbes
Director: Guy Green
Screenplay: Bryan Forbes
Original source: Michael Craig
Leading actors: Richard Attenborough, Pier Angeli, Michael Craig, Bernard Lee

The League of Gentlemen (1960), 109 min.

Allied Film Makers/Rank
Producer: Michael Relph
Director: Basil Dearden
Screenplay: Bryan Forbes
Original source: John Boland
Leading actors: Jack Hawkins, Richard Attenborough, Bryan Forbes, Nigel Patrick, Roger Livesey, Kieron Moore, Robert Coote

Séance on a Wet Afternoon (1964), 111 min.

Allied Film Makers/Beaver Films/Rank
Producers: Richard Attenborough, Bryan Forbes
Director: Bryan Forbes
Screenplay: Bryan Forbes
Original source: Mark McShane
Leading actors: Richard Attenborough, Kim Stanley, Nanette Newman, Patrick Magee

Films as producer only

Whistle Down the Wind (1961), 94 min.

AFM/Beaver Films/Rank
Producer: Richard Attenborough
Director: Bryan Forbes
Screenplay: Keith Waterhouse and Willis Hall
Original source: Mary Hayley Bell
Leading actors: Hayley Mills, Bernard Lee, Alan Bates

The L-Shaped Room (1962), 110 min.

Romulus/British Lion
Producers: Richard Attenborough and James Woolf
Director: Bryan Forbes
Screenplay: Bryan Forbes
Original source: Lynn Reid Banks
Leading actors: Leslie Caron, Tom Bell, Bernard Lee, Cicely Courtneidge, Pat Phoenix, Emlyn Williams

Films as director or producer/director

Oh! What a Lovely War (1969), 138 min.

Accord/Paramount
Producers: Richard Attenborough, Brian Duffy
Associate Producer: Mack Davidson
Screenplay: Len Deighton (uncredited)
Original source: Theatre Workshop and Charles Chilton
Cinematography: Gerry Turpin
Production Designer: Don Ashton
Costume Design: Anthony Mendleson
Choreography: Eleanor Fazan
Editor: Kevin Connor
Music: Alfred Ralston
Titles: Raymond Hawkey
Leading actors: Ralph Richardson, John Gielgud, Kenneth More, John Clements, Paul Daneman, Joe Melia, Jack Hawkins, Ian Holm, Mary Wimbush, Colin Farrell, Angela Thorne, John Mills, Jean-Pierre Cassel, Michael Redgrave, Corin Redgrave, Vanessa Redgrave, Dirk Bogarde, Susannah York, Paul Shelley, Gerald Sim

Young Winston (1972), 146 min.

Open Road/Hugh French/Columbia-Warner
Producer: Carl Foreman
Associate Producer: Harold Buck
Screenplay: Carl Foreman
Original source: Winston S. Churchill
Cinematography: Gerry Turpin
Production Design: Don Ashton, Geoffrey Drake
Costume Design: Anthony Mendleson
Editor: Kevin Connor
Music: Alfred Ralston
Leading actors: Simon Ward, Robert Shaw, Anne Bancroft, Colin Blakely, Jack Hawkins, Ian Holm, Clive Morton, Robert Flemyng, Patrick Magee, Edward Woodward, Russell Lewis, Michael Audreson, John Mills, John Woodvine

A Bridge Too Far (1977), 169 min.

Joseph E. Levine Presents/United Artists
Producers: Joseph E. Levine, Richard P. Levine
Screenplay: William Goldman
Original source: Cornelius Ryan
Cinematography: Geoffrey Unsworth
Production Design: Terence Marsh
Production Manager: Terence A. Clegg
Costume Design: Anthony Mendleson
Editor: Anthony Gibbs
Music: John Addison
Leading actors: Dirk Bogarde, James Caan, Michael Caine, Sean Connery, Edward Fox, Elliott Gould, Gene Hackman, Anthony Hopkins, Hardy Kruger, Laurence Olivier, Ryan O'Neal, Robert Redford, Maximilian Schell, Liv Ullmann

Magic (1978) (USA), 102 min.

Joseph E. Levine Presents/20th Century-Fox
Producers: Joseph E. Levine, Richard P. Levine
Screenplay: William Goldman
Original source: William Goldman
Cinematography: Victor J. Kemper
Production Design: Terence Marsh
Editor: John Bloom
Music: Jerry Goldsmith
Leading actors: Anthony Hopkins Ann-Margret, Burgess Meredith, Ed Lauter

Gandhi (1982), 183 min.

Indo-British Films in association with International Film Investors, Goldcrest Films
International, National Film Development Corporation of India/Columbia–EMI–Warner
Producer: Richard Attenborough
In charge of Production: Terence A. Clegg
First Assistant Director: David Tomblin
Screenplay: John Briley
Original source: Louis Fischer
Cinematography: Billy Williams, Ronnie Taylor
Production Design: Stuart Craig
Editor: John Bloom
Music: George Fenton and Ravi Shankar
Leading actors: Ben Kingsley, Candice Bergman, Edward Fox, John Gielgud, Trevor Howard, John Mills, Martin Sheen, Ian Charleson, Roshan Seth, Saeed Jaffrey, Alyque Padamsee, Rohini Hattangady

A Chorus Line (1985) (USA), 113 min.

Embassy Films Associates/Polygram Pictures/Rank
Producers: Cy Feuer, Ernest H. Martin
Screenplay: Arnold Schulman
Original source: James Kirkwood, Nicholas Dante
Cinematography: Ronnie Taylor
Production Designer: Patrizia von Brandenstein
Editor: John Bloom
Music: Marvin Hamlisch
Lyrics: Edward Kleban
Choreography: Jeffrey Hornaday
Leading actors: Michael Douglas, Alyson Reed, Terence Mann, Audrey Landers, Vicki Fredericks

Cry Freedom (1987), 151 min.

Marble Arch Productions/Universal
Producer: Richard Attenborough
Co-producers: Norman Spencer and John Briley
In charge of Production: Terence Clegg
Assistant Director: David Tomblin
Screenplay: John Briley
Original source: Donald Woods
Cinematography: Ronnie Taylor
Production Design: Stuart Craig
Editor: Lesley Walker

Music: George Fenton and Jonas Gwangwa
Leading actors: Denzel Washington, Kevin Kline, Penelope Wilton, Josette Simon, John Thaw

Chaplin (1992), 139 min.

Carolco-Le Studio Canal + RSC Video Japan Satellite Broadcasting/Lambeth Production/Guild
Producers: Richard Attenborough, Mario Kassar
Co-producer: Terence Clegg
Assistant Director: David Tomblin
Associate Producer: Diana Hawkins
Screenplay: William Boyd and Bryan Forbes and William Goldman
Story: Diana Hawkins
Original source: Charles Chaplin, David Robinson
Cinematography: Sven Nykvist
Production Design: Stuart Craig
Editor: Anne V. Coates
Music: John Barry
Leading actors: Robert Downey Jr., Dan Aykroyd, Geraldine Chaplin, Kevin Kline, Paul Rees, Anthony Hopkins, Moira Kelly, Kevin Dunn

Shadowlands (1993), 126 min.

Shadowlands Productions/Spelling Films International in association with Price Entertainments/Savoy Pictures
Producers: Richard Attenborough, Brian Eastman
Executive Producer: Terence Clegg
Co-producer: Diana Hawkins
Screenplay: William Nicholson
Original source: William Nicholson, C.S. Lewis.
Cinematography: Roger Pratt
Production Design: Stuart Craig
Editor: Lesley Walker
Music: George Fenton
Leading actors: Anthony Hopkins, Debra Winger, Edward Hardwicke, John Wood, Joseph Mazzello

In Love and War (1996), 108 min.

New Line Productions in association with Dimitri Villard Productions/Entertainment
Producers: Dimitri Villard, Richard Attenborough
Co-producer: Diana Hawkins
Screenplay: Allan Scott, Clancy Sigal, Anna Hamilton Phelan

Original source: Henry S. Villard and James Nagel
Cinematography: Roger Pratt
Production Design: Stuart Craig
Editor: Lesley Walker
Music: George Fenton
Leading actors: Sandra Bullock, Chris O'Donnell, Ingrid Lacey, Mackenzie Astin, Emilio Bonucci

Grey Owl (1999), 113 min.

Largo Entertainment/Transfilm/Beaver Productions/20th Century-Fox
Producers: Richard Attenborough, Jake Eberts, Claude Léger
Co-producer: Diana Hawkins
Screenplay: William Nicolson
Original source: Donald B. Smith
Cinematography: Roger Pratt
Production Design: Anthony Pratt
Editor: Lesley Walker
Music: George Fenton
Leading actors: Pierce Brosnan, Annie Galipeau, Stephanie Cole, Renée Asherson

Closing the Ring (2007), 113 min.

Closing the Ring/Prospero Pictures and Scion Films
Producers: Richard Attenborough, Jo Gilbert
Screenplay: Peter Woodward
Cinematography: Roger Pratt
Production Design: Tom McCullagh
Editor: Lesley Walker
Music: Jeff Danna
Leading actors: Shirley MacLaine, Christopher Plummer, Mischa Barton, Neve Campbell, Pete Postlethwaite, Brenda Fricker, Stephen Amell, Martin McCann

Bibliography

Primary sources

Archival and unpublished document sources

British Film Institute Special Collections
Ann Skinner Collection (AS)
David Lean Collection (DL)
Michael and Aileen Balcon Collection (MEB)
BECTU Oral History Tapes: no. 500, 'Lord (Richard) Attenborough'

British Film Institute unpublished scripts

A Bridge Too Far by William Goldman (S11081), Combined Continuity Script (undated).
'Charlie' (*Chaplin*) by William Boyd (S17786), Shooting Script (January 1991).
Cry Freedom by John Briley (S13419), Combined Continuity Script (1987).
Gandhi by John Briley, Shooting Script (S14493) (November 1979).
Gandhi by Briley, Dialogue Script (S11547) (undated).
Gandhi by Briley, Shooting Script (S18597) (undated).
'Gandhiji' by Robert Bolt. Dated only by an accompanying letter from Margaret Ramsey, 27 January 1976 (DL 17/2).
Magic by William Goldman (S6098) Release Script (September 1978).
Magic by Goldman (September 1977) (AS Box 12).
Oh! What a Lovely War by Len Deighton (14 March 1968) (AS Box 4).
Shadowlands by William Nicholson (S18338) Second Draft (22 October 1991).
Shadowlands by Nicolson (S19308) Shooting Script) (undated).
'The Young Mr Churchill' by Bryan Forbes (S11697) (10 February 1963).
Young Winston by Carl Foreman, Revised Draft (4 December 1970) (AS Box 70).
Young Winston by Foreman (S137890) US version (undated).
Young Winston by Foreman (S13610) Release Script – US version (undated).
Young Winston by Foreman (S13611) First Draft (20 October 1969).
Young Winston by Foreman (S13612) Second Draft (15 June 1970).
Young Winston by Foreman (S15232) Release Script (July 1972).

208 BIBLIOGRAPHY

British Library Department of Manuscripts

Lord Chamberlain's Correspondence Files, Readers Reports
  File: 1963/3308, *Oh What a Lovely War!*
  File: 1969/3553, *Oh What a Lovely War!*

National Archives, London

FCO 26/188: *Oh! What a Lovely War*, 1 Jan. 1969–31 Dec. 1969.
DEFE 68/85: *A Bridge Too Far*, 8 Apr. 1975–17 Aug. 1976.
DEFE 24/974: *A Bridge Too Far*, 19 Mar.–29 July 1976.
DEFE 24/1248: *A Bridge Too Far*, 1 Jan. 1976–31 Dec. 1983.

Data sources

Nielsen, AC, Nielsen EDI Ltd 2004, Entertainment Data International, Source for UK Box Office Returns.
Niclsen, AC Nielsen EDI Ltd 2004, Entertainment Data International, Source for USA Box Office Returns.

Newspapers and periodicals

Many film reviews are taken from the British Film Institute Library's microfiche collection (page numbers not always provided). These include: *Daily Express, Daily Herald, Daily Mail, Daily Sketch, Daily Telegraph, Daily Worker, Evening News, Evening Standard, Financial Times, Glasgow Herald, Guardian, Independent, Independent on Sunday, Irish Times, Mail on Sunday, Mirror, Morning Star, News of the World, News Chronicle, Observer, People, Radio Times, Scotsman, Spectator, Sun, Sunday Dispatch, Sunday Express, Sunday Mirror, Sunday Telegraph, Sunday Times, The Times, Times Educational Supplement, Times of India, Time Out, Times Tribune, TV Times, Voice, Western Mail* and *What's on in London*.

American newspaper sources include: *Atlanta Journal, Chicago Sun Times, Daily News of Los Angeles, Georgia Straight, International Herald Tribune, Los Angeles Times, Newsweek, New York, New York Times, New Yorker, San Francisco Chronicle, Saturday Review, Time, Village Voice* and *World Press Review*.

Canadian newspaper sources include: *Calgary Sun, Globe and Mail, Montreal Gazette, Ottawa Citizen, Toronto Star, Toronto Sun* and *Vancouver Sun*.

Dutch newspaper sources include: *Gooi en Eemlander, Trouw, Twentsche Courant* and *De Waarheid*.

Indian newspaper sources include: *The Times of India*.

Trade papers and film periodicals

The trade journals, fan magazines and film periodicals include: *Action, American Cinematographer, American Film, Black Filmmaker, Black Film*

Review, Brighton Film Review, Broadcast, Cahiers du cinéma, Cineaste, Cinema Papers, Cinema (UK), *Cinema* (US), *Cinema Quarterly, CinemaTV Today, Dialogue on Film, Daily Cinema, Empire, Eyepiece, Film Comment, FilmFacts, Film Review, Film Weekly, Filmmakers Monthly, Films and Filming, Films Illustrated, Films in Review, Framework, Hollywood Reporter, Indian and Foreign Review, Kinematograph Weekly, Listener, Monthly Film Bulletin, Motion Picture Herald, Movie Maker, Photoplay, Premiere, Screen, Scoop, Screen Finance, Screen International, Show, Sight and Sound, Stills, Today's Cinema* and *Variety*.

Interviews and meetings

Richard Attenborough (with the author) 26 May 2001, 15 June 2003, 30 April 2004, 16 February 2007.
Richard Attenborough and Terence Clegg (with the author) 16 June 2003.
Charles Chilton (with the author) 9 March 2004.
Major-General Ian Gill (with the author) 18 September 2005.

Published screenplays

Briley, John, *Gandhi: The Screenplay* (New York, Grove Press, 1982).
Goldman, William, *Five Screenplays with Essays: All the President's Men, Magic, Harper, Maverick, The Great Waldo Pepper* (London, A&C Black, 1997).

Memoirs and autobiographies

Attenborough, Richard, *In Search of Gandhi* (London, Bodley Head, 1982).
Attenborough, Richard, *Richard Attenborough's Cry Freedom: A Pictorial Record* (New York, Alfred A. Knopf, 1987).
Attenborough, Richard and Diana Carter, *Entirely Up to You, Darling* (London, Hutchinson, 2008).
Balcon, Michael, *Michael Balcon Presents ... A Life Time of Films* (London, Hutchinson, 1969).
Carter, Diana, *Richard Attenborough's Chorus Line* (London, Bodley Head, 1985).
Eberts, Jake and Terry Ilott, *My Indecision Is Final: The Rise and Fall of Goldcrest Films* (London, Faber and Faber, 1990).
Eberts, Jeremy, Dane Lanken and Anthony Hobbs, *The Making of Richard Attenborough's Grey Owl* (Ottawa, Ajawaan Books, 1999).
Forbes, Bryan, *Notes for a Life* (London, Collins, 1974).
Gandhi, M.K., *An Autobiography or The Story of My Experiments with Truth* (London, Penguin, 1982, originally published in two volumes in 1927 and in 1929).
Goldman, William, *Adventures in the Screen Trade* (London, Abacus, 1996).

Goldman, William, *Which Lie Did I Tell?: More Adventures in the Screen Trade* (London, Bloomsbury, 2001).
Goorney, Howard, *The Theatre Workshop Story* (Oxford, Oxford University Press, 1981).
Gresham, Douglas, H., *Lenten Lands: My Childhood with Joy Davidman and C.S. Lewis* (New York, Macmillan, 1988).
Hagen, Louis, *Arnhem Lift* (London, Hammond, 1977).
Hawkins, Jack, *Anything for a Quiet Life: The Autobiography of Jack Hawkins* (London, Hamish Hamilton, 1973).
Littlewood, Joan, *Joan's book: The Autobiography of Joan Littlewood* (London, Methuen, 2003).
Mills, John, *Up in the Clouds, Gentlemen Please* (London, Orion, 2001).
Shirer, William, *Gandhi: A Memoir* (London, Abacus, 1981).
Woods, Donald, *Biko* (London, Penguin, 1987).
Woods, Donald, *Asking for Trouble: Autobiography of a Banned Journalist* (London, Penguin, 1987).
Woods, Donald, *Filming with Attenborough: The Making of Cry Freedom* (London, Penguin, 1987).

Television and video recordings

'Attenborough at 80' Arena, BBC2, 24 and 28 August 2003.
'Fifty Years of Acting in the Cinema', Lord Attenborough, St Catherine's College Oxford, 5 February 1996.
Shadowlands, BBC, Worldwide 1987.
The Great War, 30 May–22 November 1964, BBC.
The Truth about Len Deighton, BBC4, 7 January 2006.

Radio

True Brit: Richard Attenborough's view of British Cinema, Radio 4, 18 and 25 April 2002.
Charles Chilton – Radio Producer – The Archive Hour, BBC Radio 4, 21 February 2004.

Source material for films

Chaplin, Charles, *My Autobiography* (London, Penguin, 1992, originally published 1964).
Churchill, Winston, *The Dream* (Cambridge, Churchill College, 1987, originally published in the *Daily Telegraph*, 30 January 1966).
Churchill, *My Early Life* (London, Eland, rev. edn, 2000).
Churchill, *The World Crisis, 1911–1918* (London, Penguin, 2007, originally published 1931).
Fischer, Louis, *The Life of Mahatma Gandhi* (London, HarperCollins, 1997).
Goldman, William, *Magic* (London, Macmillan, 1976).

Hemingway, Ernest, *A Farewell to Arms* (London, Arrow Books, 2004).
Johnstone, Iain, *The Arnhem Report: The story behind A Bridge Too Far* (London, W.H. Allen, 1977).
Nicholson, William, *Shadowlands: A Play* (London, Samuel French, 1992).
Robinson, David, *Chaplin: His Life and Art* (London, Penguin, 2001).
Ryan, Cornelius, *A Bridge Too Far* (Hertfordshire, Hamish Hamilton, 1999).
Sibley, Brian, *Shadowlands: The True Story of CS Lewis* (London, Leslie Frewin, 1974).
Smith, Donald, B, *From the Land of Shadows: The Making of Grey Owl* (Saskatoon, Western Producer Prairie Books, 1991).
Theatre Workshop, Charles Chilton and members of the original cast, *Oh What a Lovely War* (London, Eyre Methuen, 1974).
Villard, Henry S. and James Nagel, *Hemingway in Love and War: The Lost Diary of Agnes von Kurowsky* (Boston, Northeastern University Press, 1989).
Woods Donald, *Asking for Trouble: The Autobiography of a Banned Journalist* (London, Penguin, 1987).
Woods, Donald, *Biko* (London, Penguin, 1979).

Secondary Sources

Books and monographs

Aldgate, Anthony, *Censorship and the Permissive Society: British Cinema and Theatre 1955–1965* (Oxford, Oxford University Press, 1995).
Aldgate, Anthony and Jeffrey Richards, *Best of British: Cinema and Society from 1930 to the Present* (London, I.B. Tauris, rev. edn, 1999).
Allon, Yoram, Del Cullen and Hannah Patterson (eds), *Contemporary British and Irish Film Directors: A Wallflower Critical Guide* (London, Wallflower Press, 2001).
Ambrose, Stephen, E., *Pegasus Bridge: 6 June 1944* (London, George Allen Unwin, 1984).
Barr, Charles (ed.), *All Our Yesterdays: 90 Years of British Cinema* (London, British Film Institute, 1986).
Barr, Charles, *Ealing Studios* (Moffat, Cameron & Hollis, rev. edn, 1998).
Battlefront: Operation Market Garden (Public Record Office, Richmond, 2000).
Blake, Robert (ed.), *The Private Papers of Sir Douglas Haig 1914–1919* (London, Eyre & Spottiswood, 1952).
Bond, Brian (ed.), *The First World War and Military History* (Oxford, Clarendon Press, 1991).
Booker, Christopher, *The 1970s: Portrait of a Decade* (Penguin, Middlesex, 1980).
Brownlow, Kevin, *David Lean* (London, Faber and Faber, 1997).
Carpenter, Humphrey, *That Was Satire That Was: The Satire Boom of the 1960s* (London, Phoenix, 2002).

BIBLIOGRAPHY

Castell, David, *Richard Attenborough: A Pictorial Film Biography* (London, Bodley Head, 1984).
Chapman, James, *The British at War: Cinema State and Propaganda, 1939–1945*, (London, I.B. Tauris, 1998).
Chapman, James, *Licence to Thrill: A Cultural History of the James Bond Films* (London, I.B. Tauris, 1999).
Chapman, James, *Past and Present: National Identity and the British Historical Film* (London, I.B. Tauris, 2005).
Chapman, James, Mark Glancy and Sue Harper (eds), *The New Film History: Sources, Methods, Approaches* (Basingstoke, Palgrave Macmillan, 2007).
Chibnall, Steve, *J. Lee Thompson* (Manchester, Manchester University Press, 2001).
Clark, Alan, *The Donkeys* (London, Pimlico, 1991).
Cohen, M.J. and John Major, 'History in Quotations, Reflecting 5000 Years of World History: An Extract', *History Today*, 53:10 (October 2003).
Coldstream, John, *Dirk Bogarde* (London, Phoenix, 2004).
Connelly, Mark, *The Charge of the Light Brigade* (London, I.B. Tauris, 2003).
Dickinson, Margaret and Sarah Street, *Cinema and State: The Film Industry and the British Government 1927–1984* (London, British Film Institute, 1985).
Dorsett, Lyle W., *Joy and C.S. Lewis: The Story of an Extraordinary Marriage* (London, HarperCollins, 1994).
Dougan, Andy, *The Actors' Director: Richard Attenborough behind the Camera* (Edinburgh, Mainstream Publishing, 1994).
Durgnat, Raymond, *A Mirror for England: British Movies from Austerity to Affluence* (London, Faber and Faber, 1970).
Dyja Eddie (ed.), *BFI Film and Television Handbook* (London, British Film Institute, 1995, 1996, 1997, 1998).
Falk, Quentin, *Anthony Hopkins: The Authorised Biography* (London, Virgin Publishing, 2000).
Forbes, Bryan, *Notes for a Life* (London, Collins, 1974).
Forbes, Bryan, *A Divided Life* (London, William Heinemann, 1992).
Forster, Margaret, *Daphne du Maurier* (London, Chatto & Windus, 1993).
Friedman, Lester, *Fires Were Started: British Cinema and Thatcherism* (Minnesota Press, Minneapolis, 1993).
Gifford, Denis, *The British Film Catalogue, vol.1, Fiction Film, 1895–1994*, (London, Fitzroy Dearborn Publishers, 3rd edn, 2000).
Gilbert, Martin, *Churchill: A Life* (London, Heinemann, 1991).
Goorney, Howard, *The Theatre Workshop Story* (Oxford, Oxford University Press, 1981).
Guinness Book of Records of 1998 (London, Guinness Publishing, 1977).
Hacker, Jonathan and David Price, *Take 10: Contemporary British Film Directors* (Oxford, Clarendon Press, 1991).
Harper, Sue, *Women in British Cinema: Mad, Bad and Dangerous to Know* (London, Continuum, 2000).
Harper, Sue and Vincent Porter, *British Cinema of the 1950s: The Decline of*

Deference (Oxford, Oxford University Press, 2003).

Harper, Sue and Justin Smith (eds), *British Film Culture in the 1970s: The Boundaries of Pleasure* (Edinburgh, Edinburgh University Press, 2012).

Hewison, Robert, *Too Much: Art and Society in the 1960s, 1960–75* (London, Methuen, 1986).

Higson, Andrew, *Waving the Flag: Constructing a National Cinema in Britain* (Oxford, Clarendon Press, 1995).

Higson, Andrew (ed.), *Dissolving Views: Key Writings on British Cinema* (London, Cassell, 1996).

Hill, John, *Sex, Class and Realism: British Cinema 1956–1963* (London, British Film Institute, 1997).

Hill, John, *British Cinema in the 1980s: Issues and Themes* (Oxford, Clarendon Press, 1999).

Jenkins Roy, *Churchill* (London, Pan Books, 2002).

Johnstone, Iain, *The Arnhem Report: The Story Behind A Bridge Too Far* (London, WH Allen, 1977).

Kelly, Andrew, *Cinema and the Great War* (London, Routledge, 1997).

Laffin, John, *On the Western Front: Soldiers' Stories from France and Flanders, 1914–1918* (Gloucester, Sutton Publishing, 1985).

Lancelyn Green, Roger and Walter Hooper, *C.S. Lewis: A Biography* (London, HarperCollins, 2003).

Lewis, C.S., *The Problem of Pain* (London, HarperCollins, rev. edn, 2002).

Lloyd, Ann (ed.), *Movies of the 1960s* (London, Orbis Publishing, 1983).

McFarlane, Brian, *An Autobiography of British Cinema* (London, Methuen 1997).

Mackenzie, S.P., *British War Films: 1939–1945* (London, Hambledon and London, 2001).

Mackillop, Ian, and Neil Sinyard, *British Cinema of the 1950s: A Celebration* (Manchester, Manchester University Press, 2003).

Marland, Charles J., *Chaplin and American Culture* (New Jersey, Princeton University Press, 1989).

Marwick, Arthur, *British Society since 1945* (London, Penguin, rev. edn, 2003).

Maschler, Tom (ed.), *Declaration* (London, MacGibbon & Key, 1957).

Mast, Gerald, *A Short History of the Movies* (New York, Macmillan, 1986).

Middlebrook, Martin, *Arnhem 1944: The Airborne Battle* (London, Penguin, 1994).

Milward Oliver, Edward, *Len Deighton: An Annotated Bibliography 1954–1985* (London, Sammier Press, 1985).

Milward-Oliver, Edward, *The Len Deighton Companion* (London, Grafton Books, 1987).

Monk, Claire and Amy Sargeant (eds), *British Historical Cinema* (London, Routledge, 2002).

Moore-Gilbert, Bart (ed.), *The Arts in the 1970s: Cultural Closure?* (London, Routledge, 1994).

Munn, Michael, *Gene Hackman* (London, Robert Hale, 1997).

Murphy, Robert, *1960s British Cinema* (London, British Film Institute, 1997).

Murphy, Robert (ed.), *British Cinema of the 90s* (London, British Film Institute, 2000).
Murphy, Robert, *The British Cinema Book* (London, British Film Institute, 2nd edn, 2001).
Neale, Steve, *Genre and Hollywood* (London, Routledge, 2000).
Nichols, Bill (ed.), *Movies and Methods* (London, University of California Press, 1976).
Nowell-Smith, Geoffrey (ed.), *The Oxford History of World Cinema* (Oxford, Oxford University Press, 1995).
Paget, Derek, *True Stories? Documentary Drama on Radio, Screen and Stage* (Manchester, Manchester University Press, 1990).
Paris, Michael (ed.), *The First World War and Popular Cinema* (Edinburgh, Edinburgh University Press, 1999).
Perry George, *The Great British Picture Show* (London, Pavilion Books, 2nd edn, 1985).
Ramsden, John, *Man of the Century: Winston Churchill and His Legend since 1945* (London, HarperCollins, 2003).
Reisz, Karel, *The Techniques of Film Editing* (London, Focal Press, 1953).
Richards, Jeffrey, *Thorold Dickinson: The Man and His Films* (Beckenham, Croom Helm, 1986). Republished as *Thorold Dickinson and the British Cinema* (London, Scarecrow Press, 1997).
Richards, Jeffrey, *Films and British National Identity: From Dickens to 'Dad's Army'* (Manchester, Manchester University Press, 1997).
Richards, Jeffrey, *A Night to Remember: The Definitive Titanic Film* (London, I.B. Tauris, 2003).
Robertson, Patrick (ed.), *The Guinness Book of Film Facts and Feats* (London, Guinness, 1985).
Robinson, David, *Richard Attenborough* (London, British Film Institute, rev. edn, 2003).
Ryall, Tom, *Alfred Hitchcock and the British Cinema* (London, Athlone Press, 1996).
Ryan, Cornelius, *The Longest Day* (London, Four Square, 1962).
Shail, Robert (ed.), *British Film Directors: A Critical Guide* (Edinburgh, Edinburgh University Press, 2007).
Sheffield, Gary, *Forgotten Victory: The First World War: Myths and Realities* (London, Review, 2002).
Sherman, William L., *Gandhi: A Memoir* (London, Abacus, 1982).
Smith, Donald B., *From the Land of Shadows: The Making of Grey Owl* (Saskatchewan, Western Producer Prairie Books, 1990).
Spicer, Andrew, *Sydney Box* (Manchester, Manchester University Press, 2006).
Stewart, Ian and Susan Carruthers (eds), *War Culture and the Media: Representation of the Military in 20th Century Britain* (Trowbridge, Flicks Books, 1996).
Street, Sarah, *British National Cinema* (London, Routledge, 1997).
Street, Sarah, *Transatlantic Crossings: British Feature Films in the USA* (London, Continuum, 2002).

Taylor, A.J.P., *The First World War: An Illustrative History* (London, Penguin, 1966).
Terraine, John, *The Great War* (Hertfordshire, Wordsworth, 1977).
Terraine, John, *Douglas Haig: The Educated Soldier* (London, Hutchinson, 1963).
Threadgall, Derek, *Shepperton Studios: An Independent View* (London, British Film Institute, 1994).
Turner, Adrian, *Robert Bolt: Scenes from Two Lives* (London, Hutchinson, 1998).
Walker, Alexander, *Hollywood England: The British Film Industry in the 1960s* (London, Michael Joseph, 1974).
Walker, Alexander, *National Heroes: British Cinema in the 1970s and Eighties* (London, Orion Books, rev. edn, 2005).
Walker, Alexander, *Icons in the Fire: The Rise and Fall of Practically Everyone in the British Film Industry, 1984–2000* (London, Orion, 2005).
Walker John (ed.), *Halliwell's Who's Who in the Movies* (London, HarperCollins, 1999).
Walker, John (ed.), *Halliwell's Film and Video Guide 2001* (London, HarperCollins, 16th edn, 2000).
Wilson, A.N., *C.S. Lewis: A Biography* (London, William Collins, 1990).
Wolff, Leon, *In Flanders Fields* (Middlesex, Penguin, 1958).
Wood, Linda (ed.), *British Film Industry* (London, British Film Institute, 1980).
Yule, Andrew, *Sean Connery: Neither Shaken Nor Stirred* (London, Warner Books, 1994).

Articles and chapters

Ambrose, Stephen E., 'The Longest Day (1962): "Blockbuster" History', *Historical Journal of Film, Radio and Television*, 14:4 (1994), pp. 421–31.
Anderson, Lindsay, 'The Director's Cinema?', *Sequence*, 12 (autumn 1950), pp. 6–11 and 37.
Anderson, Lindsay, 'Get Out and Push', in Tom Maschler (ed.), *Declaration* (London: MacGibbon & Key, 1957), pp. 154–78.
Badsey, Stephen, The Great War since the Great War', *Historical Journal of Film, Radio and Television*, 22:1 (March 2002), pp. 37– 45.
Badsey, Stephen, '*Blackadder Goes Forth* and the "Two Western Fronts" Debate', in Graham Roberts and Philip M. Taylor (eds), *The Historian, Television and Television History* (Luton, University of Luton Press, 2001) pp. 113–25.
Barber, Sian, 'Government Aid and Film Legislation: "An Elastoplast to Stop a Haemorrhage"', in Sue Harper and Justin Smith (eds), *British Film Culture in the 1970s: The Boundaries of Pleasure* (Edinburgh, Edinburgh University Press, 2012), pp. 10–21.
Bittner, John R., 'The Hemingway Biography on the Silver Screen: The Critical Reception of Richard Attenborough's film, *In Love and War*', *Hemingway Review*, 19 (spring 2000), University of Idaho, n. p.

Burton, Alan, 'Death or Glory? The Great War in British film', in Claire Monk and Amy Sargeant (eds), *British Historical Cinema* (London, Routledge, 2002), pp. 31–46.

Chapman, James, '"The Yanks Are Shown to Such Advantage": Anglo-American Rivalry in the Production of *The True Glory* (1945)', *Historical Journal of Film, Radio and Television*, 16:4 (1996), pp. 523–54.

Chapman, James, 'Our Finest Hour Revisited: The Second Wold War in British Feature Films since 1945', *Journal of Popular British Cinema*, 1 (1998), pp. 63–75.

Christie, Ian, 'As Others See Us: British Film-making and Europe in the 90s', in Robert Murphy (ed.), *British Cinema of the 90s* (London, British Film Institute, 2000), pp. 68–79.

Connelly, Mark, 'The Great War, Part 13: The Devil is Coming', *Historical Journal of Film Radio and Television*, 22:1 (2002), pp. 21–8.

Danchev, Alex, 'Bunking and Debunking: The Controversies of the 1960s', in Brian Bond (ed.), *First World War and Military History* (Oxford, Clarendon Press, 1991), pp. 263–88.

Dux, Sally, 'Allied Film Makers: Crime, Comedy and Social Concern', *Journal of British Cinema and Television*, 9:2 (April 2012), pp. 198–213.

Dyer, Richard, 'Feeling English', *Sight and Sound*, 4:3 (March 1994), pp. 16–19.

Elsaesser, Thomas, 'Images for Sale', in Lester Friedman (ed.), *Fires Were Started: British Cinema and Thatcherism* (Minneapolis, University of Minnesota Press, 1993), pp. 52–69.

Harper, Sue, 'History and Representation: The Case of 1970s British Cinema' in James Chapman, Mark Glancy and Sue Harper (eds), *New Film History: Sources, Methods, Approaches* (Basingstoke, Palgrave Macmillan, 2007).

Higson, Andrew, 'A Diversity of Film Practices: Renewing British Cinema in the 1970s', in Bart Moore Gilbert (ed.), *The Arts in the 1970s: Cultural Closure?* (London, Routledge, 1994), pp. 217–39.

Higson, Andrew, 'The heritage Film and British Cinema', in Higson (ed.), *Dissolving Views: Key Writings on British Cinema* (London, Cassell, 1996), pp. 232–48.

Hutchings, Paul, 'Beyond the New Wave: Realism in British Cinema, 1959–63', in Robert Murphy (ed.), *The British Cinema Book* (London, British Film Institute, 2001), pp. 146–52.

Jarvie, Ian, 'Fanning the Flames: Anti-American reaction to *Operation [sic] Burma* (1945)', *Historical Journal of Film, Radio and Television*, 1:2 (1981), pp. 117–37.

Lovell, Alan, 'The British Cinema: The Known Cinema?', in Robert Murphy (ed.), *The British Cinema Book* (London, British Film Institute, 2001), pp. 235–43.

Maschler, Tom (ed.), *Declaration* (London: MacGibbon & Key, 1957).

Miller, Toby, 'The Film Industry and the Government', in Robert Murphy (ed.), *British Cinema of the 90s* (London, British Film Institute, 2000), pp. 37–47.

Paris, Michael, 'Enduring Heroes: British Feature Films and the First World War, 1919–1997', in Michael Paris (ed.), *The First World War and Popular Cinema* (Edinburgh, Edinburgh University Press, 1999), pp. 51–73.

Porter, Vincent, 'Methodism versus the Market-place: The Rank Organisation and British Cinema' in Robert Murphy (ed.), *The British Cinema Book* (London, British Film Institute, 2001), pp. 85–92.

Ramsden, John, 'The Great War: The Making of the Series', *Historical Journal of Film Radio and Television*, 22:1 (2002), pp. 7–19.

Richards, Jeffrey, 'Transatlantic Rainbows', in Ann Lloyd (ed.), *Movies of the 1960s* (London, Orbis Publishing, 1983), pp. 85–7.

Schatz, Thomas, 'The New Hollywood', in Ava Collins, Jim Collins and Hillary Radner (eds), *Film Theory Goes to the Movies* (London, Routledge, 1993), pp. 8–36.

Sharma Shailja, 'Citizens of the Empire: Revisionist History and the Social Imaginary in Gandhi', *Velvet Light Trap: A Critical Journal of Film and Television*, 35 (spring 1995), pp. 60–8.

Sheffield, G.D., '"Oh! What a Futile War": Representations of the Western Front in Modern British Media and Popular Culture', in Ian Stewart and Susan Carruthers (eds), *War, Culture and the Media: Representations of the Military in 20th Century Britain* (Trowbridge, Flick Books, 1996), pp. 54–74.

Smither, Roger, 'A Wonderful Idea of the Fighting: the Questions of Fakes in "The Battle of the Somme"', *Historical Journal of Film, Radio and Television*, 13:2 (1993), pp. 149–68.

Sorlin, Pierre, 'War and Cinema: Interpreting the Relationship', *Historical Journal of Film, Radio and Television*, 14:4 (1994), pp. 357–66.

Sorlin, Pierre, 'Cinema and the Memory of the Great War', in Michael Paris (ed.), *The First World War and Popular Cinema: 1914 to the Present* (Edinburgh, Edinburgh University Press, 1999), pp. 5–23.

Todman, Dan, 'The Reception of the Great War in the 1960s', *Historical Journal of Film, Radio and Television*, 22:1 (2002), pp. 29–36.

Wenden, D. J. and K.R.M. Short, 'Winston S. Churchill: Film Fan', *Historical Journal of Film, Radio and Television*, 11:3 (1991), pp. 197–215.

Unpublished Papers and Theses

Lovell, Alan, 'The British cinema: the unknown cinema', paper presented to the British Film Institute Education Department, 13 March 1969 (held by BFI National Library).

Paget, Derek, '*Oh What a Lovely War* and the broken tradition of documentary theatre', 1988 (sm D77811), Ph.D. thesis, British Library, London.

Index

Addison, John, 81
Allan, Ted, 39, 45
Anderson, Lindsay, 9, 67
Angry Silence, The, 13, 20, 21–5, 27, 31, 32
Ann-Margret, 90–2
Associated British Picture Corporation (ABPC), 9
Attenborough, David, 5, 153, 157
Attenborough, Michael, 114
Attenborough, Sheila (Sim), 7, 8, 9, 194

Baker, Leslie 26, 32
Balcon, Michael, 25, 107
Barnett, Correlli, 51–2
Barton, Mischa, 190, 191
Belaney, Archie (Grey Owl), 138, 153–5
Biko, Steve, 105, 124, 125, 126, 127, 128, 129, 130, 131
Bludhorn, Charles, 44
Bogarde, Dirk, 49, 58, 77, 78, 79, 81–2, 88, 89
Bolt, Robert, 64, 109, 110, 111, 112, 113
Boulting, John, 6, 7, 9, 12, 20, 21
Boulting, Roy, 7, 8, 9, 12, 20, 21
Boyd, William, 143, 144, 149
Briley, John, 90, 112–13, 128, 130–1
British Lion, 10, 22, 25
Brosnan, Pierce, 157, 159–160, 161, 162, 163, 164
Browning, Lt-General Frederick 74, 77, 81, 82, 88, 89
Bryanston Films, 20, 25, 34
Bullock, Sandra, 184, 187
Burton, Alan, 48

Carolco Pictures, 143, 144–5, 148
Carpenter, Humphrey, 42, 179–80
Castell, David, 40, 65, 117
Chaplin, Charles, 138, 140, 141–2, 146–7, 148, 152–3
Chaplin, Geraldine, 145, 152, 153
Chaplin, Oona, 142, 153
Chapman, James, 83
Charge of the Light Brigade, The, 38, 57
Chilton, Charles, 38–9, 47
Churchill, Winston, 62, 63, 64, 65, 66, 108, 181, 189
Clegg, Terence, 80, 144, 145, 191
Connelly, Mark, 40
Connery, Sean, 79
Coward, Noël, 1, 5, 6, 110
Craig, Michael, 13, 20, 21, 22

Danchev, Alex, 38, 43
Davis, John, 26, 110
Dearden, Basil, 1, 11–12, 27, 28, 29, 30, 31, 32, 40
Deighton, Len, 40, 43, 44, 45, 50–1
Dougan, Andy, 81
Douglas, Michael, 120–1
Downey, Robert, Jr, 143, 150, 152
Duffy, Brian, 40, 43, 44, 50–1

Du Maurier, Daphne (Browning), 87, 88–9
Dyer, Richard, 171

Eady Levy, 10, 106, 139
Eberts, Jake, 113, 121, 128, 158, 161

Fenton, George, 156, 177, 180
Fischer, Louis, 109–10, 112, 113, 116
Forbes, Bryan, 1, 21, 22, 24, 25, 26, 27, 28, 29, 30–1, 32, 33–4, 65–6, 91, 111, 142–3, 149, 158
Foreman, Carl, 62, 66–9, 70–1, 72, 127, 182
French, Philip, 17, 18, 47, 86, 92, 124, 148, 151, 178, 179, 200

Gallipeau, Annie, 157, 160, 164
Gandhi, Mohandas, K., 1, 105, 108, 109, 119, 129, 181
Goldcrest, 106, 113, 114–15, 120, 128
Goldman, William, 75, 79, 82, 83, 84, 85, 90, 91, 92, 142–3, 144, 149
Gough, Colonel Frederick, 71, 87
Gough, General Hubert, 71
Great War, The, (TV) 42–3
Green, Guy, 1, 13, 20
Gresham, Douglas, 17, 174, 176, 179
Gresham, Joy, (Lewis), 168, 169, 176, 179, 180

Haig, Field Marshal Sir Douglas, 39, 42, 52
Hawkey, Raymond, 45
Hawkins, Diana (Carter) 14, 124, 142, 149, 156, 183, 186, 191
Hawkins, Jack, 1, 26, 28, 48
Hemingway, Ernest, 168, 180–1, 183, 188, 189
Higson, Andrew, 62, 70, 156, 171
Hill, John, 20, 106
Hopkins, Anthony, 70, 79, 90, 92, 93, 145, 171, 174, 176, 178, 180
How I Won the War, 38, 57

In Which We Serve, 15, 43, 46, 49, 110

Jennings, Humphrey, 7
Johnstone, Iain, 81, 85, 124

Kelly, Moira, 145
Kemp, Philip, 188
King and Country, 38, 43, 57–8
Kingsley, Ben, 3, 114, 116, 150, 158
Kline, Kevin, 128, 132, 145, 153
Kothari, Motilal, 108–9, 110, 111–12, 116, 124

Lacey, Ingrid, 184
League of Gentlemen, The, 14, 27–9, 31
Lean, David, 1, 5, 43, 77, 109, 110, 123, 170
Levine, Joseph E., 62, 63, 73, 74–5, 77–9, 81, 89–90, 91, 93, 111, 112, 113
Levine, Richard, P., 84
Lewis, C.S. (Jack), 168, 169–70, 172–3, 175, 176, 177, 179, 180
Life for Ruth, 27, 32
Littlewood, Joan, 37, 39, 54
Lovell, Alan, 37, 55
L-Shaped Room, The, 27, 32–3

MacLaine, Shirley, 190, 192, 194
Man in the Moon, 27, 29
Mandela, Winnie, 127–8
McCarthy, Senator Joe/House Un-American Activities Committee (HUAC), 69, 153
Mills, John, 5, 6, 11, 30, 40, 45
More, Kenneth, 22, 30, 48, 50
Mountbatten, Earl, 62, 85, 108, 110, 115–16
Murphy, Robert, 41

Nairn, Tom, 55
National Film Finance Corporation (NFFC) 10, 106
Neale, Steve, 2

New Line, 182, 183, 184, 189
Nicholson, William, 125, 158, 170, 172–3, 174, 175, 176
Norman, Barry, 67

O'Donnell, Chris, 184, 187
Olivier, Laurence, 9, 44, 48, 56, 64, 79

Paget, Derek, 40
Paris, Michael, 47
Phelan, Anna Hamilton, 183
Powell, Michael, 7, 109
Pratt, Roger, 185, 186, 191, 192
Pressburger, Emeric, 7
Puttnam, David, 139, 140, 148

Ragtime Infantry, The (TV), 50
Ralston, Alfred, 70
Rank Organisation, 9, 10, 25–6, 27, 31, 32, 110
Ray, Satyajit, 16, 114
Redford, Robert, 78, 83–4
Redgrave, Michael, 9, 44, 90, 170
Relph, Michael, 1, 27, 30, 31
Richards, Jeffrey, 45, 82, 146
Robinson, David, 54, 117, 142, 146, 153
Robinson, Edward, G., 7
Rushdie, Salman, 118
Ryan, Cornelius, 72, 73–4, 83

Séance on a Wet Afternoon, 27, 31–2
Sibley, Brian, 172
Spencer, Norman, 128
Spielberg, Steven, 16–7
Stanley, Kim, 31–2
Street, Sarah, 41, 65, 120

Taylor, A.J.P., 39, 43
Terraine, John, 43, 52
Thatcher, Margaret/Thatcherism, 106–7, 119, 125, 139, 140
Turpin, Gerry, 68, 186

Unsworth, Geoffrey, 81

Victim, 30, 31
Villard, Demetri, 182–3, 188–9
Villard, Henry, 182, 183, 188
Von Kurowsky, Agnes, 168, 180–1, 182, 183, 188–9

Walker, Alexander, 14, 21, 24, 25–6, 31, 32, 54, 151, 163, 178, 179, 188
Ward, Simon, 3, 68, 70, 72
Washington, Denzel, 129, 132
Whistle Down the Wind, 27, 30
Winger, Debra, 174, 176, 178, 180
Woolf, James, 32–3
Woods, Donald, 105, 124, 125, 126, 127, 128, 129, 130, 134